ROGER O'REILLY
LEGENDARY LIGHTHOUSES OF BRITAIN
AN ILLUSTRATED GUIDE TO THE SENTINELS THAT GUARD OUR SHORE

LEGENDARY LIGHTHOUSES OF BRITAIN

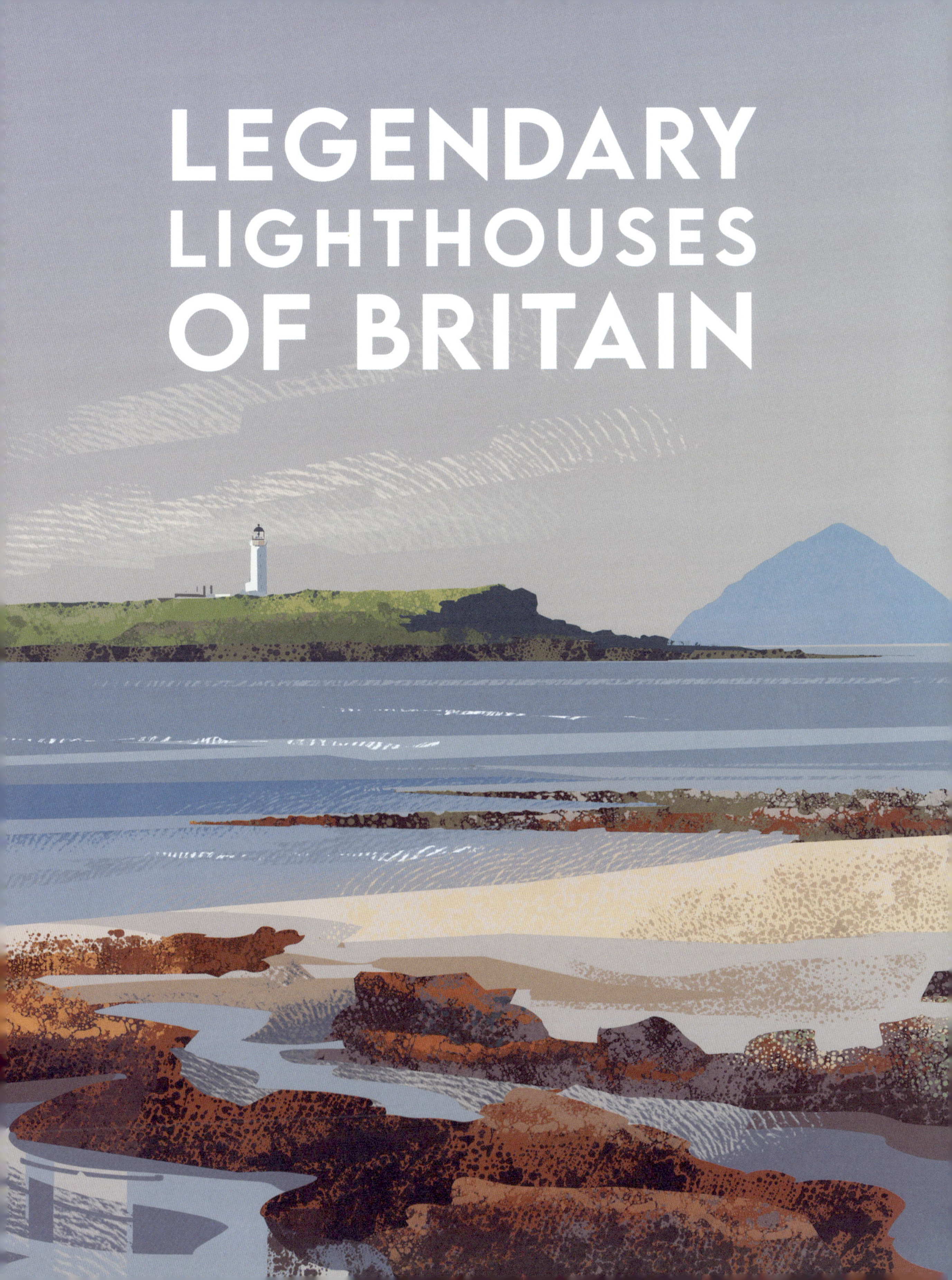

ROGER O’REILLY

LEGENDARY LIGHTHOUSES OF BRITAIN

AN ILLUSTRATED GUIDE TO THE SENTINELS THAT GUARD OUR SHORE

WATKINS

Legendary Lighthouses of Britain
Roger O'Reilly

First published in the UK and USA in 2024 by Watkins, an imprint of Watkins Media Limited Unit 11, Shepperton House, 83–93 Shepperton Road, London N1 3DF

enquiries@watkinspublishing.com

Publisher: Fiona Robertson
Editorial Manager: Daniel Culver
Copyeditor: Joanne Osborne
Head of Design: Karen Smith
Designers: Alice Claire Coleman, Sneha Alexander
Production: Uzma Taj

A CIP record for this book is available from the British Library

ISBN: 978-1-78678-811-5 (Hardback)
ISBN: 978-1-78678-812-2 (eBook)

10 9 8 7 6 5 4 3 2

Printed in China

www.watkinspublishing.com

The manufacturer's authorised representative in the EU for product safety is eucomply OÜ - Pärnu mnt 139b-14, 11317 Tallinn, Estonia, hello@eucompliancepartner.com, www.eucompliancepartner.com

To the keepers of the light

"I CAN THINK OF NO OTHER EDIFICE CONSTRUCTED BY MAN AS ALTRUISTIC AS A LIGHTHOUSE. THEY WERE BUILT ONLY TO SERVE."
— GEORGE BERNARD SHAW

CONTENTS

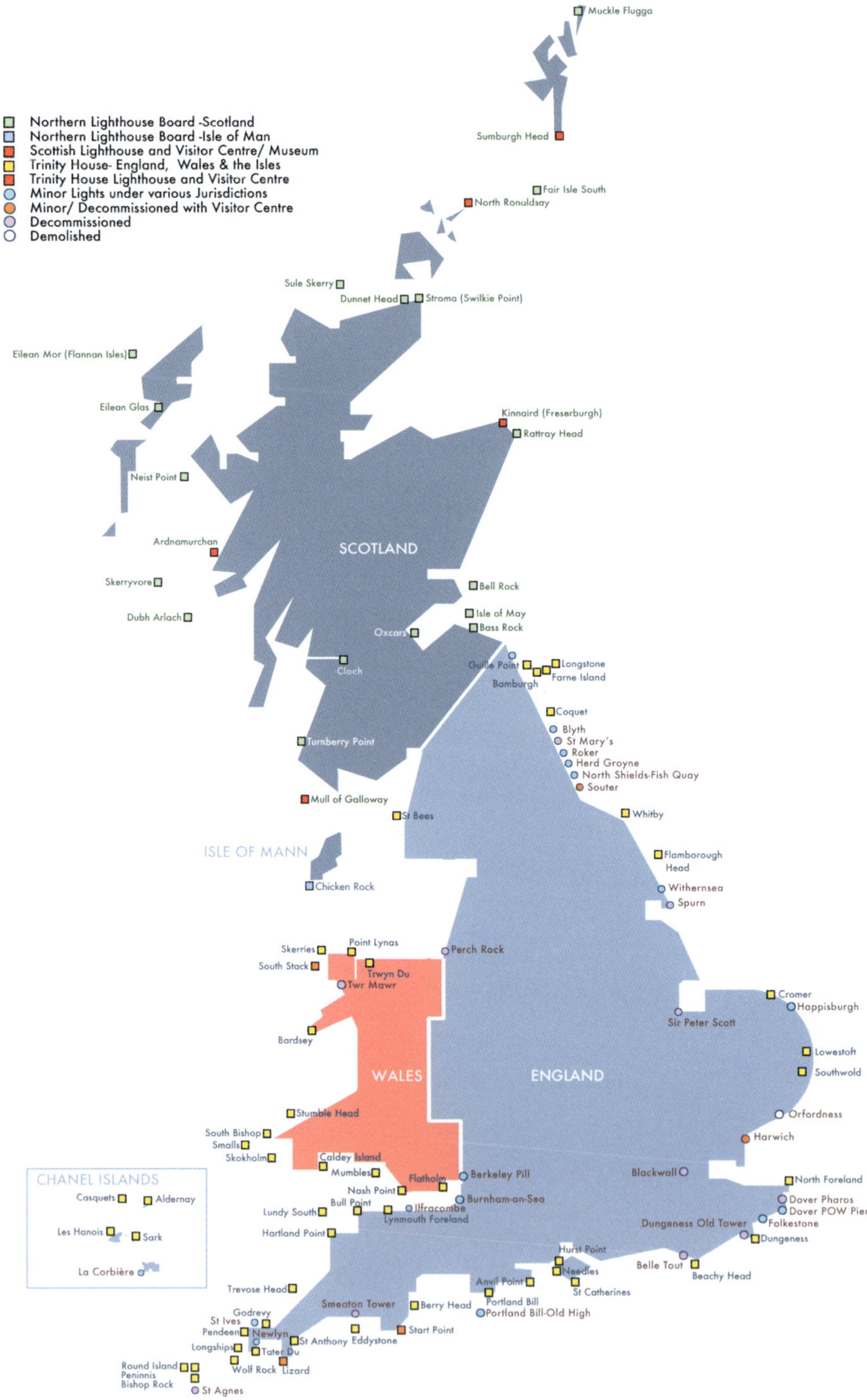
Northern Lighthouse Board -Scotland
Northern Lighthouse Board -Isle of Man
Scottish Lighthouse and Visitor Centre/ Museum
Trinity House- England, Wales & the Isles
Trinity House Lighthouse and Visitor Centre
Minor Lights under various Jurisdictions
Minor/ Decommissioned with Visitor Centre
Decommissioned
Demolished
Muckle Flugga
Sumburgh Head
Fair Isle South
North Ronaldsay
Sule Skerry
Dunnet Head
Stroma (Swilkie Point)
Eilean Mor (Flannan Isles)
Eilean Glas
Kinnaird (Freserburgh)
Rattray Head
Neist Point
Ardnamurchan
SCOTLAND
Skerryvore
Bell Rock
Dubh Arlach
Isle of May
Bass Rock
Oxcars
Cloch
Gullie Point
Longstone
Farne Island
Bamburgh
Coquet
Blyth
St Mary's
Roker
Herd Groyne
North Shields-Fish Quay
Souter
Turnberry Point
Mull of Galloway
St Bees
Whitby
ISLE OF MANN
Flamborough Head
Chicken Rock
Withernsea
Spurn
Skerries
Point Lynas
Perch Rock
South Stack
Trwyn Du
Twr Mawr
Cromer
Happisburgh
Sir Peter Scott
Bardsey
Lowestoft
Southwold
WALES
ENGLAND
Stumble Head
Orfordness
South Bishop
Smalls
Skokholm
Harwich
Caldey Island
Mumbles
Flatholm
Berkeley Pill
Blackwall
North Foreland
CHANEL ISLANDS
Casquets
Aldernay
Les Hanois
Sark
La Corbière
Nash Point
Burnham-on-Sea
Bull Point
Ilfracombe
Lynmouth Foreland
Lundy South
Hartland Point
Dover Pharos
Dover POW Pier
Folkestone
Dungeness Old Tower
Dungeness
Hurst Point
Needles
Belle Tout
Beachy Head
Anvil Point
St Catherines
Trevose Head
Smeaton Tower
Berry Head
Portland Bill
Portland Bill-Old High
Godrevy
St Ives
Pendeen
Newlyn
Start Point
St Anthony
Eddystone
Longships
Tater Du
Round Island
Peninnis
Bishop Rock
Wolf Rock
Lizard
St Agnes

INTRODUCTION

As kids growing up on the carefree beaches of East Meath in Ireland, my friends and I would regularly cycle the short distance to the unspoiled sand dunes that tumbled down to the mouth of the River Boyne and to the imposing "Maiden's Tower", which has stood sentinel on this site for over four centuries. The 18m (59ft) high tower was built during the reign of Queen Elizabeth I (hence the "Maiden" in the name) and used as a beacon to aid ships navigating their way into the port of Drogheda. At that time the doorway to the tower, 2m (6ft) off the ground, was open to all and sundry and we would shimmy up the spiralling stone staircase to the lookout platform at the top where we had a 360-degree view of the Boyne Estuary, the distant town and the beaches stretching toward Skerries to the south and the Mourne Mountains to the north. We also had an enviable view of the shipping approaching the river mouth and it was easy to imagine what it must have been like 400 years ago, watching as merchant schooners and barques took bearings on the tower and cautiously navigated their way past the ever-shifting sandbar that obstructed passage into the estuary.

By the late 20th century, the tower no longer served its original purpose as a daymark to guide shipping to shore. It had been superseded almost 100 years earlier by three unusual lighthouses situated among the dunes. The north, east and west lights were truncated towers that stood like Daleks on stilts, gazing forlornly out to sea and only coming to life as dusk crept in and we reluctantly set our bikes toward home. The sense of composure and reassurance that I felt in the warm glow of those beacons as they ultimately illuminated those summer nights was an almost tactile experience that has remained with me ever since.

A few years ago, I was driving my own small kids along the Hook Peninsula to visit Loftus Hall, reputedly the most haunted house in Ireland, for a Halloween tour. In the failing light, the distant Hook Head lighthouse had just come into view when its flash broke through the evening gloom. I drove past my turn and kept going until I could find a spot to pull in and watch the distant sweep

The Maiden's Tower at Mornington, Co Meath, guarding the mouth of the River Boyne.

of its beam. Loftus Hall could wait.

Whether at home on sea or on land, we have a special affinity to lighthouses. Maybe it's the idea of strength and resilience, a guiding light in the darkness, that feels so relevant in our challenging times, perhaps it's just a childlike fascination with tall towers and spiral staircases, with splendid isolation and romantic seascapes, but everyone seems to have a favourite.

While at their core, they are simply towers topped with beacons, these structures have captured the imagination in a way that few other types of building have managed. The lighthouse represents a unique part of our maritime history and an aesthetically pleasing part of our built heritage. Long may they continue to shine.

The east and west lights at Mornington guided ships past the drifting sandbar that obstructed smooth passage into the mouth of the River Boyne. The lights were decommissioned in 2002.

The history of the lighthouse goes back almost as far as that of seaborne trade itself. The need to protect the value of a ship's cargo, as much as the lives of its crew, has long inspired the positioning, where possible, of markers to enable craft to plot a safe passage into port.

The earliest recorded lighthouses were built on the shores of Upper Egypt. These navigational aids were often pyres set on the upper levels of temples and attended to by priests or adherents who were also versed in the arts of seafaring. As early as the third century BC, Alexander the Great's successor, King Ptolemy I, had commissioned the construction of probably the greatest of all lighthouses and one of the seven wonders of the ancient world, the Pharos of Alexandria. Incredibly, this structure, which took 12 years to build during the reign of Ptolemy's son, Ptolemy II, survived a millennium and a half of storms, tides and wars, eventually succumbing to an earthquake in the 14th century. The Pharos, which gives us the term "pharology", meaning the study of lighthouses, was named after the island on which it was built, a thin strip of land connected to Alexandria at low tide by a causeway. Soaring into the heavens to a height of 120m (394ft), the lighthouse both illuminated the approach to the port and displayed to all who saw it the commercial might of this great Mediterranean city.

The Pharos of Alexandria.

As the light faded on the Egyptian dynasties and the Roman Empire began to expand, Roman engineers and merchants quickly grasped the importance of lighthouses to their ever-expanding trade. In Britain, the Pharos of Dover, once one of a pair that stood on either side of the port, survives in the grounds of Dover Castle. The structure, built in the second half of the first century AD, illustrates how highly the Romans valued this southeastern English port. In northern Spain, the Tower of Hercules outside A Coruña in Galicia dates to a similar time. The tower was restored in the 16th century, eradicating most of its Roman vestiges, but it retains its Latin core and is regarded as the world's oldest continuously functioning lighthouse.

With the fall of the Roman Empire, however, maritime trade both literally and figuratively entered the dark ages; the few lights that had sporadically illuminated the trade routes into Britain were doused, and for the next millennium the coasts of Albion and Scotia were blanketed in darkness.

The late medieval period saw a modest resurgence in maritime trade, but the next attempts to provide guiding lights came primarily from ecclesiastical quarters and were mostly of philanthropic intent without any commercial consideration. On the north Norfolk coast, for example, St Edmund's Chapel was a familiar marker on the approach to King's Lynn and here a hermit, a Mr Thomas Cooke, was tasked with maintaining a light on the gable after dark. Shortly thereafter, however, Mr Cooke inconsiderately keeled over and died, and for a long spell no light shone forth. The search for a new hermit to take his place presumably proceeded with all due haste. Hermits were in fact in high demand as coastguards and lightkeepers at these lonely stations and, among others, there are records of ascetic lightkeepers at St Margaret's at Cliffe on the South Foreland near Dover, and at Spurn Point at the mouth of the Humber.

During this time, one particular light was established in unusual circumstances. In 1328, Walter de Godyton, a landowner on the Isle of Wight, was threatened with excommunication by the Pope on account of having been found guilty of fencing a large amount of wine from a ship that had been wrecked at St Catherine's Point. Had the wine been some run of the mill plonk, the matter would probably have been overlooked. However, it had originated from a well-connected monastic vineyard in Picardy and the nobleman was given the choice of either financing the building of a lighthouse and oratory at the Point or accepting eternal damnation. Predictably, he demurred at the latter.

Spurn Point off the Yorkshire coast.

In Ireland in the fifth century, to warn approaching ships of the treacherous waters nearby, St Dubhán established a beacon on the headland then known as Hy-Kinsellagh and now called Hook Head. The light would have been a brazier or metal cage of burning wood, turf or whatever he could get his hands on, probably set on a small tower of stones, though there are also suggestions that he may have suspended the cage from a mast on the cliffs. William Marshall, Earl of Pembroke, subsequently established a permanent tower on the site in the 12th century. It is now the oldest operating lighthouse in these isles. As well as the lights provided by monasteries and churches, some private structures were built. These, however, were expensive to construct and maintain, and often required royal intervention to get the necessary permissions. Consequently, they were somewhat rare.

Lowestoft low lighthouse circa 1850.

Before the development of large-scale maritime commerce in the 18th century, there was no guarantee that establishing a light would be profitable, and collecting fees from shipping presented its own set of problems. Most early British lighthouses were situated on the southern and southeastern coasts to serve the predominant trade routes to mainland Europe. However, the situation was soon to change. As the Industrial Revolution picked up speed, coal was suddenly in high demand and now colliers in vast numbers plied the waters between the northeastern ports and a prosperous and expanding capital. The explosion of Atlantic trade in the 18th century benefited west coast ports such as Liverpool and Glasgow, which now asserted themselves as new behemoths of maritime commerce.

Moving all this merchandise by sea presented myriad potential dangers and difficulties. Reefs, skerries, headlands and sandbanks hindered safe passage to ports and harbours. Storms and gales could force vessels off course, and racing tides and uncharted currents catch out the unwary. Even for those seamen fortunate enough to have rudimentary charts or local knowledge, plotting a safe channel toward port or around a stormy headland would be a challenge during daylight hours. After nightfall, only the bold or the foolhardy would attempt it.

In response to concerns about unregulated pilots on the Thames, "the Brethren of the most glorious and undivided Trinity, and of St Clement in the Parish of Deptford-Strond in the County of Kent" was founded in 1514. Now known by the more manageable name of Trinity House, this organization's mission was to "make, erect, and set up such, and so many beacons, marks, and signs for the sea ... whereby the dangers may be avoided and escaped, and ships the better come into their ports without peril". Henry VIII's younger daughter, Elizabeth I, officially recognized the importance of seamarks in a law that punished anyone guilty of "removal, alteration or defacement" of these structures. The fine was £100 – equivalent to approximately £37,000 today. This law was targeted at the notorious "wreckers" on the southern shores of England, who made a profit from luring floundering ships toward the rocks with decoy beacons and then looting the cargo. Though the scale of their activities is probably exaggerated, the wreckers would not have been above sabotaging genuine markers.

The original Smalls lighthouse off the Pembrokeshire coast stood precariously on nine oak pillars. Remarkably, it remained intact for 80 years before being replaced by a more permanent structure.

Over the next 200 years, a hodgepodge of systems of providing shore lights and markers existed in Britain, but there was no effective regulation or oversight. Private franchisees and operators ran lighthouses that were often inefficient, poorly lit or sometimes simply not lit at all due to cost-cutting or negligence. In the 1830s, the keeper of Lowestoft lighthouse would regularly light the lamp, then lock up the building and head into town to ply his second trade as a waiter in nearby hostelries for five shillings a night. More worrying still was that on occasion keepers subcontracted their duties to others. In one case a keeper hired an elderly woman who lived quite a distance from the lighthouse. In bad weather, when the light was most needed, she simply stayed at home. The situation was only brought to a head when a ship struck the rocks below the tower with the loss of a costly cargo and all lives on board.

Oystercatchers in the Plym Estuary to the east of Plymouth.

As a result, Trinity House was empowered from 1836 to buy out the remaining 12 private lighthouses. This they mostly managed without too much fuss from their war chest of over £1 million. There were, however, some holdouts, most notably the leaseholders of the Skerries lighthouse off Anglesey in Wales. The operators were understandably reluctant to relinquish an average annual profit of £12,525 and, since they had been issued a lease "in perpetuity", they held out until 1841 when they were finally tempted by the sum of £444,984 (an astonishing £37 million in today's money!). That small matter out of the way, Trinity House pressed ahead with an ambitious building programme. Eminent engineers including Thomas Matthews, James Walker, James and William Douglass and Henry Norris were commissioned to build iconic stations such as Beachy Head, Wolf Rock and Souter.

In Scotland, apart from some minor lights on the Clyde and Tay, the only permanent light was a coal brazier on the Isle of May in the Firth of Forth. There was, it became apparent, such a confusion of chancers, speculators and the downright inept, that if further tragedies were to be averted, a body with the authority to regulate responsibility for the provision of navigational aids was urgently required. Following an Act of Parliament in 1786 and largely at the behest of the politician "Honest George" Dempster, the Commissioners of Northern Light Houses (now the Northern Lighthouses Board) was founded with responsibility for lighthouses in Scotland and, since 1854, the Isle of Man.

Today the revenue for Trinity House and the Northern Lighthouses Board is collected as light dues levied on all shipping that arrives in British ports. The fees, which are based on the net tonnage of each vessel, are collected by the Customs Authority and then paid into a general lighthouse fund.

A ship founders on a hidden reef.

Long before GPS, radio transmission and radar, lighthouses served two primary purposes. The first was to guide shipping through waterways made treacherous by shoals, reefs and rocks as they left the open ocean and headed to port. Most lighthouses also included a sonic fog signal to warn of hazards at times of reduced visibility. The second purpose was to act as a reference point. An individual lighthouse distinguishes itself with its daymark – the colour schemes and patterns on the tower – and its light signature. For example, three white flashes every 15 seconds tells a sailor that they are near Smalls lighthouse off the Pembrokeshire coast. A white flash every five seconds means that they are further north, approaching the South Bishop in the St George's Channel. Today, in the event of GPS failure, crews can still refer to light lists to plot a course using lighthouses and their distinguishing traits.

From the start the new bodies tasked with provisioning Britain's lighthouses had to accommodate complex engineering systems and devices as well as lightkeepers to maintain the buildings and equipment in perfect working order. In addition to the light itself, a full lighthouse station might include housing for a fog signal, living quarters for the keepers and their families and fuel stores and workshops.

Early lighthouses used whatever materials were available locally: wood, brick, stone, concrete or cast iron. The life of these early lighthouses was predictably short, especially if they were offshore. However, the rebuilding of the Eddystone lighthouse off Plymouth

Four lighthouses have stood on the Eddystone Rocks. From left: Henry Winstanley's pioneering if whimsical wooden structure, which lasted a mere five years; John Rudyard's brick, stone and timber edifice, nearly 50 years; John Smeaton's tower, which outlasted the rock it was built upon and which now gazes out to sea from Plymouth Hoe; and the current tower, designed by James Douglass, as it appeared before a helicopter landing stage was fixed above the lantern.

Sound on England's southern coast by the 18th-century engineer John Smeaton set a new standard in lighthouse design. Previous attempts at placing a warning on these wave-swept rocks, a major hazard to shipping, had been decidedly temporary. Smeaton's version of the Eddystone lighthouse remained in use for over 100 years and the lessons learned were implemented in countless offshore lighthouses constructed over the next two centuries.

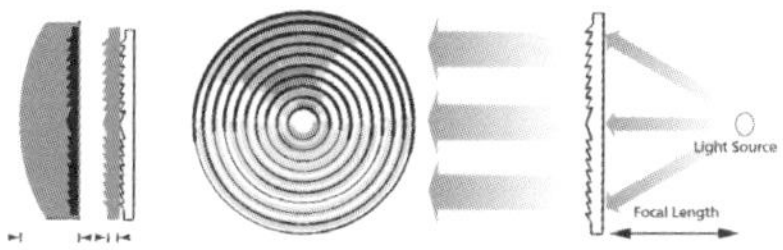

Centre thickness of a Fresnel lens compared with a contemporary convex lens of equivalent power.

Scotland's most celebrated lighthouse engineer, Robert Stevenson, might, under different circumstances, have become a minister. Instead, fate intervened when his widowed mother married Thomas Smith, a mechanic and inventor who had the previous year been appointed engineer to the Northern Lighthouse Board. Stevenson became Smith's ever attentive and ambitious apprentice and was so highly regarded that, at age 19, he was entrusted with the supervision of the new lighthouse on the island of Little Cumbrae on the River Clyde. His thirst for knowledge was unbounded and he took every opportunity to study the subjects that pertained to his profession. From 1797 to 1843 Robert acted as engineer to the Northern Lighthouse Board. During this time, he oversaw the construction of many lighthouses, the most famous of which was the Bell Rock.

Stevenson married his stepsister Jean Smith and they had 13 children, of whom only 5 survived into adulthood. Three of his sons also became lighthouse engineers, and his grandson, Robert Louis, went on to enjoy fame and fortune as a writer of classics such as *Kidnapped* and *Treasure Island*. Between them, the Stevenson dynasty was responsible for designing and building over 80 "major" lighthouses, 112 minor lights and scores of beacons and buoys in Scotland and the Isle of Man during the years from 1811 to 1937.

Maintaining the foghorn at Inchkeith lighthouse on the Firth of Forth. The last foghorn was decommissioned in 2004.

The 18th and 19th centuries saw major advances not only in the construction of the lighthouse tower but also in the design of the lighting mechanism itself. The method of illumination for the ancient lighthouses had generally been a fire fed by coal, charcoal or wood. Vast quantities of fuel – in some cases as much as 400 tons per annum – were needed to keep these beacons burning. This was obviously expensive and extremely cumbersome to deliver and manoeuvre on site. Subsequently, candles and oil lamps magnified by concave mirrors were experimented with as an alternative – with varying results. Smeaton's Eddystone was illuminated by 24 candles, and numerous other lighthouses adopted the technology despite the light being rather feeble at best. The candles were made on site from tallow and each one would last a maximum of three hours.

Getting on and off a rock station in stormy weather was a hair-raising business. Here the keeper is being hoisted ashore by derrick and relief provisions will be unloaded by the same means.

With the invention in 1782 of the Argand lamp, which provided a steady, smokeless flame, the technology of lighthouse illumination took a leap forward. The lamp had a sleeve-shaped candlewick mounted so that air could pass around the wick before being drawn into a central chimney. It first used whale oil, and later colza oil as a cheaper alternative, and became the standard for lighthouses for over a century.

Sometime later, in Ireland, John Richard Wigham was pioneering a system of gas illumination for lighthouses. His new gas "crocus" burner was fitted at the Baily lighthouse on Dublin's Howth Head, and gave an output four times stronger than oil lights of a comparable size and rate of consumption. An improved "composite" design, installed in the Baily light in 1868, was 13 times brighter than the most powerful light of the time. In 1870, the light at Wicklow Head was fitted with Wigham's intermittent-flashing mechanism, which used clockwork to turn the gas supply on and off as required. This mechanism was combined

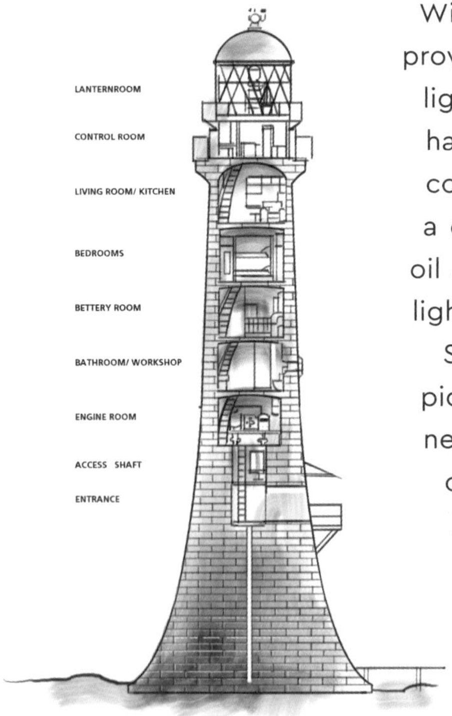

Bell Rock lighthouse, Arbroath, designed and built by Robert Stevenson between 1807 and 1810.

Davaar lighthouse lights up at the mouth of Campbeltown Loch on Scotland's east coast.

with a revolving lens in the Rockabill lighthouse to produce the world's first lighthouse with a group-flashing characteristic.

With its steady illumination, the Argand lamp initiated the development of optical lenses designed to increase and focus the light intensity. The first practicable system used paraboloidal reflectors to concentrate the light into a beam, thereby making it visible from distances never previously achieved. However, the lens was extremely heavy and expensive. While numerous propositions for alternative lenses were proposed, the multi-part Fresnel lens, developed by the French engineer of the same name in 1822, soon became the standard fitting. Fresnel's design allowed for lenses of large aperture and short focal length without the weight of glass that would be required of a conventional lens. It also projected the beam over longer distances. The first Fresnel lens was fitted on the Cordouan lighthouse on the west coast of France and could be seen from a distance of 32km (20 miles). Some beautiful examples of early optical lenses can be seen at the Museum of Scottish Lighthouses in Fraserburgh.

The technology of projecting light across vast distances and of reducing the work of the lightkeepers was in constant flux and new inventions and techniques were continually being developed. While the first electrically illuminated tower appeared in Dungeness in Kent as early as 1862, most lighthouses had to wait until the mid-20th century to convert to electricity; some did not fully make this change until the early 1970s. Al Hamilton, a keeper on Rathlin East lighthouse off the North Antrim coast, related how in July 1969 he prepared the paraffin lamp and wound up the clockwork mechanism to keep the lens rotating while watching Neil Armstrong take his first steps on the moon on the black and white screen of the television in the corner of the service room below the lantern room.

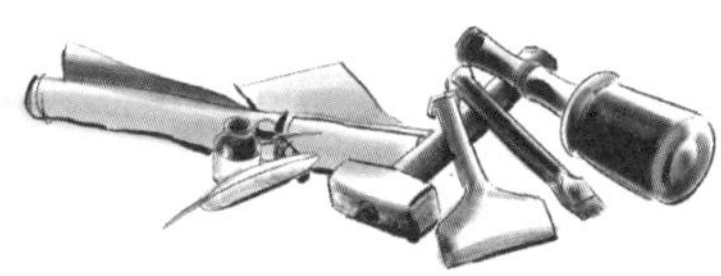

The lantern room, the uppermost space of a lighthouse tower, is where its most important function is performed. Generally, this is a single- or double-storey chamber constructed of metal and glass and mounted on the masonry tower. In the centre is the lens assembly, which can weigh several tons. Traditionally, it was supported on a bath of mercury, which kept the lamp perfectly level and reduced friction so the whole arrangement could be rotated quite easily, though due to safety considerations these are gradually being replaced. Today, the movement is powered by an electric motor, but originally it would have been operated by a clockwork mechanism like that at Rathlin East, using a weight running through a tube at the centre of the lighthouse tower. This was wound up half hourly and regulated the speed at which the optic rotated.

The last iteration of the Lowestoft low lighthouse, built in 1866. The light was discontinued in 1923 when the Stanford Channel became unnavigable and the structure was demolished soon after.

The lantern room is glazed with storm panes and these are set into metal frames. Generally, as in the Lizard lighthouse, the panes are divided diagonally, but less frequently they are set as rectangular panes, such as at Belle Tout above Beachy Head. The diagonal or vertical members of the frames are called astragals and have handles fitted on the exterior side for the keeper to hold while standing on a ladder to clean the outside of the storm panes. These would be accessed from the circular balcony or gallery that surrounds the lantern room.

Above the lantern is the cupola, or dome. This consists of a metal frame, clad, usually, in copper and surmounted by a ball vent. A lightning rod and sometimes a wind vane tops the vent. Below the lantern room is the watch room or service room where the clockworks for rotating the optics are positioned along with various fuel tanks and vents. The service room is also where the keeper would clean the lamp chimneys and prepare the lantern for the coming night.

The Trinity House flagship THV Patricia also carries passengers as she patrols the coasts of England, Wales and the Channel Islands. This unique experience allows guests to observe her crew carrying out statutory duties such as maintaining buoys and lightvessels, attending and refuelling offshore lighthouses and on occasion dealing with emergencies at sea.

Cleaning the lens.

On the offshore or "rock" lighthouses as they were known, there were three keepers on duty sharing six four-hour shifts between them. The early morning watch started at 6 am and ended at 10 am. The second was from 10 am to 2 pm, and so on. The keeper on the early shift prepared the light for the day ahead. This entailed oiling up the mechanism, cleaning the retort and getting the lantern ready for the evening. Breakfast would then be had by all and the relieving keeper would clean up the mess room and get everything ship shape.

Before the advent of electricity, the lens required a lot of care and attention, especially as the paraffin lamp fumes created a build-up of black oily residue on the glass of the optic. This would be cleaned using water and vinegar during the day, with one keeper on the inside and another on the outside. Whoever was on the inside would need to keep moving around as the magnification of the lens was so powerful that on a sunny day it could seriously singe your clothes. After all this shining and polishing, linen curtains would be drawn over the lens to shield it from the sun. Since automation, the lens is allowed to revolve all day long so the sun doesn't have the chance to build up heat in any one spot.

On a rock station, the keepers were kept busy with routine work such as polishing floors, and maintenance duties such as painting and mending. Cooking was generally shared, though the divvying out of such chores might depend on the keepers' abilities. You ordered your groceries from the nearest town or village every fortnight or so. With the dawn of the 20th century, the lighthouse might have a deep freezer powered by paraffin oil or, later, electricity, but shortages of fresh food were always a potential problem on the offshore postings. With bad weather you could be stranded on a rock for weeks before getting eggs, milk or bread, and emergency rations had to take this into consideration.

For keepers on the mainland or sizeable islands, there were kitchen gardens to tend and, in many cases, they kept livestock, generally chickens or goats. Rabbits and, of course, fish also supplemented their diets. Potable water was a vital consideration. Unless the station had a well or large water tank, this was collected off the roofs. Fresh water was a finite commodity and had to be used for washing as well as drinking. The keepers had to be sure it hadn't been contaminated with seawater. To test it they would boil off a small amount in a pan; if there was no tell-tale salt mark left behind, it would generally be regarded as fit to drink.

Up until the 1940s, an offshore posting meant that you were completely cut off from society until the end of your term, when, weather permitting, you could return to the mainland and your family. The arrival of radio telephones after World War II was a boon as it meant that you could now communicate with other lighthouses, with ships and on occasion with your nearest and dearest back on shore.

Advances in technology, especially in the area of remote monitoring in the 1960s and 1970s, made it inevitable that the business of providing navigational aids would increasingly be conducted in unmanned stations. The first part of the lighthouse estate to be automated were the lightships that primarily dotted the east and southeast coasts in locations where the water was either too deep to build a lighthouse or where the ground was unsuitable, such as the Goodwin Sands off the Deal coast.

The first modern lightship was moored on the Nore sandbank in the mouth of the Thames in 1732. By 1819 there were nine lightvessels around Britain's coast. This shows the Nore lightship, circa 1870.

The first lightship dates back as far as 1734 when a vessel called the Nore was placed near the mouth of the Thames. This was a business venture between a former barber, Robert Hamblin, and a small-time venture capitalist called David Avery. Their genius idea was to moor an out of commission ship, probably a Dutch galliot, with a prominent light in it to act as a navigational aid and then collect fees from passing ships. Unfortunately for the pair, they were opposed by Trinity House and ultimately their licence was revoked. They did at least gain financial compensation for the discontinuation of their pioneering scheme and the small consolation that their innovation would go on to save countless lives.

Held in position using 3-ton mushroom anchors, the ships displayed a light in a tall mast or tower. They usually also had a day marker, typically a large painted globe mounted on a rear mast. Life for the crew was uncomfortable and often dangerous; there were numerous instances of lightships being sunk in fog by unwitting shipping.

By the 1980s most lightships along Britain's coast were being converted into Automatic Light Floats (ALFs), and there currently remain about eight of these around the coast, all operated by Trinity House, all unmanned and powered by solar energy. The first lights were candles, or lamps that burned sperm whale oil. Occasionally, the early ships were fitted with sails in case they broke adrift, but lightvessels are not designed for travel and the later craft generally had no means of propulsion. By the early 1900s most lightships had a crew of 11. This consisted of a master and six ratings on board, and a master and three ratings ashore. The masters were changed every month, while the rest of the crew served a month afloat followed by two weeks of shore leave. The crews were qualified seamen who had normally served at least two years on deck. When a man started, he would serve as a general seaman before being promoted to Fog Signal Driver and Lamplighter. After 15 to 20 years of service, he could become a master.

The LANBY or Large Automatic Navigation BuoY was first used in the United States and adapted for use in British waters in the early 1970s.

The cost of running and repairing even unmanned lightships was substantial, and by the late 1960s a potential replacement was being tested on the seas. The LANBY or Large Automatic Navigation Buoy was intended to perform the same function as a lightship but at a tenth of the cost. Adapted for use in British waters in the early 1970s, they consisted of a circular hull with a central light to provide all-round visibility, along with a foghorn and various antennae and beacons. The navigation buoy was intended to be monitored remotely and to run for extended periods without repair. However, they proved unreliable in rough seas and were difficult for staff to maintain as, even in a light swell, they would rotate on one axis while pitching on another, making concentrating (and avoiding severe seasickness) almost impossible. The LANBY was eventually regarded as unsuitable for British waters and today the main aid to navigation employed by Trinity House and the Northern Lighthouses Board is the smaller Type A buoy. Fitted with a tail tube to keep them stable in the water, the buoys are held on the seabed by cast-iron sinkers weighing 3–5 tons. These buoys can be either lighted or unlighted, have a focal height in excess of 5m (16ft) and are fitted with a racon (radar beacon) and Automatic Identification System (AIS). Even though they stand 15m (49ft) high and can weigh 10 tons, they come in at a fraction of the size of their big brother.

Familiar to anyone who as a kid was a fan of Airfix model kits, the South Goodwin lightship was used to mark the Goodwin Sands, a 16km (10-mile) long shifting sandbank located off the easternmost tip of the Kent coast.

There are currently over 300 lighthouses dotted around the shores of Great Britain and its island dependencies. They vary in size from the colossus that is Skerryvore to the diminutive Berry Head – Britain's shortest at 5m (16ft) tall – and along the way take in more modest harbour and breakwater lights. Their architecture varies considerably, due mainly to the particular demands of their location rather than to any design trends of the day. Some sought to be contemporary, pioneering structural marvels, while others were happy to replicate the building styles of previous generations. All have sought to protect seafarers no matter their nationality or origin. Indeed, in times of war, lighthouses are neutral. As an island nation, Britain has always striven to make its coastline as safe as possible for the shipping plying its waters. The proliferation of lights that dot these islands' Atlantic shores, the Irish Sea and the English Channel, alongside the eastern ones that welcome shipping returning across the North Sea, bears testimony to this concern for safe passage into and out of European waters and further afield.

The collection of lighthouses contained within this book was never intended to be comprehensive. Five volumes would hardly contain the histories of the scores of lighthouses both operational and retired to be found on these shores. Instead, the primary criteria for inclusion were: "Are the lighthouse and the landscape visually engaging?" and "Does it have an interesting tale to tell?"

Choosing where to start our journey has been a difficult decision. Because of where I grew up, I have a fondness for that diverse environment of both human and ornithological life that you find in an estuary, and so I found it hard to resist the broad expanse of the Humber at Spurn Point. That it has now become a tidal island only adds to its attraction. This deactivated but restored lighthouse points to an optimistic future for these treasures of our maritime heritage. Today the 39m (128ft) of steps is regularly climbed by families, bird-watchers and day trippers; in fact, everyone bar lightkeepers. The building's future, inasmuch as coastal erosion will allow, is assured, and, although its beam no longer sweeps across the ebb and flow of the Humber, Spurn Point lighthouse remains a steadfast reminder of the central role these structures have played in our seafaring history.

Despite my obvious partiality for this stretch of silt, sand and marram grass, there is one outstanding edifice in the story of British lighthouses that simply cannot be ignored. In the world of pharology, the various incarnations of the Eddystone lighthouse stand out for the bravery, ingenuity and sheer daring of their pioneering designers and builders. To contemplate building on an often submerged reef 14km (9 miles) offshore takes guts and imagination. To do so using only hand tools after rowing the distance out from shore with a window of only a few short hours before the tides and swells made continuing impossible, is unimaginable. For observers in the 18th century, it must have seemed as unlikely as a man landing on the moon. If the lighthouse at Alexandria was one of the wonders of the ancient world, then the Eddystone is the wonder of the modern pharological world.

So, the start point is set. Onward to Plymouth Hoe.

I hope you enjoy the journey. It's been quite the adventure.

TERMS AND ABBREVIATIONS USED IN THE BOOK

ELEVATION: the height above high water of the light. Given in metres.

CHARACTER: the pattern of flashes distinct to that lighthouse plus the colour of the light.

PATTERN:
FL – flashing
GR FL – group flashing
OC – Oculating (time of light intervals are longer than those of dark)
Q – quick flashing
ISO – Isophase (intervals of light and dark are the same).

COLOURS:
W – white
R – red
G – green

TIME:
S – seconds

As an example: Fl W 10s means flashing white once every ten seconds.

CATOPTRIC: refers to the reflection of light. Mirrors are used to focus and magnify the lighthouse beam.

CATADIOPTRIC LENS: a lens that uses both a lens (dioptrics) and curved mirrors (catoptrics) to combine refraction and reflection in the focusing process.

DIOPTRIC: refers to the refraction of light. Where the lens is convex, it is referred to as a dioptric lens.

RACON: a radar transmitter that by providing a distinctive mark on a ship's radar screen, indicates distance as well as bearing.

LEADING LIGHTS: a pair of lights separated by a distance and that indicate safe passage for vessels navigating a shallow or dangerous channel. When viewed from the vessel, the lights should align, signalling that the right approach to enter the channel is being taken.

BUOYS: TYPES AND USES

Travelling around the coast or in and out of harbours, you will see a wide variety of buoys floating in the water. Their forms and colours are varied and diverse and from a distance they can look quite small. When you get up close, however, or see them brought ashore for repair, you can see just how big they actually are. Some are as tall as a house. Shown above are the main types of buoys you'll encounter along the British coast. Traditionally, conical buoys ('nuns'), with or without a painted top, always referred to starboard in a channel, while 'can' buoys, with a flat top, were port-hand buoys. Staffs and globes were used on starboard buoys, while staffs and cages were used on port-hand buoys. The silhouette of a buoy is important as the colour may not be apparent at a distance.

On the cardinal buoys above, the two cones at the top indicate what direction it advises. Similarly, triangles, crosses and Xs help identify the marker when outlined against the horizon. At night, each buoy type has a distinctive light pattern which helps sailors identify the marker.

THE LIGHTHOUSES

EDDYSTONE
LIGHTHOUSE
EDDYSTONE ROCKS
DEVON

EDDYSTONE

LOCATION: 50°11′02″N, 4°16′05″W
OS GRID: N/A
ELEVATION: 41m (135ft)
CHARACTER: Fl (2) 10s
RANGE: 32km (20 miles)

Eddystone lighthouse perches on the Eddystone Rocks, about 14km (9 miles) south of Cornwall's Rame Head, slap bang in the middle of the English Channel's shipping lanes. Although Eddystone is nearer to Cornwall, this reef of igneous rock falls under the jurisdiction of Devon.

Dating from 1882, the present tower is the fourth to protect these waters. The first lighthouse on Eddystone Rocks, and the first offshore lighthouse in the world, was an octagonal wooden structure built almost two centuries earlier by Henry Winstanley, an engineer, artist and inventor who latterly became a merchant. Having lost two ships on the rocks, he undertook to build where no man had attempted before. The rocks are submerged at high spring tides and, even today, landing on them, especially in the predominant swells that wash the reef, is not for the fainthearted.

Construction started in earnest in 1696. However, at this time Britain and France were at war and one foggy afternoon a French privateer loomed out of the mist, took Winstanley and his crew prisoner, and destroyed the work down to its foundations. When he heard of the seizure, the French king, Louis XIV, ordered Winstanley's release with the words 'France is at war with England, not with humanity.' The captain of the privateer was rewarded with new accommodation at the Bastille, and the tower was completed in 1698.

While its foundations were embedded in solid stone, Winstanley's edifice was in other respects a curious affair. This wooden structure over-embellished with weathervanes, carved balustrades and balconies looked more like a fairground attraction or a Disney castle than a lighthouse designed to withstand waves, tides and storms. Regrettably for Winstanley, despite no ships being lost during its lifespan, the structure ultimately proved inadequate. Determined to show that his lighthouse was sturdy enough to cope with the worst that nature could throw at it, Winstanley expressed a desire to be in the tower during "the greatest storm there ever was". He got his wish. While he was visiting the Eddystone on the night of 27 November 1703, the lighthouse was entirely destroyed during a tempest so severe that Daniel Defoe wrote a whole book about it. No trace was ever found of Winstanley, or of the five men with him.

The second lighthouse on the rock was a more robust affair. Designed by John Rudyard and completed in 1709, it consisted of a brick and concrete core pinned to the rock with 36 iron spikes. This central structure was skinned in wood and covered in pitch, much like the hull of a ship. Rudyard's structure lasted for 50 years, which, given its location and the technology of the day, was no mean feat. Its eventual undoing was by an internal fire rather than the action of the waves.

The third tower was the real game-changer and the reason Eddystone is probably the most famous lighthouse in the world apart from the Statue of Liberty (yes, it's officially a lighthouse!). John Smeaton's revolutionary design mimicked the shape of an oak trunk. The base flared out in a curve, which helped to break up the energy of the waves crashing onto the structure. Granite blocks were joined together using a system of dovetail joints, while below the waterline Smeaton pioneered a new type of concrete that cured when it was immersed in brine. His final innovation was to make the structure as weighty as possible, which ensured it was robust enough to stand up to the fiercest storms. First lit in October 1759, the lighthouse was finally decommissioned in 1877 when erosion of the rocks it was built on caused it to shake when hit by large waves. However, it remained in use until its replacement was completed in 1882.

The current structure was designed by James Douglass. Complete new foundations had to be painstakingly prepared in the four-hour windows between ebb and flood tide. Bit by bit the tower rose and within three years the new 49m (161ft) tower was complete. First lit in 1882, it was automated in 1982, two years after a helipad was constructed on Eddystone.

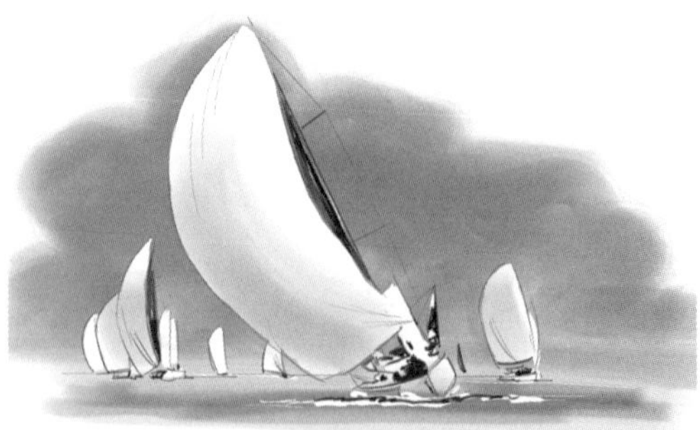

The Eddystone charity sailing pursuit takes place each summer from Plymouth Sound to the lighthouse and back.

Winstanley's original tower stood for five years before being washed from the rocks.

SMEATON
TOWER
PLYMOUTH HOE
DEVON

SMEATON TOWER

LOCATION: 50°21′52″N, 4°08′31″W
OS GRID: SX477537
DEACTIVATED: 1882

John Smeaton's Eddystone lighthouse was disassembled and rebuilt on Plymouth Hoe as a memorial, although the foundations and stub of the tower, which were too difficult to dismantle, remain on the Eddystone near to the more solid foundations of the current lighthouse.

Now standing 22m (72ft) high, Smeaton Tower is open to visitors. You can climb the 93 steps, including the final stepladder to the lantern room, and take in fantastic views of Plymouth Sound and the city.

A much-loved centrepiece on Plymouth Hoe, Smeaton Tower has become one of the southwest's best-known landmarks.

Statue of Walter Raleigh with the Plymouth Hoe war memorial in the background.

The Mayflower Steps, from which the Pilgrims are believed to have boarded the Mayflower on 6 September 1620 to journey across the Atlantic Ocean and settle in North America.

LIZARD

LOCATION: 49°57′37″N, 5°12′8″W
OS GRID: SW704116
ELEVATION: 70m (230ft)
CHARACTER: Fl 3s
RANGE: 48km (30 miles)

The area around the Lizard peninsula has an unenviable reputation for strong winds and dangerous currents. Lurking below the waves are the Manacles, an escarpment of razor-sharp rocks lying in wait for any wayward vessel or ship's master unfamiliar with the coast and shoreline. As well as the unwitting and the incautious, this seabed is also believed to have claimed numerous victims of the "wreckers" who operated along this stretch of the south coast. Opportunists with a reputation for wilfully luring ships to their doom for plunder's sake, the wreckers were probably far less prolific than is often supposed. Their legend was helped along by the fact that local houses often featured a mishmash of salvaged ship parts and the tendency of the chattering classes to portray their Cornish cousins as wild and lawless.

Lizard lighthouse stands at the southernmost point of mainland Britain.

By the end of the 16th century, the need for some marker for shipping was apparent and Sir John Killigrew, who himself was descended from several generations of alleged pirates, managed to obtain a patent to build a lighthouse on the peninsula. As you can imagine, suspicion was rife and there was considerable opposition to the project, especially from the newly established Trinity House, which had been charged by Henry VIII with managing England's lighthouses. Sir John endured, however, and despite the expense and difficulty of building the tower, it was ready by Christmas 1619. Theoretically, running a lighthouse could make you very rich, but collecting fees from ship owners was a task in itself. Despite James I intervening and slapping a halfpenny charge per ton on passing vessels, Sir John soon ran out of money and patience; the fires were

LIZARD
LIGHTHOUSE
LIZARD POINT
CORNWALL

extinguished and the tower eventually demolished. Darkness ensued.

Lizard Point remained in darkness until over a century later when Thomas Fonnereau was successful in obtaining a patent. By August 1752 he had completed the bones of the present structure with a tower at each end of the compound and a small cottage in between. Here, like a pasha, the superintendent reclined on his couch, glancing left and right to make sure his subordinates were stoking the coal fires sufficiently. If either flame dimmed, he simply took out his cow's horn and bellowed into it and order was restored. No doubt, Turkish delights were also taken, but this is not recorded. By 1812, the coal fires had been replaced by oil lamps and just over 50 years later electric arc lights lit up the night sky "with the brightness of a summer's day", according to one local reporter.

The Lizard lifeboat station lies at the foot of a 45m (148ft) cliff near Church Cove.

The next major development occurred in 1903 when a revolving first-order optic was fitted to the eastern tower, making its western sister redundant. The new light was so bright that it could be seen over the horizon and local fishermen were worried that it would scare away the schools of pilchard!

ST ANTHONY

LOCATION: 50°08′28″N, 5°00′57″W
OS GRID: SW846311
ELEVATION: 22m (72ft)
CHARACTER: Iso WR 15s
RANGE: 30km (19 miles)

One of Cornwall's best-known lighthouses, thanks to its appearance during the credits of the 1980s children's TV show *Fraggle Rock*, St Anthony lighthouse guards the eastern side of the entrance to Falmouth harbour and the Carrick Roads, guiding vessels clear of the Manacles (see page 40) on its southern approaches and the Black Rock at the centre of the channel. Boasting the deepest natural harbour in Europe and being positioned close to the English Channel, Falmouth has long been regarded as a strategically important refuge and point of departure.

The local Killigrew family, whom we previously met at Lizard Point, saw to it that a red flag flew from an elm tree near shore to act as a daymark and an indicator of wind direction. At night the Killigrews kept a beacon burning as a signal for their own vessels, but it was a measure that was also appreciated by other boatmen navigating the harbour. However, with the outbreak of the Anglo-French War in 1778, these aids were temporarily removed for fear of offering assistance to an invading fleet.

By December 1830, the ship owners of Falmouth were petitioning for a lighthouse to be built at St Anthony, which in conjunction with Lizard Point would ensure a safe passage for shipborne trade. A design was prepared by Trinity House's consultant engineer James Walker and construction started in 1834. As land access to the site was so difficult, the granite was cut and shaped in Penzance and then transported to St Anthony by boat.

Walker's design consisted of a 19m (62ft) white octagonal tower built into the rock just 3m (10ft) above sea level with a raised area at the back for the keeper's cottage.

Great Molunan and Little Molunan beaches near the lighthouse.

St ANTHONY
LIGHTHOUSE
St ANTHONY HEAD
CORNWALL

Light was provided by eight Argand lamps and reflectors mounted on a revolving frame driven by a set of weights that descended a 12m (40ft) deep shaft. In 1865, an additional lamp and reflector were installed in the living room of the principal keeper, which shone a fixed beam through a square window in the direction of the Manacles. This light was later moved to a shed outside the lighthouse.

In the early 20th century, the lighthouse was modernized. A fixed optic and a clockwork occulting mechanism changed the pattern so that a red sector was now added to the main lamp to warn shipping of the Manacles, and the subsidiary light that had fulfilled this role was discontinued.

Electricity came to the lighthouse in 1954, at which time an experimental fog signal that sounded from 35 Tannoy emitters was tested. It was deemed a success and installed at more than a dozen other stations. The fog bell, which had hung from the gallery at the front of the tower, was decommissioned and donated to the nearby Penwerris church. However, there were no funds to build a bell tower, so, after many years of sitting on the church front lawn, the bell was taken away to be melted down.

NEWLYN

LOCATION: 50°06′11″N, 5°32′34″W
OS GRID: SW467285
ELEVATION: 10m (33ft)
CHARACTER: Fl 5s
RANGE: 14km (9 miles)

Enjoying natural protection thanks to an area of calm water in Mount's Bay called the Gwavas Lake, Newlyn has been known as a fishing port since at least the 13th century. At that time it was recorded as Nulyn or Lulyn, deriving from the Cornish term meaning "a pool for boats".

The town's fate is interlinked with the sea, for good or bad. Newlyn was one of four neighbouring Cornish settlements (the others being Penzance, Mousehole and Paul) that succumbed to the only successful major landing on English soil by the Spanish during the Anglo-Spanish War of 1585–1604. Ever since the Prayer Book Rebellion, which took place in Devon and Cornwall in 1549, the Spanish had hoped that many Cornish people might return to the Catholic faith. On 2 August 1593, a force of 400 Spanish men sailed into Mount's Bay and, in the manner of all emancipating armies, immediately opened fire on the inhabitants, burning churches and putting villagers to the sword. Within two days, they had scarpered, promising to return and build a church on the Western Hill outside Penzance, but that never happened.

In 1620, another religiously-inspired group would pass through the port when the Pilgrims aboard the *Mayflower* made their last stop at Newlyn to pick up supplies before setting course to the New World.

By the end of the 17th century, Newlyn's fleet of fishing barques had outgrown the cramped anchorage. However, those with the means to advance the fortunes of the port seemed reluctant to invest despite the obvious potential and it was another two centuries before the harbour was expanded. The 180m (600ft) long south pier was completed in 1884 and the lighthouse built at the end was first exhibited in

Old style hand-woven lobster pots on Newlyn quay.

NEWLYN
LIGHTHOUSE
NEWLYN PIER
CORNWALL

March 1887. The lantern displayed a quick-flashing white light, visible for 11km (7 miles). However, in January 1896, tragedy struck when a fire broke out within the lighthouse. The keeper, William Maddern, tried to drain the oil supply to starve the fire but the pipes melted and he was splashed with oil, suffering terrible burns as a result.

In 1914, the south pier was extended by 30m (100ft) and a new circular cast-iron lighthouse was built, coming into operation on 29 April 1915. A small building was added next to the lighthouse tower at the same time. This houses the Ordnance Survey's Newlyn Tidal Observatory, from which mainland Great Britain's mean sea level was gauged based on hourly measurements from 1915 to 1921. This datum is the starting point for every height measurement on Ordnance Survey maps.

The Fishermen's Rest on Newlyn's old quay. The building served as a sanctuary for fishermen to chat, play cards and drink tea, regardless of their faith, while also hosting prayer meetings and services for the fisherfolk of Newlyn.

TATER DU

LOCATION: 50°03′08″N, 5°34′39″W
OS GRID: SW440230
ELEVATION: 34m (112ft)
CHARACTER: Fl (3) 15s
RANGE: 37km (23 miles)

The Cornish coast, it is estimated, has ensnared at least 6,000 shipwrecks over the last 800 years, more than any other comparable coastline in the British Isles. The area around Tater Du is no exception. Although the Runnelstone Rocks have been signalled by a buoy and Gwennap Head marked by beacons since the 18th century, it took a more recent tragedy to finally galvanize support for a lighthouse on this part of the coast. In 1963, the Spanish trading ship *Juan Ferrer* floundered off Boscawen Point and sank with the loss of 11 lives. The Newlyn and Mousehole Fishermen's Association petitioned Trinity House to locate a lighthouse on the Tater Du headland and it was decided that a general navigational light, rather than a small local light, was required. Construction commenced in June 1964 to a design by Michael H Crisp. As well as a rotating lamp, Crisp's design also incorporates 72 fog signal speakers set directly in the wall of the lighthouse tower. The lighthouse was officially opened by the Duke of Gloucester on 7 July 1965.

Lamorna Cove just up the coast from Tater Du.

The name Tater Du doesn't refer to potatoes, but rather comes from the Cornish *torthel du*, meaning "black loaf", and refers to the rounded greenstone cliffs that are unlike the granite cliffs to be found elsewhere on this part of the coast. The area is rich in history and the walk to the lighthouse from Lamorna Cove along the South West Coast Path is very pleasant (in good weather) and not too difficult. Nearby stands the Merry Maidens

TATER DU
LIGHTHOUSE
St BURYAN
CORNWALL

Neolithic stone circle, where legend tells us that 19 maidens were turned to stone for the misdeed of dancing on a Sunday. Two fields away is a pair of ancient megaliths called the Pipers, which represent two fleeing musicians who provided the music for this debauchery.

A short distance from the lighthouse is the famous Logan Rock at Treen. The precariously balanced boulder weighs about 90 tons and legend had it that no force or lever could dislodge it. This proved too much of a temptation for Lieutenant Hugh Goldsmith and a dozen of his crew back in 1824 when his ship, the HMS *Nimble*, was docked nearby. The group used bars, levers and brute force to rock the huge boulder from its perch. Needless to say, the locals were not amused and the Admiralty ordered the rock be put back. It took more than 60 men and a block and tackle to restore the rock to its original position.

Scuba divers entering the water at Lamorna Cove. The area around Tater Du is a popular diving spot.

WOLF ROCK
LIGHTHOUSE
LAND'S END
CORNWALL

WOLF ROCK

LOCATION: 49°55'34"N, 5°45'26"W
OS GRID: N/A
ELEVATION: 34m (112ft)
CHARACTER: Fl 15s
RANGE: 30km (19 miles)

Lying 15km (9 miles) off the most southwesterly point of Great Britain, halfway between the Lizard and the Isles of Scilly, is Wolf Rock. It takes its name from the howling sound the wind makes as it whistles through the fissures of the phonolitic lava that makes up this ridgeback shelf and which is particular to this part of the Cornish coast.

Behind the posing seal you can see the enormous conical iron beacon which took five years to build.

Attempts to build a navigational aid on Wolf Rock have a long history. The rock was surveyed in 1791 by Lieutenant Henry Smith, the builder of the Longships lighthouse (see page 55), who concluded that it was beyond his or anyone's capability to build on such a small reef. He did erect a 6m (20ft) mast with a model of a wolf on it as a daymark, but this was soon washed away by the tides.

From 1836 to 1840, James Walker supervised the construction of another daymark, a cone-shaped beacon made of iron plates and filled with concrete rubble. Though it has survived the pounding of the waves to this day, it is almost invisible out in the wild ocean. The fact that it took four years to transport and erect even this simple structure (it was recorded that only 300 workable hours were available during the whole of the construction period) gave some idea of the difficulties that would face anyone foolhardy enough to consider building a more substantial edifice.

However, in 1861 Walker himself returned to take up this challenge. His design for a 36m (118ft) tower was inspired by John Smeaton's Eddystone lighthouse (see page 35), which had recently celebrated its centenary. The granite blocks were cut and shaped in Penzance and shipped out to the rock. Progress was painfully slow. The hours available to work on this isolated, wave-lashed reef were few and it is hard to imagine a more perilous building site.

James Walker was now 80 years old. His enthusiasm was undiminished, but supervising such a Herculean task must have put a great strain on him. In 1862, he succumbed to a heart attack and James Douglass stepped into his role as chief engineer. These were obviously men of iron will. Douglass had nearly drowned when, on a visit to the site, he had been thrown from his boat in rough seas, but now he was determined to see the project to completion.

On 1 January 1870, Wolf Rock lighthouse was illuminated for the first time. It had taken eight long years to complete and swallowed four and a half thousand tons of granite. To begin with, there was no landing stage on the rock and so one of the workmen had been forced to dive in and swim to shore to secure the boat. Yet despite all the hazards, the tower now stood proud and tall, its glittering beam visible 30km (19 miles) away.

In 1972, the lighthouse became the first to be fitted with a helicopter pad, which became the template for others around the coast, and in 1988 the station was finally automated.

The Wolf Rock helideck was trialled at Trinity House's Blackwall depot before being installed at the lighthouse.

LONGSHIPS

LOCATION: 50°06'11"N, 5°32'34"W
OS GRID: N/A
ELEVATION: 35m (115ft)
CHARACTER: Fl (2) WR 10s
RANGE: 28km (17 miles)

The seas surrounding Cornwall's most westerly point, Land's End, have a perilous reputation when the weather turns sour. Along this coastline, the swells and currents merge and, in the teeth of a storm, the sea can resemble a boiling cauldron with waves battering the granite cliffs relentlessly. Combine this with a headland that is encircled by submerged reefs and it's little wonder that countless ships have foundered on this stretch of coast down through the ages.

In 1700, Trinity House issued a lease to Lieutenant Henry Smith to survey and build a lighthouse on either the Longships islets or Wolf Rock. With the increase in shipping on the south coast, the issue had become urgent. Smith sailed out to survey Wolf Rock but was dismayed by what he regarded as the impossibility of building on the wave-washed stone. He instead recommended the Longships and got to work on putting up several beacons. These were soon swept away, and Smith was on the verge of calling it a day and surrendering the lease when he commissioned Samuel Wyatt, an architect with experience of working with Trinity House, to look at the project. Wyatt chose Carn Bras, the largest of the Longships rocks, as the site on which to build a tower. Completed in 1795, the lighthouse consisted of a tapered circular tower of three storeys, with a copper-clad wooden lantern room at top which utilized 18 parabolic metal reflectors and Argand lamps projecting an estimated 23km (14 miles) out to sea.

At this stage, the hapless Lieutenant Smith was declared incapable of managing the concern and found himself in debtor's jail. Trinity House took over the manning of the lighthouse, but remitted the profits

Enys Dodnan sea arch, visible after walking just a short distance from the Land's End car park. Beyond it in the distance lies the Longships lighthouse.

LONGSHIPS
LIGHTHOUSE
CARN BRAS, LAND'S END
CORNWALL

due Smith to his family through the courts before buying out the lease almost 40 years later for the incredible sum of £40,676.

With the lighthouse in place, there was a steep decline in fatalities along that stretch of the coast. However, the shortcomings of this squat tower would soon become apparent. During particularly violent storms, waves would crash over the lighthouse, obscuring the light. In fact, the opaque veil of foam would often cause the fixed beam to look like an occulting flash, which would mislead vessels into believing they had strayed from their course and were approaching a different lighthouse; and they would subsequently alter direction, with disastrous consequences.

In 1869, Trinity House commissioned William Douglass, at that time putting the finishing touches to Wolf Rock, to design and build a new tower for the Longships. This new lighthouse would place the lantern almost 35m (115ft) above high water. Because they were building 12m (40ft) above the tide, work proceeded rapidly and by December 1873 a new light was shining from the tower.

The ever-popular Land's End sign.

The lighthouse can be seen clearly from the keepers' cottages at Sennen Cove on the mainland. However, although only a short distance away, landing at the station could be fraught with danger due to the swells and swirling currents that surge around the Longships rocks. One way the keepers kept in touch with their families was by semaphore. A broad white border was painted around the entrance door to the tower and the keeper would stand within this frame and signal to his loved ones on shore in a 19th-century version of texting.

Despite being 35m (115ft) above high water, the tower is only 20m (66ft) tall, so living conditions in the lighthouse were always cramped. This wasn't helped by the damp, especially during winter storms when the tower was battered relentlessly by waves and the shutters had to be kept closed, further exaggerating the sense of isolation and claustrophobia. With the arrival of a helideck in the 1970s, the keepers were at least no longer reliant on calm weather for shift relief, but this period of easy access would soon be over for the keepers as automation loomed. By 1988, the last of the keepers had retired and the lighthouse is now remotely monitored from Trinity House Control Centre in Harwich, Essex.

BISHOP ROCK

LOCATION: 49°52′22″N, 6°26′44″W
OS GRID: SV807064
ELEVATION: 44m (144ft)
CHARACTER: Fl (2) 15s
RANGE: 37km (23 miles)

A helicopter approaches the lantern-top landing pad with maintenance crew aboard.

The rocks and reefs around the Isles of Scilly were justly feared for the ferocious toll they took on shipping in centuries past. The islands notoriously have one of the highest concentrations of shipwrecks anywhere in the world – over 900 in total have been recorded. In 1707, one of the most tragic disasters in maritime history saw four naval warships founder in atrocious weather with the loss of some 2,000 lives.

At that time, the islands were marked by the sole lighthouse at St Agnes, and because of topography, the light did not give adequate warning to vessels approaching from the west. The Elder Brethren of Trinity House (as they were still referred to then) resolved to build a lighthouse on the most westerly of the aquatic hazards, the Bishop Rock.

James Walker was charged with the task and his preference was to build a cast-iron screw-pile construction, which he was confident would offer minimal resistance to surf and waves and would therefore remain secure on the rocks. Days before the lantern was to be fitted to the structure, a storm tore two years of work straight off the reef and into the inky waves. Undeterred, but surely dismayed, Walker now considered the altogether more difficult task of building a granite tower on a tiny island in the middle of the ocean.

The Bishop Rock rises sheer from the ocean from a depth of 45m (148ft) and is exposed to the power of the Atlantic and its storms. Whatever was built on that rock would need to be extremely strong. As soon as the spring weather and the tides permitted, work on the new tower got underway. Time would be short on the rock, so the workmen were billeted on nearby Rosevear Island, barely big enough to accommodate two huts – the gable ends of the houses remain to this day, along with the tiny slip the men built into the rocks.

The base of the new tower was to be 10m (33ft) in diameter. First the rock was hewn to accommodate the massive granite blocks, each dovetailed to its neighbour to

BISHOP ROCK
LIGHTHOUSE
MEN EPSKOP
ISLES OF SCILLY

create an immovable solid base, and slowly the granite walls rose, but the difficulty of working on such an exposed site meant that the lighthouse took seven years to build. By 1 September 1858, the 35m (115ft) tower was complete.

Bit by bit, doubts about the tower started to emerge. In one notable storm, waves lashed the side of the lighthouse and ripped the 250kg (550lb) fog bell loose from its fastenings on the gallery. The keepers reported concerns about the steadiness of the tower in storms and the condition of the foundations. In 1881, the civil engineer and lighthouse designer James Douglass inspected the building and recommended strengthening the tower and increasing its height to 47m (154ft). The plan was essentially to build a new tower around the old one, which was duly constructed between 1883 and 1887. By the time it was finished, it had swallowed 5700 tons of granite. Just the task of bringing all that stone by boat from shore in every sort of weather is heroic!

The flashing white light, visible for 39km (24 miles), was first illuminated in October 1887. Electrification arrived in 1973 and two years later a helipad was added to the roof.

When Bishop Rock lighthouse was converted to automatic operation in 1991, the last keepers left the lighthouse the following year, on 21 December 1992. The fog signal was discontinued on 13 June 2007. Today, the lighthouse is controlled from Trinity House's Planning Centre in Harwich, Essex.

Basking in the sun
at Bishop Rock.

PENINNIS

LOCATION: 49°54′14″N, 6°18′13″W
OS GRID: SV911093
ELEVATION: 36m (118ft)
CHARACTER: Fl 20s
RANGE: 17km (11 miles)

Peninnis lighthouse is located on the boulder-strewn outer headland of Peninnis Head, the most southerly point of St Mary's, the largest of the Isles of Scilly. It was built to replace the St Agnes light and helps vessels enter Hugh Town harbour via St Mary's Sound. Coming into service in 1911, the tower is a circular, 14m (45ft) tall metal structure consisting of a black steel open-lattice foundation, white gallery and black domed top.

The station has never been manned, nor was that ever the intention, being one of the first gas-powered lighthouses to use a sun valve to control the flow of acetylene. The valve uses the heat of the sun to minutely expand a rod, cutting off the supply of acetylene to the lamp. As the rod cools down in the evening, the supply is resumed and the light ignites again. The sun valve was invented by the Swedish engineer Gustaf Dalén, who won the Nobel Prize in Physics for his device in 1912. Nobody believed it would work . . . until it did!

Dalén will be a familiar to many of us for another of his inventions, one that sits at the heart of the idealized British country kitchen: the Aga cooker. Although Dalén developed his invention in his own kitchen at Villa Ekbacken at Lidingö, he never got to see his most famous appliance in action, having been blinded a decade earlier while carrying out experiments with acetylene for the sun lamp. We can be thankful for this most persistent of inventors. The sun lamp enabled lighthouses to operate independently in locations that previously couldn't have been countenanced and

The St Mary's lifeboat station.

PENINNIS
LIGHTHOUSE
PENINNIS HEAD
ISLES OF SCILLY

contributed considerably to the safety of mariners around the coast.

Peninnis station was converted to electricity in 1992 and in recent years the light has been converted to LED illumination.

On a spring or summer's day, the walk around the headland with its tors and cliffs is recommended; if you're lucky you might spot some dolphins close to shore. The Manx shearwater is also a common sight, and in April the puffin makes a return to the island.

Peninnis Head and other nearby headlands are rich in wild plants such as sorrel, thrift, red fescue and early meadow grass, but these have been encroached upon by gorse and bracken due to a lack of grazing animals. The Wildlife Trust has now introduced Ruby Red Devon cattle to graze the area in spring and autumn so that coarse grasses are kept in check and native wildflowers have room to seed and germinate.

Rock formation at Peninnis Head.

ROUND ISLAND
LIGHTHOUSE
ROUND ISLAND
ISLES OF SCILLY

ROUND ISLAND

LOCATION: 49°58'45"N, 6°19'23"W
OS GRID: SV902177
ELEVATION: 55m (180ft)
CHARACTER: Fl 10s
RANGE: 33km (21 miles)

At the time that Round Island was being considered for a lighthouse by Trinity House in the late 19th century, the Isles of Scilly were served by only two lighthouses. St Agnes guided vessels on the southern approach, while Bishop Rock did the same to the west. The unlit northern limits were hazardous, especially in fog, and accordingly William Douglass was tasked with building the lighthouse on Round Island, a small granite islet 10km (6 miles) northeast of Bishop Rock and 4km (2.5 miles) north of St Mary's.

Round Island is a considerable size, but it rises 40m (130ft) above sea level, with the ground falling steeply away on all sides, and the only access for Douglass's team was up a flight of steps cut out of the rock. This made getting materials to the site quite the challenge. Supplies were shipped out and then taken up the rock face using an aerial hoist, a 120m (394ft) zip line of sorts strung between Round Island and an adjacent, lower-lying islet.

Regrettably, during the building process a cairn, or burial chamber, dating back to the Bronze Age was destroyed. At that time, 5,000 years ago, sea levels were lower and Round Island would probably have been a peninsula accessible by land from one of the larger islands.

When the tower was completed in 1887, it had a red light flashing at intervals of 30 seconds. Because the colour red projects less robustly than white, the light had to be intensified by means of a huge hyperradial lens similar to that installed at Bishop Rock the year before. This optic was replaced in 1967, and once again when the lighthouse was automated in 1987. In 1912, the lighthouse was provided with a fog siren in the form of two large trumpets mounted

The 12m (40ft) high St Martin's daymark is the earliest surviving beacon in the British Isles. It was built by Thomas Ekins, an island steward working for the Godolphin family, in about 1680.

on the roof of the foghorn house next to the lighthouse itself. The keepers also had a small vegetable garden. However, the rockiness of the island meant that the soil for the plot had to be shipped in along with everything else.

The island was designated a Site of Special Scientific Interest in 1995 on account of its large colonies of breeding seabirds, especially the European storm petrel. A seabird survey in 2000 also found 34 occupied nests of Manx shearwater. Puffins have been frequent visitors here since at least 1850 when Isaac North, the chaplain of the Isles of Scilly, first wrote about the colony on Round Island. Nevertheless, during the construction of the lighthouse it was said that: "They [the puffins] were extremely tame and used to walk in and out of the kitchen of the workmen who built the tower. This tameness, and the edibility of their eggs, proved their undoing, for none survive now."

The Isles of Scilly Wildlife Trust has a non-intervention policy to ensure that seabirds can breed with minimal disturbance, and therefore permission is needed from Trinity House to land on the island.

Sails at dusk.

ST AGNES

LOCATION: 49°53′33″N, 6°20′43″W
OS GRID: SV880082
ELEVATION: 23m (75m)
DEACTIVATED: 1911

The isle of St Agnes is only about a mile wide – one of the smallest of the five inhabited islands in the Scilly archipelago – and it is joined at low tide to the island of Gugh by a sandbar. It is an isle rich in contrasts, with rocky outcrops on its exposed west side and coves with fine white beaches.

St Agnes's most obvious landmark, standing as it does on the island's highest point, is the lighthouse built by Trinity House in 1680. It was the second lighthouse to be erected in Cornwall (after the Lizard lighthouse of 1619). A plaque attests that it was constructed by Captains Hugh Hill and Simon Bayly, who were also builders of the 1676 Lowestoft lighthouse.

The four-storey structure is located 23m (75ft) above the ground and 42m (138ft) above mean high water. It is a rare surviving example of an early post-medieval coal-burning lighthouse tower, although it has been modified to some extent, and it is quite unique in containing gun ports. While defensive measures are rare in a lighthouse, in the 17th century the isolated Isles of Scilly were at the mercy of buccaneers and pirates and a lighthouse served as a decent lookout and defensive tower.

St Agnes was a rare example of a lighthouse with an enclosed coal fire. Usually these were hung in a brazier from a timber support suspended over the ridge of an open tower. Here, a funnel through the roof was provided to let smoke escape, but as anyone who has stoked an open hearth knows, there are a dozen reasons why a room can suddenly start to fill with fumes. In the event, the windows of the lighthouse were inclined to become blackened with soot – and the keepers seemed disinclined to keep them clean, rendering the light almost invisible out to sea. The concept of

St Agnes viewed from scenic Porth Conger, Isles of Scilly.

ST AGNES
LIGHTHOUSE
MIDDLE TOWN, ST AGNES
ISLES OF SCILLY

an indoor coal-fired beacon didn't catch on. In 1790, an oil lamp was introduced. This had a parabolic reflector (which the keepers were no doubt instructed to keep polished) and the new flashing white light had a range of 29km (18 miles).

Although the original lantern has been replaced, the form of the early light source is known about in detail, thanks to the survival nearby of one of the braziers used in this tower, together with accurate 18th-century illustrations of the lighthouse. St Agnes lighthouse and the daymark on St Martin's demonstrate well the nature and form of navigational aids developed in the later 17th century. The lantern that remained after the lighthouse was decommissioned is also significant in that it was never updated, unlike the apparatus of working lighthouses, so is a perfectly intact surviving example of early 19th-century lighting technology.

With the construction of Bishop Rock in 1858 and Peninnis in 1911, St Agnes was suddenly surplus to requirements and was decommissioned in 1911. It now serves simply as a daymark for shipping.

One of the guns from St Agnes lighthouse.

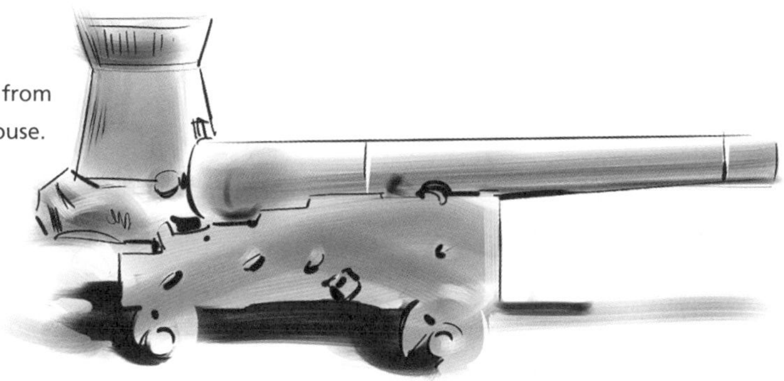

PENDEEN WATCH
LIGHTHOUSE
St JUST, PENZANCE
CORNWALL

PENDEEN WATCH

LOCATION: 50°09′53″N, 5°40′17″W
OS GRID: SW379359
ELEVATION: 59m (194ft)
CHARACTER: Fl (4) 15s
RANGE: 30km (19 miles)

The lantern at Pendeen.

Northeast by east of Cape Cornwall, the Wra, also known as the Three Stone Oar, is a group of three rocks lying off Pendeen. The entrance to St Ives Bay is a further 13km (8 miles) along the shore. With the treacherous Gurnard's Head also still to navigate, this stretch of coastline has sent many a ship's crew to a watery grave.

Matters were made worse by the high cliffs that obscured sight of both Trevose Head lighthouse to the east and Longships to the west. Unable to accurately determine their position, many ships got lost and then foundered on the rocks off Pendeen. Despite this, it wasn't until the 19th century that a lighthouse was given serious consideration for this part of the Cornish coast. In the meantime, mariners had to rely on an antiquated and inefficient rocket apparatus based at the coastguard station or, in an emergency, the lifeboats from Hayle, St Ives or Sennen Cove.

Above the lighthouse are the remains of the Levant tin mine, part of the Cornish Mining World Heritage Site and home to a working 1840 steam-powered beam engine dating from 1840.

In 1891, Sir Thomas Matthews, a renowned Trinity House engineer, was assigned the task of designing the lighthouse; the construction contract was awarded to Arthur Carkeek of Redruth. First the headland needed to be flattened and a retaining wall built. Once this was complete, work could begin on the 17m (56ft) tall tower. Because this wasn't a wave-washed position, the walls of the tower could be built of rubble and plaster. By mid-1900 the lighthouse was ready to receive its lantern. On 26 September, Pendeen Watch lighthouse was officially put into commission.

The lighthouse was automated in 1995 and the keepers left the station on 3 May that year. A new electric lamp was fitted, but the original optic was retained and remains in use. As with all lighthouses, the reassuring boom of the fog signal was eventually silenced, in this case in 2014.

ST IVES

LOCATION: 50°12′48″N, 5°28′36″W
OS GRID: SW520406
ELEVATION: 8m (26ft)
CHARACTER: 2 fixed vertical green – no longer operational.

By the early 14th century, St Ives was a thriving fishing port. It continued to flourish and by 1490 had been granted a charter to hold a market. Less than a century later, in 1558, the town was declared a borough, being represented by two members of parliament, and it was now west Cornwall's main port of departure for Ireland. The town's patron saint, Ia, who several centuries earlier had travelled in the opposite direction, certainly seemed to be answering her petitioners' prayers. However, one invocation that had so far gone unanswered was for a harbour, which, despite the huge numbers of fish being unloaded by the town's fleet of boats, St Ives would lack for another 200 years or more.

Originally intended as a breakwater, Smeaton's Pier was built between 1767 and 1770. Some 60 years later, a lighthouse was added at what was then the pier's end. The building consisted of a square granite base with an octagonal stone gallery room rather than the more usual lantern room. This area was used as an observation point. The structure was completed with a domed roof and weathervane. The light was powered by gas, giving a range of 11km (7 miles) when the lighthouse was in service. The pier and lighthouse were a boon to the town, which by the mid-19th century had more than 400 boats and 700 men employed in the pilchard fishing industry alone.

With the expansion of the fishing fleet, a new wooden pier was built to accommodate the additional vessels. However, this pier lasted for only 20 years and all that can be seen of it now are a few timbers that are revealed at low water.

Time for a long cool drink!

It was apparent that the original pier needed to be extended and so foundations were laid in 1888. Among the novel features built into the new part of the pier were a

SMEATON PIER
LIGHTHOUSE
ST IVES
CORNWALL

reservoir at its base which fills up at high tide to limit wave action in the harbour, as well as three arches that function as sluice gates to prevent sand build-up. Unfortunately, this action was as likely to dislodge stationary boats as sand and so temporary timber beams had to be fitted to resolve the problem.

Losing my way wandering the winding streets of St Ives.

A second lighthouse, a 10m (32ft) octagonal cast-iron tower, was mounted on a black base at the end of the new extension. This light shows fixed red, with a white sector to the south when there is more than 3m (10ft) of water. When the level is below this, the light changes to green. The lighthouse is no longer operational.

Across from Smeaton's Pier is the much shorter West Pier, which was built in 1894 to load stone from local quarries and which hosts the lifeboat slipway, completed exactly a century later.

GODREVY

LOCATION: 50°14'33"N, 5°24'01"W
OS GRID: SW577436
ELEVATION: 28m (92ft)
CHARACTER: Fl WR 10s
RANGE: 15km (9 miles)

Beyond Godrevy Island lies a dangerous reef known as the Stones, which extends into St Ives Bay. Countless ships have met their doom here, including one that was wrecked in 1649. Following the execution of King Charles I, his loyal followers attempted to send some of the dead king's lace-trimmed clothing and belongings abroad for safe keeping as relics. The ship was quickly loaded with booty, passengers and crew. Sails were hoisted and off she went, straight into the teeth of a storm. The vessel hit the Godrevy rocks and was quickly overwhelmed and capsized in the surf, the only survivors being a man, a boy and his dog. The king's wardrobe was presumed resting in Davy Jones's locker until some weeks later, when ornate garments of lace and velvet began to be washed up on the shore. They were quickly seized upon as salvage, and we can only imagine that the area's wreckers enjoyed a very distinct dress style for a season or two.

Two centuries were to pass before the loss in 1854 of the iron-hulled screw steamer the SS *Nile*, which sank on the reef with the loss of all 40 of her passengers and crew. This disaster finally persuaded Trinity House to commence construction of a lighthouse on the island.

By December 1857, James Sutcliffe had been appointed as the engineer for the project and the lighthouse was built to the design of consultant engineer James Walker. Construction took a year, not helped by storms over the winter of 1858, which kept the builders trapped on the island for weeks at a time; while hordes of curious visitors got in the way when the weather was fine. The building was finished

The Hungry Horsebox - purveyors of replenishments and refreshments for those in need after a long day toiling in the sun.

GODREVY
LIGHTHOUSE
St IVES BAY
CORNWALL

at a cost of £7,082 15s 12d, and the light began operating on 1 March 1859.

The lighthouse consists of a 37m (121ft) high white octagonal tower built of rubble and cement, with two keepers' cottages adjoining it. The original optic revolved on rollers rather than the more usual mercury bath, and was operated by a clockwork motor which was in turn wound using a weight running through a cavity in the lighthouse wall. Until it was automated in 1939, there was a 3cwt bell used as a fog signal. This was struck once every five seconds.

The name Godrevy comes from the Cornish *go-dref*, meaning "little huts or little homesteads", which described the scattered small holdings of the headland. In 1622, the naturalist John Ray described it as: "Godreve Island, which is nothing but a rock, upon which, in time of year, build great store of birds." Today, it is still a haven for birdlife, and the National Trust describe it as a birdwatcher's paradise. Species recorded here include storm petrels, peregrines, skylarks, gannets and fulmars. Gulls, oystercatchers and pipits also live on the island, which is partly covered with grass.

In 1995, the lighthouse was converted to operate with solar power. It is now monitored and controlled from the Trinity House Operations Control Centre at Harwich in Essex. A review in 2005 proposed closure, but following a campaign this decision was overturned, and the light continues to provide a warning to mariners. The light was moved in 2012 from the lighthouse tower to a new structure made of steel.

Surfers at St Ives Bay.

TREVOSE HEAD
LIGHTHOUSE
TREVOSE HEAD
CORNWALL

TREVOSE HEAD

LOCATION: 50°32′57″N, 5°02′06″W
OS GRID: SW850765
ELEVATION: 62m (203ft)
CHARACTER: Fl 7.5s
RANGE: 39km (24 miles)

To the west of Padstow, Trevose Head lighthouse sits on the rugged headland jutting into the Atlantic. It was constructed in the mid-19th century to bridge the gap in navigational assistance into the Bristol Channel between the Longships lighthouse near Land's End and Lundy Island off the north Devon coast. Two more lighthouses were built at Godrevy and Pandeen on Cornwall's north coast, to create a converging system of navigational aids for shipping along this hazardous coastline.

One of the residents of this part of the world.

On a more local level, the light was designed to help mariners making the difficult approach into Padstow itself, before negotiating the treacherous Doom Bar sandbank and the many reefs facing them at Stepper Point to the west and Pentire Point to the east. Folklore has it that a mermaid fell in love with a man from Padstow and tried to lure him beneath the waves. Waking from her spell, he eventually escaped but not before fatally wounding her. As she breathed her last, the mermaid cursed the harbour with the ever-shifting "bar of doom", which stretches from Hawker's Cove to Trebetherick.

The accurate identification of a lighthouse is a necessary part of any mariner's skillset. During the day, it's the kind of thing that any old sea dog might be expected to manage, but at night, with a running tide and the roar of the surf breaking across reefs, the speedy recognition of the correct lighthouse could be a simple matter of life or death. When Trevose Head lighthouse was first illuminated, it quickly became apparent that it could too easily be mistaken for other lights along the coast and the judicious solution of adding a lower light to change its character was carried out straight away. As time went by, there were still complaints that it wasn't distinctive enough, so the upper light was changed to occulting (a type of flash – the light was obscured for three seconds, three times a minute) and the lower one retired.

In 1912, the light was again updated when the current rotating optic, weighing 3.6 tons, was floated on a bed of mercury, itself weighing in at 1.5 tons. The optic was then driven by a weight-driven clockwork rotation system that had to be rewound every 90 minutes. Before the advent of precision electrically operated rollers, this was the preferred method of ensuring a smooth rotation of the light. The following year the fog signal got an overhaul. In an area bedevilled by sea mist, the latest type of system was a necessity. This came in the form of a huge trumpet, 11m (36ft) in length with an aperture measuring 2m by 61cm (ft by 2ft), devised to give it a wide horizontal spread. Fifty years later this was replaced by an air-driven signal with eight horns. The fog signal was finally decommissioned in 2012.

The lighthouse was automated in 1995 and the remaining keepers left. The colour red was removed from the light and the rotation speed of the optic was slowed. Today, the former keepers' cottages (arranged in two semi-detached pairs) have been carefully updated and sympathetically decorated, and are available to rent as holiday accommodation.

The Padstow RNLI lifeboat station.

The area around Trevose Head is home to dozens of shipwrecks. The Quies, a group of rocks about a mile offshore, and the Bull, off Dinas Head, have probably contributed more than most, but there was a time when shipwrecks in this part of the world would have been unimaginable as far as the locals were concerned. In about 6500 BC, sea levels were much lower than now, and flint tools have been found along the shore that are believed to have originally been shaped out of pebbles from the chalk deposits that run up to 100 miles offshore at the bottom of the Irish Sea!

HARTLAND POINT

LOCATION: 51°01′19″N, 4°31′33″W
OS GRID: SS229277
ELEVATION 30m (98ft)
CHARACTER: Fl (6) 15s
RANGE: 15km (9 miles)

The radar station is utilized by the Civil Aviation Authority for air traffic control.

Hartland Point is a high, rocky outcrop of land on the northwest tip of the Devon coast. It sits 5km (3 miles) northwest of the village of Hartland and indicates the western limit of the English side of the Bristol Channel and the passage between the Devon coast and Lundy Island. The location was known to the Romans as the "promontory of Hercules". The change in the nature of the coast is quite dramatic at this sharp turn from the sheltered north-facing cliffs to the rugged Atlantic coastline. The Point marks the end of what is sometimes referred to as the Hartland Peninsula, Devon's own Land's End.

A short distance south of the lighthouse sits the old Rocket House. This building was used to store a lifesaving device that in this day and age seems hardly feasible or advisable. The rocket "apparatus" fired a small cannonball, with a double line attached, out to a vessel in trouble. The line was then to be tied to the mast and pulled fast; and one by one the crew were coaxed into a breeches buoy harness, to be pulleyed across from the stricken craft to shore. The harness, which looked for all the world like a pair of extra-baggy trousers sewn onto a life ring and then attached by a pair of braces to a pulley, may not have preserved the passengers' dignity, but it was so effective in saving lives that the apparatus continued to be used around the country until the late 20th century, when helicopter rescue made it redundant.

Hartland Point lighthouse, situated on the tip of the promontory, has over the years been threatened by the undermining of the headland by wave action. An attempt to tackle this was made by breaking away rock from above and behind the tower, and letting this roll down to the beach below

HARTLAND POINT
LIGHTHOUSE
HARTLAND POINT
DEVON

to act as a barrier. Unfortunately, whenever a northwesterly gale coincided with a high spring tide, these efforts were swiftly washed away and, in 1925, the decision was taken to build a sea wall 6m (20ft) high and 3m (10ft) long to provide a more permanent barrier.

The cliffside walk to the lighthouse from Hartland Quay is stunning, revealing a seldom seen side of Devon. On the coast north of the quay, the jagged, stratified rock reaches out into the waves like gnarly witch's fingers. It's on these rocks that a French vessel ran aground one summer's day in 1879. The ship was bound for Cardiff with a cargo of pit props, when the unfortunate Captain Bidhout mistook Hartland Point lighthouse for one of its sisters on the Welsh coast and his craft wound up high and dry on the rocks. Luckily, no one was injured, but the suspicious captain was convinced that the locals would plunder his cargo and could not be persuaded to leave the ship. Eventually, the vicar's wife managed to assure him in her halting French that the locals presented less of a danger than a night spent camped out on a shipwreck and he reluctantly accepted their invitation to come ashore.

The station was manned for many years by four keepers, who lived with their families in cottages adjoining the lighthouse, until the lighthouse was automated in 1984. The empty dwellings were eventually demolished to make way for the construction of a helipad next to the tower. A review of aids to navigation in 2010 proposed that Hartland Point be discontinued, as GPS had made this and other lighthouses redundant, but local enthusiasm for the tradition of the light persuaded Trinity House to reduce the light's power to 14km (9 miles) instead, using a solar-powered system mounted on an alternative structure, thus preserving the tower and remaining buildings as a landmark in the area.

Along the Hartland Peninsula walk - a great place to get some sea air and admire the dramatic coastal views.

LUNDY SOUTH
LIGHTHOUSE
LUNDY ISLAND
DEVON

LUNDY SOUTH

LOCATION: 51°09′41″N, 4°39′26″W
OS GRID: SS143436
ELEVATION: 53m (174ft)
CHARACTER: Fl 5s
RANGE: 28km (17 miles)

The original Lundy lighthouse stood at Chapel Hill, the highest point in the centre of this island off the coast of north Devon. Built in 1820, the lighthouse soon revealed serious operational failings and so plans were made to replace it with lighthouses at the northern and southern extremities of the island. Lying as it does in the entrance to the Bristol Channel, Lundy – or rather the ability of shipping to avoid Lundy – was vital to Bristol's trading success.

The island has also seen plenty of its own trade in its time, much of it less than legal. It was occupied by Barbary pirates during the 1600s, and the following century Lundy became infamous as the base of Thomas Benson, MP for Barnstaple, who became Devon's most notorious smuggler.

Benson, who held the lease on the island, was awarded a contract to transport convicts to Maryland and Virginia, but instead of taking them to the New World, he shipped them the short distance to Lundy. Once there, they were worked as slaves, building infrastructure for Benson's smuggling operations, including a tobacco processing plant. When 14 desperate convicts escaped to the mainland in a small boat, his scheme came to light. To pay his fines from the scandal, Benson came up with another ruse. He bought a ship called the *Nightingale* and had it loaded up with a valuable cargo of pewter and linen, which he insured. Once the ship had sailed out of sight of port, it made for Lundy, where the booty was unloaded and stored in a cave built by the convicts. It then set sail again, rendezvousing with another of Benson's ships. The sailors boarded the second ship and scuttled the *Nightingale*, and Benson claimed for his supposed losses.

This new scheme was undone, however, when some disgruntled members of the crew let the cat out of the bag. Captain John Lancey, the master of the ship, was

South pier, Lundy.

hanged for his part in the operation, but Benson managed to escape to Portugal, where it is said he built up a thriving business in trade.

When it was built, the south lighthouse inherited the equipment from the old Lundy lighthouse, including the 1857 optic, which remained in use until 1962. The light displayed a single flash every 30 seconds.

The south lighthouse (but not its northern counterpart) also had an explosive fog signal, which used to be detonated manually from the lantern gallery. However, in 1908 the signal was automated and moved to a separate building. When the signal was taken out of service, the building was demolished to make space for a helipad.

The south lighthouse was automated and converted to solar power in 1994. As part of this process, the fourth-order optic – the sizes go from sixth order (the smallest) to first order (the largest) – which had been in use since 1962, was removed and later installed in Dungeness lighthouse, where it still gives service.

The "landing place" plaque that Trinity House placed on Lundy ruffled a few feathers as it was seen as staking a claim to part of the island. The inhabitants responded in the early 20th century by displaying their own plaque, which read: "This island is entirely private property. There are no public roads, footpaths or rights of ways whatever hereon." Happily, good sense endured and lighthouse staff were left to carry out their work unimpeded.

BULL POINT

LOCATION: 51°11′56″N, 4°12′05″W
OS GRID: SS463467
ELEVATION: 54m (177ft)
CHARACTER: Fl (3) 10s
RANGE: 37km (23 miles)

Once the haunt of smugglers and wreckers, the coastline stretching from the delightfully named Morte Point to Bull Point and onward to the village of Lee is a great place to get away from the crowds and enjoy dramatic scenery, with jagged cliffs, rocky headlands and hidden bays. One of the notorious points for landing contraband lay at Sandy Beach, just west of Lee. The authorities had their work cut out keeping an eye on the comings and goings along this coast and, more often than not, they arrived too late to catch the smugglers red-handed. Anything attracting duty was game. A typical haul was that of June 1786, when the customs men came across a catch of 66 bottles of gin, 13 gallons of Portuguese wine, 113kg (250lbs) of salt and 73 packs of playing cards, all of them missing the ace of spades!

The plans for Bull Point lighthouse were drawn up in 1876, when two engineers from the Board of Trade surveyed the coastline around Morte to find the most serviceable spot to position a lighthouse. They favoured Bull Point, and a roadway was duly planned to run from Morte to there. Had the Maritime Corporations of the Bristol Channel seaboard had their way, however, the lighthouse would have been

The impressive and slightly menacing Morte Point along the Bull Point cliff walk.

BULL POINT
LIGHTHOUSE
BULL POINT, MORTEHOE
DEVON

The foghorn at Bull Point.

situated offshore on Morte Stone, one of the shipping hazards along this stretch of coast.

When it was eventually built, the original Bull Point lighthouse tower was 9m (30ft) high and situated only 21m (70ft) from the cliff edge. At the top, it had a cylindrical lantern that housed a six-wick oil lamp within a revolving first-order optic. A fixed red sector light also shone from a window in the tower, marking the Morte Stone. Beside the tower, there was accommodation for the keepers, some outbuildings and a long engine room that housed machinery for the foghorn and the light. These were all contained behind a tall whitewashed retaining wall, giving the station a cosy atmosphere not unlike that of a small fortified village.

All continued as expected until one fateful day in 1972, when the principal keeper felt tremors underfoot and noticed large cracks appearing in the ground. Suddenly, the floor dropped an inch or two and a strange rumbling sound was heard, followed by a crash. It transpired that about 15m (50ft) of the cliff had sheared off and dropped into the sea, and now a further 15m (50ft) had subsided. Cracks started to appear all over the station and the fog signal station had partly collapsed, putting the fog horn out of action. While the keepers escaped unharmed, the stability of the whole station was now in question.

After assessing the damage to buildings and determining that almost all the equipment was unharmed, the decision was made that a brand-new station would be built. A temporary light tower, which had originally been used at Braunton Burrows, Devon was repurposed with the Bull Point optic installed on top. This continued in use for almost two years, until the new lighthouse was constructed further inland. The new Bull Point lighthouse was designed in such a way that the equipment from the old lighthouse could be utilized after certain modifications. It was automated in 1975 and is now controlled from Trinity House's Planning Centre in Harwich, Essex. Use of the fog signal was discontinued in 1988.

ST NICHOLAS CHAPEL, ILFRACOMBE

LOCATION: 51°12′40″N, 4°06′47″W
OS GRID: SS525478
ELEVATION: 39m (128ft)
CHARACTER: Fl (2) G 5s
RANGE: 11km (7 miles)

Dating back to 1321, St Nicholas Chapel is set on a rock known as Lantern Hill, positioned between the harbour and the sea. For centuries, the chapel was used by the seafaring folk of Ilfracombe, which has the largest harbour in north Devon. It was built by order of the Bishop of Exeter, Walter Stapleton, to serve as a place of worship for mariners and was named after the patron saint of sailors. In this capacity, it served the community until 1540, when Henry VIII dissolved the monasteries and St Nicholas ceased to be used for prayer.

A boat tour aboard the Ilfracombe Princess is a great way to see the coast and its seals, porpoises and dolphins.

Although the current tower only dates to about 1800, the chapel is reputed to display the oldest continuously lit navigation beacon in the country, guiding ships since 1522. From 1650, a larger lantern was used and a light was also illuminated at its western end, to warn of rocks near the harbour entrance.

Ilfracombe harbour has fairly safe access; however, at the western entrance to the port there are a number of rocky outcrops which have signalled the end of many a ship. The number of wrecks along this stretch of the coast are numerous. In the winter of 1895 alone, the *Arabella* and the *Llanisley* went down offshore. While the four crew of the *Llanisley* managed to abandon ship when their schooner foundered near Lundy Island, they were subsequently lost at sea while attempting to reach Ilfracombe. In the 50 years preceding this, there were almost 20 wrecks within sight of the chapel itself.

In the early 1900s, the Welsh ports were extremely busy, sending more than 300 ships a day past Ilfracombe. On 28 January 1914, while on her way from Milford

ST NICHOLAS CHAPEL
LIGHTHOUSE
ILFRACOMBE
DEVON

to Avonmouth, the SS *Collier* sent out a distress signal. By 2.30am the coastguards had been alerted and the lifeboat from Ilfracombe was on its way. By the time the rescue party arrived, the seven crewmen, ship's dog, cat and goldfinch had managed to board the ship's dinghy and were hauled to safety. The S.S. *Collier* had been one of the first steamers to carry mail to Australia and her wreckage can still be found among the sands at Rockham Bay.

In 1819, Trinity House took over responsibility for the light in the chapel and added a lantern to the roof. The light was later converted to gas power and the 11m (36ft) tall lantern displays a green flashing light.

Between 1835 and 1871, John Davie served as the lighthouse keeper. He, his wife, Elizabeth, and their 14 children lived together within the chapel's cramped confines, where Elizabeth and 2 of their daughters also took in laundry. In addition to housing the family, it served as a reading room for visiting dignitaries. Following the family's departure, the chapel drifted into a period of slow decline and by the end of the World War II was in serious need of attention. In 1962, the local Rotary Club undertook the care of the chapel and, though they continue to staff it as custodians, today North Devon Council owns and maintains the building. The chapel is open to the public between Easter and October.

The remains of a shipwreck on the north Devon coast.

LYNMOUTH FORELAND

LOCATION: 51°14′43″N, 3°47′12″W
OS GRID: SS753510
ELEVATION: 67m (220ft)
CHARACTER: Fl (4) 15s
RANGE: 33km (21 miles)

The rocky headland of Foreland Point near Lynmouth is the most northerly location on the Devon coast. The lighthouse here, sometimes referred to as the Countisbury Foreland lighthouse and originally simply called the Foreland lighthouse, was built, along with its cottages, on terraces carved out of the hillside. Access from the service road is by a flight of 58 steps down to the upper terrace. Although the squat white tower is only 15m (49ft) high, it stands at an elevation of 67m (220ft) above high-water spring tides.

The first lights to serve the southern approaches to the Bristol Channel were those at Hartland Point, built in 1874, and Bull Point, which followed less than a decade later. In 1900, Trinity House decided to add a third lighthouse at Foreland Point, 32km (20 miles) east of Bull Point, and the difficult task of carving the base for the station two thirds of the way down an almost sheer 275m (900ft) hillside commenced. Because of its position the lighthouse was designed with the unusual configuration of having the tower below the accommodation.

The "upside down" lantern at Lynmouth.

LYNMOUTH
FORELAND LIGHTHOUSE
FORELAND POINT
DEVON

The station was always an unpopular posting for keepers because, as a result of being built on this steep northern slope, the buildings only received sunshine during the three months of high summer. It was also a problematic place for families to live. Because of the dramatic way the hillside plunges to the sea, a very close eye had to be kept on any small children. Even for adults it was treacherous. If you tripped, you were a goner.

Lynmouth Foreland was electrified in 1975 when diesel generators were installed to provide power and it was eventually connected to the National Grid. The station was automated in 1994.

The lighthouse's first-order dioptric lens flashes 4 times every 15 seconds. Although originally intended as part of the original station, the fog signal was built later and abutted the tower on the north side below the lantern, sounding 3 blasts every 30 seconds. The fog signal has since been taken out of service.

The Blue Ball Inn at Lynmouth, a welcome diversion off the South West Coast Path for thirsty ramblers.

The headland is now owned by the National Trust. Some areas are open to the public as part of the South West Coast Path, while access to other areas is restricted. The lightkeeper's cottage is now a National Trust holiday cottage.

There is a path to the foreland from the Blue Ball Inn on Countisbury Hill. It is a stunning clifftop walk along the headland but requires a head for heights.

BURNHAM
HIGH & LOW LIGHTS
BURNHAM-ON-SEA
SOMERSET

BURNHAM-ON-SEA

The old Round Tower lighthouse, inactive since 1832. Originally four storeys tall, it was reduced in height so that it wouldn't be confused with the high light.

LOCATION: 51°14′54″N, 3°00′21″W
OS GRID: ST298503
ELEVATION: 7m (23ft)
CHARACTER: Fl W 7.5s; directional fixed W/R/G
RANGE: White 22km (14 miles); Red/Green 19km (12 miles)

Burnham-On-Sea in Somerset has had three lighthouses over the years, all very different shapes. The nine-legged wooden Lower Lighthouse was built in 1832 and is a Grade II Heritage listed structure and is the only one of the three which is still active.

Before these, the tower of St Andrews Church was the original Burnham light. Legend has it that around 1750 a fisherman and his wife lived in a cottage close to the church. One stormy night, concerned for her husband's safety, the wife placed a candle in the window to help him navigate his way home. The light did its job and the grateful sailors put money aside so that she might continue to keep a candle lit to guide them on their homeward journeys.

Later, the sexton of the church gave the fisherman's wife five pounds for the rights to place a light on the church tower – it being higher and therefore more effective. He, in turn, was given twenty pounds by the Reverend David Davies, Curate of Burnham, who built the Round Tower.

Burnham's 'lighthouse on legs' was built to complement the separate 99-foot-tall pillar 'High' lighthouse which had been in turn built to replace the older 'Round Tower' lighthouse. This it did admirably for 137 years where the High light was visible for 30km and the Low light for 22 km, so that lining the two lights provided a safe approach course for vessels navigating up the Bristol Channel from the direction of Foreland Point and Minehead.

In 1969, a sector light was added to the High Lighthouse indicating the correct bearing for the deep-water channel, rendering the low light redundant, at which point, it was duly decommissioned. Revenge however was had 24 years later when the high light was itself decommissioned. Its flashing light and subsidiary sector light were then transferred to its leggy cousin down on the sands. In 1890, the lower lighthouse's original stripe of black was changed to red, and this band of red was replicated on the High Light making both lighthouses more conspicuous as day marks.

The lower lighthouse is very popular with walkers, but caution is advised on Burnham sands and mudflats where the tide can recede for over 2.5km, and surge back in faster than a person can run.

BERKELEY PILL
FRONT & REAR LIGHTS
SEVERN ESTUARY
GLOUCESTERSHIRE

BERKELEY PILL

LOCATION: 51°41′59″N, 2°29′24″W
OS GRID: SO662002
ELEVATION: 8m (26ft)
CHARACTER: Fixed G
RANGE: 4km (2.5 miles)

An abandoned boat by the River Severn.

You are probably wondering why these two slight and slightly worse-for-wear lights are sharing space in this book with the Bell Rocks and Eddystones of this world, but to me, though they have never flashed their beam across the rigging of a speeding clipper or guided liners to safe harbour, they are very much a part of our maritime built heritage and have played a central role in guiding traffic along the channels of the River Severn and its adjacent waterways. They are also rather cool looking!

In 1906, the Gloucester Harbour Trustees, who held responsibility for navigation on the Severn, decided that further aids were needed to indicate to shipping when to turn in the channel and to lead vessels to the entrance of Sharpness docks. The south side of Berkeley Pill was judged to be the most suitable location and two leading lights were erected while a grant of land was obtained from Lord Fitzhardinge. The cost of the work amounting to £345 was met by the Trustees.

An old buoy at the nearby Sharpness viewpoint.

The station initially comprised two fixed white lights, which had been obtained from the nearby Shepperdine installation when it was upgraded to a more powerful light. These were initially mounted on wooden poles, which were replaced in 1937 by the current metal lattice towers. The rear light stands at 12m (39ft), whereas the front light crouches slightly lower at 10m (33ft). Having originally been oil-powered and then converted to gas, the lights are now electrified. They are lit in an unusual fashion using LED tubes which remain on constantly, showing a fixed green light throughout the day and night. As with all range or leading lights, the idea is to get the two lights in line, at which point you know you are on a safe course.

The Berkeley Pill range is emblematic of cutting-edge technology of the early 20th century. They look almost like something from an H G Wells novel. They're fast being replaced by simple aluminium poles fitted with an array of LED lights and our landscape will be all the poorer for it.

FLATHOLM
LIGHTHOUSE
BRISTOL CHANNEL
CARDIFF

FLATHOLM

LOCATION: 51°22′32″N, 3°07′06″W
OS GRID: ST222646
ELEVATION: 50m (164ft)
CHARACTER: Fl (3) WR 10s
RANGE: 28km (17 miles)

In the 18th century, Flat Holm Island was a notorious base for the smuggling of contraband, including brandy and tea. A series of tunnels, accessed by an old mineshaft, provided the perfect cover for spiriting away booty, safe from the prying eyes of any officials who hadn't been bribed. Because their vessels were in such poor shape, the customs authorities struggled to keep up with the pirates, and it's said that Flat Holm's most infamous smuggler – Richard Robinson, who worked with his son, Pasco – was so confident of his ability to evade the customs men that he had his boat painted bright red, with the added flourish of a mermaid figurehead to act as the proverbial red rag to a bull.

The island of Flat Holm is the most southerly point of Wales and lies approximately 5km (3 miles) south of Lavernock Point, in the centre of the shipping lanes where the Bristol Channel meets the Severn Estuary. It's the first hazard encountered by vessels entering the channel. In April 1735, a Mr William Crispe of Bristol notified Trinity House that he had taken out a 99-year lease for the island from the Earl of Bute. His intention, he wrote, was to build a lighthouse in the name of Trinity House but at his own expense, and to charge a toll on passing ships. Perhaps his conditions were unreasonable or there might have been doubts about his ability to carry through the enterprise, but despite the evident need for an aid to navigation, his application was turned down.

Circumstances changed quickly, however, when a naval ship foundered with the loss of 60 soldiers in the winter of 1736. Now a second proposal by Mr Crispe

The foghorn at Flatholm lighthouse.

was accepted. This saw the construction of a 21m (70ft) tower for a cost of just under £900. The light was first displayed in December 1737. Despite a plethora of tolls inward and outward on both domestic and foreign shipping, the cost of repaying his loans soon had Mr Crispe in a pickle and, with bankruptcy looming, the lease was sold onward.

While the business venture hadn't exactly been a shining success, the light itself had. The coal-fired beacon had been hailed as the greatest in Wales, with only Flamborough Head on the Yorkshire coast being regarded as its superior. Yet the mighty will come crashing down mightily – and such was the case with Flatholm lighthouse, when a lightning storm left the tower in ruins in 1790 and the light had to be displayed from ground level while repairs were undertaken.

By 1819, Trinity House had acquired the lease on the tower and set about improving the station. The tower height was increased and a new oil-fired Argand lamp was installed. In 1866, the tower was again increased in height, a new galley constructed and the new, more powerful optic changed to an occulting light. In 1929, the lighthouse was redesignated as a rock station and the keepers' families were rehoused on the mainland. By 1988, the keepers had left too, as the station became automated. Today, the flashing white light is visible for 24km (15 miles), while a red sector is visible for 19km (12 miles).

Cannon from the old artillery battery on Flat Holm.

NASH POINT

LOCATION: 51°24′03″N, 3°33′08″W
OS GRID: SS921680
ELEVATION: 56m (184ft)
CHARACTER: Fl (2) WR 15s
RANGE: 39km (24 miles)

Where the Bristol Channel begins to narrow along the headlands between Porthcawl and Barry, there lie treacherous banks known as the Nash Sands.

In 1831, a major tragedy occurred when the paddle steamer *Frolic* was wrecked on the sands during a storm, with the loss of all 78 passengers and crew. The travellers included merchants, off-duty sailors, families on a connecting trip to Bristol to board a ship to the New World and some high-ranking military personnel, including a colonel and a general.

The sandbank near Nash Point.

The steamer plied a regular passenger route between Haverfordwest, Pater (now Pembroke Dock), Milford Haven, Tenby, Carmarthen and Bristol. When the wreckage was discovered, they found the captain strapped to the mast with his infant son in his arms. He was survived by a pregnant wife and eight children. A woman's body was also found with her child strapped to her, presumably to prevent the infant from being washed overboard.

Prior to the accident, Trinity House had already purchased land and designed a station consisting of a pair of range lights, but now the construction of the lighthouse took on a new urgency.

Designed by James Walker and built by Joseph Nelson, the high and low lights at Nash Point were completed in 1832, just a year after the *Frolic* tragedy. The high light to the east stands 37m (121ft) tall. Originally painted with broad black and white horizontal bands, it was repainted white when the Low Light was decommissioned in the 1920s. Between the two towers a fixed white light is displayed over safe passage and a red sector over the sands.

NASH POINT
LIGHTHOUSE
TRWYN YR AS
VALE OF GLAMORGAN

The Low Light is 25m (82ft) tall and stands about 300m (985ft) west of the High Light. The lantern was removed in the 1970s.

The station was initially built with two cottages, but a further two were added in the late 1890s and the original dwellings were extended to the rear to give additional accommodation. Though there are four keepers' cottages, only three of them were intended for keepers based at Nash Point; the fourth was reserved for the family of a keeper who might be assigned for a time to an offshore lighthouse.

Nash Point lighthouse has the distinction of being the only working lighthouse in the UK to be licensed to hold weddings and civil partnerships. With the ceremony taking place in the lantern room before a maximum of 25 guests, it makes for an unusual and intimate venue.

The old low light tower at Nash Point.

THE MUMBLES
LIGHTHOUSE
MUMBLES HEAD
SWANSEA

MUMBLES

The old lifeboat station house on the Mumbles pier.

LOCATION: 51°34′01″N, 3°58′16″W
OS GRID: SS634871
ELEVATION: 35m (115ft)
CHARACTER: Fl (4) 20s
RANGE: 52km (32 miles)

Mumbles lighthouse sits at the southeastern end of Bracelet Bay on the second of the islands at Mumbles Head, and guides shipping past Mixon Shoals half a mile to the south. The shoals and nearby Cherrystone Rock have been responsible for the loss of hundreds of vessels over the years.

In July 1792, construction started on the lighthouse, but poor design meant that by October the partially completed structure had collapsed. In 1793, new plans by local architect William Jernegan, who had also designed the Swansea light, were accepted and Trinity House gave the harbour trustees a 99-year lease on the station. The lighthouse and a pair of adjoining keepers' cottages were finally completed in 1794.

The lighthouse originally had two open coal fires to distinguish it from the two illuminated towers of St Ann's Head and Flatholm's single light. However, coal braziers are expensive and difficult to maintain, so they were replaced with a single oil light consisting of Argand lamps with reflectors within a cast-iron lantern. The two stepped galleries are a reminder of the tower's original dual-fire configuration.

The light was taken over by Trinity House in 1836, well before the expiration of the lease, at which point numerous improvements were implemented, with the fitting of a new dioptric light to increase the range of the beam. Further improvements followed in 1905 when the character was changed to an occulting light, powered by hand cranking a series of weights that raised and lowered a metal blank within the lens to give the impression of a flashing beam. In the late 1970s, the original lantern was replaced by the lantern from a retired lightship, and in 1995 the station was converted to solar power.

It's possible to walk out to the lighthouse at low tide, but the ground is wet and uneven. The views are spectacular, with plenty to explore besides the lighthouse, including an old fort built to deter invasion by France, and later additions to deter their neighbours in Germany. Check tidal timetables before you cross. You really don't want to spend the night here! You should also be aware that the fog signal still works, so if there's any mist in the air, bring earplugs with you.

CALDEY ISLAND
LIGHTHOUSE
TENBY
PEMBROKESHIRE

CALDEY ISLAND

LOCATION: 51°37′53″N, 4°41′03″W
OS GRID: SS143959
ELEVATION: 65m (213ft)
CHARACTER: Fl (3) WR 20s
RANGE: 24km (15 miles)

Caldey Island lighthouse is located at the southern end of a small island, about 4km (2.5 miles) offshore from Tenby. It stands on the summit near the old Cistercian priory, alongside the dwellings that once served as accommodation for the lighthouse keepers and their families. The island's name, Caldey, comes from the Viking term *kaldr/ey*, meaning "cold island", or *kelda/ey*, meaning "spring island". In Welsh, it is known as Ynys Bŷr and named after Abbot Pyr, a sixth-century saint.

The island was donated to the Benedictine Order in 1131 from the Abbey of Tiron near Chartres in France. In 1536, following the Reformation and the dissolution of the monasteries, the monks were expelled and the priory fell into silence for almost 400 years. In 1906, the site was purchased by the Anglican Benedictine Brotherhood, but they left their new abbey in 1925, having experienced financial problems, and moved to Prinknash Abbey in Gloucestershire.

The Order of the Reformed Cistercians subsequently bought the abbey and settled there from Scourmont Abbey in Belgium. A small community of monks remains there to this day. The Caldey Cistercians now own the island and, aside from running spiritual retreats, they facilitate tourism on the island by producing a range of wares, including ice cream, clotted cream, shortbread and yoghurt. During the winter months, they make chocolates, perfumes and hand lotions derived from wild flowers that grow on the island.

Regarding more temporal matters, the trade of coal and limestone to and from central Wales in the mid-19th century required the consideration of a lighthouse on the island, and an application to build

The ferry ticket kiosk at Tenby.

one was made in March 1827 on behalf of the traders in Carmarthen Bay.

The light was first displayed on 26 January 1829, with a fixed white beam produced by 20 Argand oil lamps mounted in polished reflectors. The tower was built of limestone and is brick lined. It is 17m (56ft) tall, with the light standing 65m (213ft) above the mean high-water mark. A cottage was built adjoining the lighthouse for the keeper and his clan, but following improvements to the station, new accommodation was constructed as the site now required two lighthouse keepers, ably assisted, their families, to run the enterprise.

Caldey Island lighthouse was designed to operate in conjunction with Lundy North, guiding ships past St Gowan Shoal to the southwest and Helwick Sands to the southeast. Because of its elevation at 48m (157ft), the beam at Lundy North was often obscured by fog, while Caldey, lower on the horizon, could still be seen.

In 1885, a clockwork mechanism was installed and the light was subsequently converted to an occulting character. The character was altered again in 1889. Then, with improvements to gas technology in the 1920s, some Trinity House lights were converted to automatic operation and Caldey Island became powered by acetylene gas, using a Dalén sun valve. At this point, the keepers and their families left the island, and an islander was employed as an attendant.

Caldey Island remained the last Trinity House lighthouse to be powered by acetylene until its modernization in November 1997, when it was converted to mains electricity operation. The lighthouse is now monitored and controlled from Trinity House's Planning Centre in Harwich, Essex.

Caldey Abbey. Monks first came to Caldey in the sixth century. In fact, the island's Welsh name, Ynys Byr, means Pyr's Island, after the name of the first abbot. Today, the small community of monks belongs to the Cistercian order, a stricter, more contemplative offshoot of the Benedictines.

SKOKHOLM

LOCATION: 51°41′38″N, 5°17′13″W
OS GRID: SM729045
ELEVATION: 54m (177ft)
CHARACTER: Fl WR 10s
RANGE: 14km (9 miles)

Lockley House, Britain's first bird observatory, rebuilt and lived in by naturalist Ronald Lockley, is now a Grade II listed building.

The small island of Skokholm, or Ynys Sgogwm in Welsh, is just over a mile long and half a mile wide. It lies off the Pembrokeshire coast, where its red sandstone cliffs rise up from the sea to well over 30m (98ft) in parts, and it is a renowned bird sanctuary.

The lighthouse is situated on the southwest point of Skokholm. With South Bishop and the Smalls, it forms the landward corner of a triangle of lights guiding ships to stay clear of this dangerous coastline, into Milford Haven and up the Bristol Channel.

Architecturally, the lighthouse is notable for being the last stone building that Trinity House erected. After the construction of Skokholm, more contemporary building systems such as poured concrete and prefabrication were employed. The structure is also unusual in that the white brick hexagonal tower is built into the two-storey keepers' accommodation, sitting on top of it, not unlike an air traffic control (ATC) tower at an airport.

The station was built during World War I to a design by Sir Thomas Matthews, but before it could be erected, a jetty had to be constructed so that building materials could be landed safely. The jetty was thereafter used for landing stores and supplies, which were then transported the mile to the lighthouse on two small wagons which rolled on a narrow-gauge railroad track. These were pulled by a donkey, who was notorious for disappearing on the day when supplies were due and would stand motionless under an overhanging rock, the colour of his grey coat blending perfectly with the landscape behind him. While the keepers wandered the island in search of him, he kept to the shadows, presumably silently sniggering at their mounting frustration. We're told he would come at a call on any other day. The donkey was replaced by a pony, who instead threw a tantrum when expected to haul the carts up the rail tracks, scattering the coal and supplies along the route. Ultimately, he was replaced by a more placid and predictable beast of burden, a small tractor. The station is now serviced by helicopter.

SKOKHOLM
LIGHTHOUSE
SKOKHOLM ISLAND
PEMBROKESHIRE

For over 200 years, from 1324, Skokholm, like many islands in the area, served as a rabbit farm. Warrening was a significant element of rural and island economies until the late 19th century. Artificial warrens were constructed of soft earth, which the rabbits could easily burrow into. Rabbits have undergone some evolutionary changes since they were first introduced to Britain, and are now relatively robust animals, well adapted to life in the wild, but when they first arrived with the Normans, they were rather delicate creatures, barely able to dig their own burrows.

The first evidence of a dwelling on the island is shown on a map dated 1693. A map of 1748, created by the self-taught hydrographer, poet and scholar Lewis Morris, also shows a house on the island. The cottage, its environs and perhaps the lime kiln were built in about 1760.

The island had various owners and tenants until the naturalist Ronald Lockley took on the lease in 1927. By this time, the house had fallen into disrepair and the other buildings were in ruins. Lockley is mainly renowned for his pioneering studies of puffins and Manx shearwaters. He also wrote many books about island life and some of the first seabird monographs, while helping to set up the West Wales Field Society, the forerunner of today's Wildlife Trust. In 1933, he established Britain's first bird observatory on the island.

The lighthouse is now owned by the Wildlife Trust of South and West Wales, who bought the property from Trinity House in 2012. This was the last piece of the jigsaw for the Wildlife Trust, who, following a public appeal, purchased the rest of the island in 2006 to secure its globally important seabird populations. The light itself is still managed by Trinity House but is fully automated.

Skokholm lighthouse lights up.

SMALLS
LIGHTHOUSE
SMALLS ROCKS
PEMBROKESHIRE

SMALLS

LOCATION: 51°43′16″N, 5°40′12″W
OS GRID: SM466088
ELEVATION: 36m (118ft)
CHARACTER: Fl (3) 15s
RANGE: 33km (21 miles)

The original Smalls lighthouse was built in 1776, based on the plans of a musical instrument maker from Liverpool called Henry Whiteside. It stood on nine oak pillars, the idea being to allow the waves to pass underneath unimpeded. Despite its precarious appearance, it remained standing for 80 years and during its lifetime was reinforced with additional struts beyond the original nine.

Barely a quarter of a century had passed before an incident occurred that would still be talked about centuries later – a gruesome event that would come to change Trinity House's policy on the manning of lighthouses.

In 1801, Thomas Griffith and Thomas Howell were both stationed at the Smalls lighthouse, 32km (20 miles) out to sea. It was well known that the two men did not get on and to have been consigned to a long, lonely tour of duty with no respite from each other must have been uncomfortable for them, to say the least. Following an accident, Griffith became unwell and his health started to deteriorate rapidly. The pair's remote location and the battering storms meant that help would not be coming any time soon. After days of suffering, Griffith keeled over and died.

Howell knew that thanks to the well-known animosity between the pair, he would likely be suspected of murder if he discarded Griffith's body into the sea, so instead he kept his cadaver in the lighthouse. At least, that is, until the stench of the decaying corpse became too much for him. He set to work on building a coffin of sorts from salvaged wood and placed Griffith inside it, then lashed it to an exterior shelf.

Provisions were now running low and Howell was beginning to despair of being rescued before he too succumbed. However, his troubles were only just beginning.

As the storms continued to batter the lighthouse and pummel at Howell's mind, the box containing Griffith's corpse broke open. Now the cadaver could be seen dangling from the coffin, with one arm swinging in the wind – as though beckoning or perhaps pointing an accusing finger at his companion inside the cramped lighthouse apartment.

In despair and half starved, Howell managed to fulfil his duty and keep the lamp lit throughout. Nobody knows exactly how long he lived with Griffith's corpse as his only company, but it may have been as much as three weeks.

Ships continued to sail past the lighthouse, unaware of the nightmare unfolding within. While Howell managed to set off a number of emergency rockets, sailors who investigated reported a shadowy figure on the lighthouse galley, but as he seemed to be waving at them, they presumed that whatever the emergency was, it had passed.

Eventually, the storms abated and a relief crew arrived at the Smalls, to find a decomposed corpse barely hanging on to the rail and an emaciated keeper barely hanging on to his mind. When Howell returned to shore, he was so severely affected by what had happened that even those closest to him struggled to recognize him.

As a result of the tragedy, lighthouse teams were thereafter changed to rosters of three men. In 1859, Trinity House, having bought out the previous leaseholders 23 years earlier, began the construction of the current tower, which was completed in 1861. Its modest claim to fame was that it was the first British lighthouse to be fitted with a toilet!

A helideck was erected above the lantern in 1978 and the lighthouse itself was automated in 1987.

A boat tour to the present-day lighthouse, which was designed by James Walker and completed in 1861.

The original wooden lighthouse, supported by nine oaken beams, stood for an astonishing 80 years.

SOUTH BISHOP
LIGHTHOUSE
EMSGER ISLAND
PEMBROKESHIRE

SOUTH BISHOP

LOCATION: 51°51'10"N, 5°24'43"W
OS GRID: SM651226
ELEVATION: 44m (144ft)
CHARACTER: Fl W 5s
RANGE: 30km (19 miles)

The islet of South Bishop, or Emsger, lies approximately 8km (5 miles) off St David's Head, the westernmost tip of the Welsh coast. An application to build a light there was first made in 1831 by the local traders of Cardigan, but remained unheeded until it was supported three years later by merchants using the Bristol and St George's channels. At this point, Trinity House tasked their primary engineer, James Walker, with designing and building a lighthouse on the summit of this barren lava rock measuring 100m (328ft) by 250m (820ft) and sitting 30m (98ft) above the tide. The elevation was high enough to ensure that works were not inundated by the surge and swell of the sea south of St David's Head, but the rock was so exposed that winter storms regularly crashed across the surface, flooding enclosures, breaking windows and making any consideration of allowing families onto the station untenable despite the layout incorporating a two-storey dwelling intended for a household.

The 11m (36ft) brick tower was complete and ready to project its beam across the channel by 1839. The lighthouse was intended primarily to act as a waymark for vessels navigating offshore but could also assist shipping navigating their way around the Bishops and Clerks group of rocks, of which South Bishop is the largest.

The station had been built in the middle of a major migratory route and the toll of birds crashing into the lantern was alarming even for a lighthouse. To address this issue, special perches were installed in consultation with the Royal Society for the Protection of Birds and this appears to have greatly reduced the number of collisions.

South Bishop boasts the oldest completely unaltered lantern in a working lighthouse in England and Wales and is one of the few remaining operating lighthouses with rectangular astragals (frames) rather than the more common diagonal style. Measuring just over 4m (13ft) in diameter, the glazed portion is 3m (10ft) high and retains its original conical roof topped with a ball vent. The upper and lower rows of glazing have original flat glass, but the middle two rows were fitted with curved panes in the early 1970s to prevent false flashes.

STRUMBLE HEAD
LIGHTHOUSE
YNYS MEICEL
PEMBROKESHIRE

STRUMBLE HEAD

LOCATION: 52°01′47″N, 5°04′25″W
OS GRID: SM892412
ELEVATION: 45m (148ft)
CHARACTER: Fl (4) 15s
RANGE: 48km (30 miles)

The increase in shipping between Wales and Ireland, especially along the route from Pembrokeshire to Rosslare in County Wexford, necessitated the upgrading of lights along this dangerous stretch of the coast. When the new north breakwater in Fishguard was completed in 1905, Trinity House reviewed all aids to navigation in the area and decided to build a lighthouse on Ynys Meicel, or St Michael's Island, off the headland at Strumble Head to replace a lightvessel previously moored in the south of Cardigan Bay.

Although the area is known as the Pencaer Peninsula, it isn't really a peninsula. Bordered by the sea on two sides and on its inland side by a line of low hills, it nevertheless has the feeling of being isolated; and the task of building the lighthouse on the rocky site that had been selected soon revealed itself to be quite the challenge. A narrow footbridge was built to connect the island to the mainland, but even then the rocky and uneven ground made the construction of the lighthouse as difficult as any at an offshore station. To get equipment and supplies across the gap, a jackstay cable was swung between winches near the clifftop on the mainland and beside the lighthouse. In a stroke of ingenuity, the handrail of the footbridge formed the pipeline that carried oil into the tower basement.

The lighthouse tower is a circular stone-built structure, 17m (56ft) high with a galley and lantern and the keepers' flat-roofed cottages attached. To one side is a wood-lined building that once housed the explosive charges used for the original fog signal. This was replaced in the mid-1960s. The original revolving lens system weighed 4.5 tons and was supported in a bath of

Looking toward Strumble Head lighthouse.

mercury to reduce friction. It was rotated by a huge clockwork mechanism, which was itself driven by a quarter-ton weight suspended on a cable. This was dropped gradually down a cylinder running from the top to the bottom of the tower and it had to be rewound every 12 hours. In 1949, the illumination of the light was modernized from paraffin to electricity, and the lighthouse was fully electrified in 1965 when the optical system was replaced by more compact equipment. Strumble Head lighthouse was fully automated in 1980 and is monitored from the Trinity House Operations Control Centre at Harwich, Essex with regular visits made by an attendant.

Venture a few miles along the coast path to the east of Strumble Head lighthouse and you will arrive at Carregwastad Point, where a force of some 1,200 French soldiers landed in 1797, the last time the British mainland was invaded. A 30m (100ft) long "Last Invasion" tapestry commemorates the event. It was commissioned as a visual legacy of the invasion for the bicentenary commemorations in 1997 and is now on permanent exhibition in the purpose-built gallery attached to the library at Fishguard Town Hall. Sewn in a style reminiscent of the Bayeux tapestry, it is a humorous and engaging account of the ill-fated invasion and took 80 local women almost four years to complete.

BARDSEY

LOCATION: 52°45′00″N, 4°47′59″W
OS GRID: SH111206
ELEVATION: 39m (128ft)
CHARACTER: Fl R 10s
RANGE: 34km (21 miles)

Bardsey Island, or Ynws Enlli, meaning "island of the tides" in Welsh, lies off the Llŷn Peninsula and marks the division between the bays of Caernarfon and Cardigan. The lighthouse occupies the southern tip of the island, guiding ships through St George's Channel and the Irish Sea.

Once regarded as one of the holiest places in Britain, today Bardsey Island has only 4 year-round human residents and a population of about 200 grey seals and 300 sheep living alongside the 310 species of bird that have been recorded on the island. Known as the "island of 20,000 saints", Bardsey is reputed to house 20,000 graves. While that sounds unlikely for an island measuring just 2km (1.25 miles) by 1km (0.6 miles), an excavation in the 1990s at Tŷ Newydd, a stone house just south of the modern-day chapel, turned up 25 medieval graves in a very small plot. One body was discovered with a tenth-century silver coin in its mouth.

Bringing the boat
ashore at Bardsey.

It was believed that the Welsh kings of Llŷn and St Cadfan founded a monastery here in the sixth century. Local lore had it that those who died on the island would be spared damnation, and as the island became a place of pilgrimage, the concessions granted to its pilgrims were broadened. Three visits to Bardsey counted the same as one to Rome; at a time when international travel was a rare occurrence, this was an especially attractive option. By the early Middle Ages, these traditions had marked Bardsey as one of the holiest places in Britain.

The story of the island is a fascinating mix of myth, fact and conjecture. One of the earliest ships to have foundered off the island is said to have belonged to King Arthur. Legend has it that his vessel, the *Gwennan*, was lost to the notorious currents of Bardsey Sound. The ancient name for Bardsey Sound is

BARDSEY
ISLAND LIGHTHOUSE
LLYN PENINSULA
GWYNEDD

Ffrydiau Caswennan or the "Streams of Caswennan". Beyond Bardsey is Porth Neigwl, or Hell's Mouth, 6km (3.5 miles) of south-facing beach bordered by cliffs to the east and west. During the frequent southwesterly gales, ships rounding the island would find themselves being unwittingly swept toward shore and faced with the choice of either beaching on the sands or attempting to navigate past the cliffs. Unsurprisingly, most opted for the latter, but were more often than not pounded to bits on the beach and then picked over by islanders for salvage.

The 33m (108ft) red and white tower and keepers' cottages were completed in 1821 for a cost of £5,470 12s 6d (about £620,000 today) under the supervision of Joseph Nelson, who was responsible for building a number of lighthouses in the Severn Estuary. The lantern was raised in height in 1910 to increase its range. Following this improvement, the lightvessel moored to the south in Cardigan Bay was retired.

St Mary's Abbey was first established in the fifth century and was re-founded as an Augustinian priory in the 11th century, becoming an important pilgrimage centre for Wales.

The lighthouse tower is unusual in being square and is currently the tallest of its kind in Britain. It's made of ashlar limestone, quarried on Anglesey. In 1956, the light was converted to electric, and automated in 1987. For almost a decade it was monitored from the Trinity House Operations Control Centre at Holyhead, before operations were centralized in Harwich, Essex.

TWR MAWR
LIGHTHOUSE
LLANDDWYN ISLAND
ANGLESEY

TWR MAWR

LOCATION: 53°08′07″N, 4°24′56″W
OS GRID: SH385625
ELEVATION: 25m (82ft)
DEACTIVATED: 1975

At Ynys Llandwyn (Island of the Blessed). The Gate was carved by storyteller and woodworker, Dafydd Davies Hugh.

My visit to Ynys Llanddwyn (the "island of the blessed") to see Twr Mawr lighthouse was on one of those "soft days" when the rain turns to a fine mist, settling on your skin like the early morning dew. Everything is seen as though through a veil and the edges of the landscape become blurred.

At times like this it's easy to imagine Anglesey as the centre of Welsh paganism in the pre-Roman era. It was famously here that the druids made their last stand against the Roman legions between ad 59 and 79. It bought Boudicca time to reorganize her armies, but for the druids the battle was a little one-sided; those who didn't manage to flee perished under the Roman sword.

With the departure of the Romans, the early, more monastic Christian church started to flourish and this damp but picturesque corner of Britain attracted its ascetic and contemplative pioneers. One of those who settled on Llanddwyn island was Dwynwen, the Welsh patron saint of lovers. One of 24 daughters of King Brychan Brycheiniog, Dwynwen was unlucky in love, but nevertheless had the ear of God and prayed for true lovers to be more fortunate than she was. Her story drew pilgrims from all over to be blessed by the waters of her magical well. The remains of her church can be seen as you approach Twr Mawr.

The island, part of the Newborough Forest nature reserve, is really a peninsula, except at high tide when the pathway is covered by the sea. Because it lies 5km (3 miles) west of the Menai Strait, it commands the approach for all vessels navigating in toward Caernarfon or Bangor. The earliest recorded presence of daymarks, probably rubble towers, on Llanddwyn goes back to 1823, but one of these was altered into the present Twr Mawr around 1845, mimicking the style of local windmills, with a light first displayed the following year. The tower was designed purely as accommodation and the light was shone from a room at ground level rather than from the top of the structure, with a range of 11km (7 miles), and consisted of a silver-plated reflector and Fresnel lens, originally illuminated by six Argand lamps. In 1975, the station was taken out of service and the light transferred to the nearby Twr Bach, where it has been converted to solar power.

SOUTH STACK
LIGHTHOUSE
YNYS LAWD
ANGLESEY

SOUTH STACK

LOCATION: 53°18′24″N, 4°41′57″W
OS GRID: SH202822
ELEVATION: 60m (197ft)
CHARACTER: Fl 10s
RANGE: 44km (27 miles)

The rocky coast of Anglesey, jutting out into the Irish Sea, has long posed a threat to vessels that negotiate its shoreline in the busy shipping lanes connecting Liverpool and Dublin. As long ago as 1645, a petition was sent to Charles I, appealing for a lighthouse to be built to illuminate this stretch of coast. This was flatly turned down and almost two centuries were to pass before Captain Hugh Evans rallied the ship owners and merchants of Liverpool to the cause of building a lighthouse at South Stack. Overseen by Evans, this Herculean task was completed in a mere nine months despite the difficulties of building on a wave-pounded rock accessed via the steep cliffs of Holy Island.

By 1809, the first array of 21 oil lamps and reflectors were in place and literally operating like clockwork in the South Stack tower. Visible from almost 50km (31 miles) away in clear weather, the lighthouse was a godsend to shipping. However, at 60m (197ft) above sea level, it could often be lost in cloud or mist. Then, in 1831, the ever-resourceful Captain Evans came up with the novel idea of building an inclined track on which he could winch a moveable wooden cabin containing lights to within 12m (39ft) of the tide. This universally lauded innovation increased visibility of the light and vastly improved safety for ships negotiating the coastline. Several decades later, it was replaced by a permanent low light at the island's western tip, which was subsequently removed altogether when the main light was later upgraded.

The Trearddur Bay Atlantic 85 lifeboat Hereford Endeavour on exercises near South Stack.

Because there was room on the island to build accommodation, South Stack was originally regarded as a shore station and families lived at the lighthouse alongside the keepers. It must have been a tough life for all concerned, growing up on a tiny island off a slightly larger island, off a bigger island, off the British mainland. The families would have had to be pretty much self-sufficient, both in food supplies and in entertainment. Being swept off the cliffs was an ever-present danger for both adults and children, most especially during the frequent storms that battered this coast.

Few storms could compare with the tempest that struck on the night of 25 October 1859. Remembered as the "Royal Charter" gale, the storm was said to have been the worst of the century, and over two days more than 200 vessels were either driven ashore or completely wrecked. In total, over 800 lives were lost, including those of the almost 500 passengers and crew aboard the steamship *Royal Charter*, which sank within sight of shore. That same evening, the assistant keeper, Jack Jones, had been fighting the winds on his way across the iron bridge on to South Stack so that he could join the principal keeper, Henry Bowen, who was already on duty. A deluge of rocks was swept from the cliffs, striking Jones on the head. Almost senseless with concussion, he managed to drag himself to the door of the lighthouse, but unable to make himself heard over the howls of the wind, he passed out where he lay, dying weeks later from a compound fracture of the skull.

It's said that during stormy nights, if you're standing in the lantern room and you listen carefully, there among the wail of the tempest, you can hear a voice pleading to be let in.

Originally, the only means of crossing the deep water channel to the island was in a basket suspended on a hemp cable. This was superseded first by a rope suspension bridge and then by an iron structure in 1827. The current aluminium span was completed in 1997.

SKERRIES

LOCATION: 53°25′16″N, 4°36′29″W
OS GRID: SH267947
ELEVATION: 36m (118ft)
CHARACTER: Fl (2) 15s
RANGE: 37km (23 miles)

Four miles northeast of Holyhead lies a small gathering of rocky islands referred to in Welsh as Ynysoedd y Moelrhoniaid, or "the Islands of Bald-headed Grey Seals". The Skerries cover barely 16ha (40 acres) of sparsely vegetated rock, yet have been the undoing of hundreds of ships over the years.

Perhaps the most famous boat to have sunk here was HMY *Mary*, the first royal yacht to sail the seas and also the first to sink beneath its waves. On 25 March 1675, disaster struck during thick fog, when the yacht hit rocks to the southwest of the Skerries while on route from Dublin to Chester. It capsized, becoming wedged in the rocks. Luckily, the collapsed mast was touching the rocky outcrop and allowed 40 of the passengers and crew to scramble ashore and make it to the main part of the Skerries, which remain above water no matter how high the tide. However, the captain bravely went back along the mast to try to save the Earl of Meath, only to lose his own life in the attempt. The remaining 39 survivors were able to make a fire using a cask of gunpowder and timbers from the wreck, on which they are reported to have roasted some mutton. A "runlet of Usquebough" as it was described (the Irish, *uisce beatha*, translating as "water of life" . . . or whiskey) was also washed ashore and they made the most of their circumstances with a few drams to wash down their hastily prepared dinner. Two days later, they were rescued. (Happily, the majesty in question, Charles II, wasn't on board at the time.) You can now see more than 1,500 artefacts rescued from the ship at the National Museums and Galleries on Merseyside.

The Holyhead Maritime Museum at Newry beach is housed in the oldest lifeboat station in Wales.

SKERRIES
LIGHTHOUSE
YNYS Y MOELRHONIAID
ANGLESEY

A light had been proposed prior to the HMY *Mary* debacle by a private speculator, Henry Mascard, who saw a lucrative opportunity to levy dues on passing shipping, but his plans had been opposed by Trinity House. They also opposed a petition from the Irish Sea Traders in 1705 and it took another nine years until William Trench, who actually held the lease of the Skerries, was granted a patent by Queen Anne. The arrangement was that Trench would levy dues of one penny per ship and twopence per ton of cargo. This should have seen him become very rich, but without a robust collection agency in place, the tolls were often evaded by ship owners, and while William Trench had been wealthy when the light was first illuminated in November 1717, by the time he died in 1729 he was a ruined man.

When Trench died, the lease passed to his daughter, and an Act of Parliament in 1730 ensured that her heirs had sole claim to the Skerries. This would come back to haunt Trinity House in 1834 when an attempt was made by the organization to purchase the patent for the lighthouse. After the Act of 1836, which empowered Trinity House to buy out the remaining privately held lighthouses, the heirs of William Trench held out for a further five years, refusing to sell because it was such a profitable light. Eventually a deal was agreed and Trinity House purchased the Skerries lighthouse, the last privately owned lighthouse in Britain, for the astronomical sum of £444,984, or about £47 million in today's money! The lighthouse was then updated and, later, remodelled by James Walker in 1848 when a freestanding keeper's cottage was added, enclosed by crenellated walls and a cobbled courtyard. The balcony was also rebuilt with castellated stonework and a new cast-iron lantern with glazed square panes installed. In 1903, a small circular tower was added to the main tower for a sector light.

The station was converted to electric operation in 1927, and 60 years later, in 1987, the lighthouse was finally automated.

An exhilarating trip aboard a RIB or Rigid Inflatable Boat along the Anglesey Coast.

POINT LYNAS
LIGHTHOUSE
LLANEILIAN
ANGLESEY

POINT LYNAS

LOCATION: 53°24′58″N, 4°17′21″W
OS GRID: SH479934
ELEVATION: 39m (128ft)
CHARACTER: Oc 10s
RANGE: 33km (21 miles)

The lighthouse at Point Lynas.

Point Lynas, or Trwyn Eilian (named after St Eilian) in Welsh, is a headland on the northeast corner of Anglesey. A pilot station was established here by the town of Liverpool in 1766 to guide ships entering and leaving the Mersey, and in 1779 the Liverpool Pilotage Service leased a house from which two lights were shown about 300m (985ft) to the south of the present lighthouse. Two reflectors enabled modest lights to be displayed to the east and the west.

Over time it became apparent that the lights in their original location were inadequate, as industrial smoke rising from below tended to obscure the beam. When consulted in 1834, the renowned Scottish lighthouse engineer Alan Stevenson suggested raising the lights by building a 21m (70ft) tower, but ultimately the decision was taken to move the whole caboodle up the hill and start from scratch.

Built a year later, the striking castellated complex is mostly to a design by Jesse Hartley, engineer to the Mersey Docks and Harbour Board, with some later additions by George Lyster. The building comprises a two-storey dwelling surmounted by a square tower 11m (36ft) high. The semi-circular lantern, located at the base on a raised plinth, dates from about 1874.

The original Argand lamp, visible for 26km (16 miles), was converted to oil in 1901. In 1951, the station was electrified and the occulting light was upgraded to achieve its current range. In 1973, Trinity House took over responsibility for the lighthouse and the light was automated in 1989 and the pilots moved to Amlwch Pier. While the light is still operational, the building and cottages have been sold for use as a private home and holiday accommodation.

Below the lighthouse is one of 56 National Coastwatch Institution (NCI) stations, which keep a manned watch around the coastline of England and Wales. The NCI was formed when two Cornish fishermen lost their lives near a recently closed coastguard lookout and locals decided to restore the visual watch. NCI watchkeepers provide eyes and ears along the coast, monitoring radio channels in poor visibility. They can then alert HM Coastguard if they detect an emergency.

TRWYN DU
LIGHTHOUSE
NO
PASSAGE
LANDWARD
PENMON
ANGLESEY

TRWYN DU

An old VW camper van parked by the café at Trwyn Du.

LOCATION : 53°18′46″N, 4°02′26″W
OS GRID: SH641814
ELEVATION: 19m (62ft)
CHARACTER: Fl 5s
RANGE: 23km (14 miles)

The island of Anglesey marks the extreme tip of north Wales and is served by a number of lights to ensure safe passage. The first of these was the Skerries lighthouse, followed by South Stack and Point Lynas.

Tragedy occurred in 1831 when the paddle steamer the *Rothesay Castle* sank near Puffin Island with the loss of 130 lives. As a result of this disaster, there was an urgent call for a lighthouse to mark the rocks at the northern entrance to the Menai Strait. A lifeboat station was duly established in 1832 at Penmon on the southeast tip of Anglesey and Trwyn Du lighthouse was built between Black Point (Trwyn Du) and Puffin Island in 1837. The lighthouse was constructed to a design by James Walker. It was his first sea-washed tower and served as a prototype for the more ambitious redesign of Smalls lighthouse, which he was to embark on in 1857.

Trwyn Du lighthouse sits on a low-lying rock surrounded by shingle beaches. The circular stone tower is distinguished by three black bands on a white background. One of the features that Walker included in this offshore sentinel is a stepped base, designed to break up immense waves, which had lashed against earlier lighthouses on the site, and to reduce the force of the water at the bottom of the tower.

The tower has a crenellated stone parapet rather than a gallery with iron railings, and becomes narrower in diameter above the halfway point. It bears the words "NO PASSAGE LANDWARD" on its north and south sides. From a short distance away and especially during calm weather, a mariner could be easily fooled into thinking that there was enough depth to pass on the landward side, but the area is shallow and littered with serrated rock.

In 1922, Trwyn Du was the first Trinity House lighthouse to be automated and was converted to operate with acetylene using a sun valve. In the same year, a 178kg (392lb) fog bell began to sound once every 30 seconds. However, Trinity House started trials of a new foghorn in August 2019. The lamp itself became solar powered in 1996, when the lighthouse was modernized extensively.

PERCH ROCK
LIGHTHOUSE
NEW BRIGHTON
MERSEYSIDE

PERCH ROCK

LOCATION: 53°26′40″N, 3°02′32″W
OS GRID: SJ308946
ELEVATION: 23m (75ft)
CHARACTER: Fl W(2) R(1)
DEACTIVATED: 1973–2016

Visible from the nearby Marine Promenade in New Brighton, New Brighton lighthouse, or Perch Rock as it's often known locally, was also called Black Rock lighthouse during its infancy in the mid-19th century. It is strategically situated at the confluence of the River Mersey and Liverpool Bay, and gets its name from the rocky outcrop that runs down to the shore.

The first beacons to light the north channel through the Mersey appeared as early as 1683 in the form of lanterns fastened to a simple timber tripod – or perch. The charge imposed on passing vessels for upkeep of the lights was sixpence for foreign vessels and half that for locals. The lanterns weren't particularly successful, however, and were easily washed away during storms. Even the pilot boat *Liver*, whose crew would have known these waters better than anyone, came a cropper on the rocks one night in 1821, when a rogue wave extinguished the lantern and the disorientated boat took out the whole caboodle, perch and all.

As the Port of Liverpool continued to develop as a major international trading hub, the perch and its primitive light were deemed inadequate navigation aids, requiring as they did constant upkeep in return for very limited illumination. A new, more permanent structure was needed, and a suitable site was quickly identified for a lighthouse. As the base of the new tower would be under water for much of the day and the tides in the bay could get quite stormy during the winter months, the planned structure would incorporate many of the features of a rock station.

Following the ceremonial laying of the foundation stone by the Mayor of Liverpool, Thomas Littledale, construction of the current lighthouse began in 1827 and was carried out by Tomkinson & Company.

Fort Perch Rock, situated at the mouth of Liverpool Bay in New Brighton, was built in the 1820s to defend the Port of Liverpool. Today it serves as a museum, concert venue and tourist attraction.

Blocks of Anglesey granite were interlocked using dovetail joints and marble dowels, a building method influenced by the construction of John Smeaton's Eddystone lighthouse. The 29m (95ft) tower is painted white with a red-hued metal lantern topping it off.

The light first shone across the Wirral on 1 March 1839, and displayed two white flashes followed by a red flash every minute. To power the light, 30 Argand lamps were mounted on a 3-sided, hand-cranked revolving array, with red glass in front of 1 side. Three bells served as a fog signal and were operated by the same clockwork mechanism that caused the lamps to revolve. The light was ultimately electrified, but in 1973, thanks to advances in marine technology and the fact that the illuminated Liverpool docks rendered the light almost invisible, Perch Rock was decommissioned.

The lighthouse was sold to the Kingham family, who undertook to restore it with the aid of some grants, and the Grade II Heritage listed structure remains a well-loved landmark in New Brighton. In 2001, an LED light source was installed, which flashed the names of those lost at sea, including the 1,517 fatalities of the *Titanic*. In 2016, the "Brighten New Brighton" project was implemented, restoring the lights at the top of the lighthouse on the landward side.

Perch Rock lighthouse and Liverpool container terminal in the background.

ST BEES

The old foghorn at St Bees.

LOCATION: 54°30′49″N, 3°38′12″W
OS GRID: NX941143
ELEVATION: 102m (335ft)
CHARACTER: Fl (2) 20s
RANGE: 34km (21 miles)

Constructed by Trinity House in 1822, St Bees lighthouse is located at the eastern extremity of the Cumbrian coast, on the high promontory of St Bees Head. It was built to guide boats sailing between the ports of Wales to the south and harbours of the Solway Firth.

In 1718, Trinity House bought land on the head but leased their patent for a lighthouse on the site to the entrepreneur Thomas Lutwige. The terms of the lease were for 99 years at an annual rent of £20, and required Lutwige to build the tower and maintain the light at his own expense. For this, however, he would be granted the licence to collect dues at a rate of three halfpence a ton on any cargo transported by vessels docking at Whitehaven, Maryport and Workington. Quite a sum at the time.

Lutwige constructed a round stone tower 9m (30ft) tall and 5m (16ft) in diameter, topped by a large metal grate on top of which a coal fire was maintained as a beacon. Copious amounts of fuel were required to keep the fire lit, especially during the long winter nights, and part of the keeper's job was to lug almost 100 tons of coal per annum up the steps to the grating. Keeping the fire blazing and smoke-free was a strenuous and dirty job, and there was no shortage of complaints from shipmasters that the fire was too low or obscured by smoke.

In 1822, tragedy struck when the tower was destroyed by fire, claiming the lives of the keeper's wife and five children. In the aftermath, the decision was taken by Trinity House to change the light from coal-fuelled to oil. This had the advantage not only of improving safety, but also the consistency of the light. With that, the last coal-fired lighthouse in Britain was no more. The old structure was replaced by a new circular lighthouse built to the design of Joseph Nelson and fitted with the latest in lighthouse technology. The new 8.2m (27ft) tall tower was fitted at a cost of £1,447 (about £175,000 in today's money), with 15 Argand lamps set in parabolic reflectors, and it was up and running within the year.

In 1865, it was decided that a new, expanded station should be established

St BEES
LIGHTHOUSE
St BEES HEAD
CUMBRIA

slightly further inland, which was to be equipped with accommodation for two keepers. Work began that May and beneath the foundation stone an early time capsule was buried: a zinc box containing a scroll signed by Henry Norris and John Glaister, the new station's engineer and builder, respectively. Also included in the box were current newspapers and journals and various coins of the realm.

The new tower stood 17m (56ft) high, equipped with a lantern originally destined for Europa Point in Gibraltar. It was fitted with a first-order catadioptric optic that included a dioptric mirror which redirected light from the landward side of the lamp out to sea. (The order number of the optic refers to the size and focal length of the lens; first order would be reserved for a major sea light, while third order was more usual for a large harbour light.)

From 1913, an explosive fog signal was sounded. When this was replaced in the 1960s by an array of Tannoys, blasting a signal every 45 seconds, a new building was built to house them near the cliff edge. The signal no longer operates, but you can visit inside the building on open days.

In 1987, the light was fully electrified with a beam showing a range of 33km (21 miles). The keepers were retired at this time and the station was automated and monitored from Trinity House's offices at Holyhead – one of only five stations controlled from the Anglesey centre. Operations were subsequently centred at Harwich, Essex, from where the station is now controlled.

The bracing walk along the clifftop path from St Bees takes in dramatic views of the Isle of Man and the Cumbrian Mountains and coastline.

CHICKEN ROCK

LOCATION: 54°02′16″N, 4°50′19″W
OS GRID: SC142639
ELEVATION: 38m (125ft)
CHARACTER: Fl 5s
RANGE: 33km (21 miles)

The original high and low lights on the Calf of Man were eventually retired due to being persistently obscured by fog. They were replaced by the light at Chicken Rock.

By the mid-19th century, due to fog persistently obscuring the two then operational lighthouses on the Calf of Man, the demand for a new light on this stretch of water could no longer be ignored. The two Calf lights acted as a transit light for the approach around Chicken Rock. If one or the other was not visible, disaster beckoned. The Board of Trade passed a resolution stating that: "The night light on Calf of Man, so often enveloped in fog and rendered useless, [is] to be removed to the Chicken Rock, one mile and a half out and is of considerable size and great danger."

After approval was granted in 1868, construction of the lighthouse began two years later. However, work was hampered by the fact that the rock was inundated by the tide for all but five hours a day. Designed by David and Thomas Stevenson, the tower was made from granite quarried near Dalbeattie in southwest Scotland. The project took almost five years to complete and the light from Chicken Rock was illuminated for the first time on 1 January 1875.

The family accommodation blocks on the Calf of Man were maintained for a time, but no food could be grown in the gardens because the rat population was out of control and so in 1886 a new shore station was built in Port St Mary.

As a measure of how easily keepers could be stranded, in January 1960 the local newspaper reported that the two lightkeepers were marooned on Chicken Rock over Christmas and New Year. They had to forgo Christmas Day and ration their provisions. That proved prescient. Three weeks later than scheduled, the relief boat from Port St Mary eventually managed to get through and the men were able to get home for a very late Christmas dinner.

The following December, a fire broke out in the lighthouse and three keepers had a narrow escape, being rescued by the Port St Mary RNLI lifeboat. When the lighthouse was repaired the following spring, it was decided that the station would be automated and the keepers withdrawn.

By 1968 Chicken Rock was reclassified as a minor light. However, when the range of the Chicken Rock lighthouse was increased in 2007, the Calf of Man station was decommissioned.

CHICKEN ROCK
LIGHTHOUSE
CHICKEN ROCK
ISLE OF MAN

MULL OF GALLOWAY
LIGHTHOUSE
DRUMMORE
STRANRAER

MULL OF GALLOWAY

LOCATION: 54°38′07″N, 4°51′27″W
OS GRID: NX156304
ELEVATION: 99m (325ft)
CHARACTER: Fl W 20s
RANGE: 33km (21 miles)

The Mull of Galloway is perched on the end of the Rhins peninsula and is Scotland's most southerly point. The lighthouse here was constructed over the course of two years by the engineer Robert Stevenson and was first lit on 26 March 1830, with the light, housed in a 26m (85ft) tower, standing some 99m (325ft) above sea level. One hundred and fifteen steps lead up to the lantern room, from where, on a clear day, visitors can see as far as the Isle of Man and even Northern Ireland.

Initially, the beam used an occulting system, in which two cylindrical shades moved up and down on a frame to block out the light at a given interval – much like someone covering the beam of a torch with their hand. In this instance, the period of darkness would last longer than the period of light. (Even on a rotating light, you'll notice that the period of dark usually lasts longer than the sudden flash of light, which helps to attract more attention to the light's location.) Over time, the arrangement for the light was changed and it eventually had a rotating beam, for which the lens was rotated on rollers rather than a bed of mercury. The rollers were so precisely fashioned that the light could be turned by hand. Behind the lens was a simple paraffin light, much as might be found on an old sailing ship – the genius of the system lay in the Fresnel lens. First developed by the Frenchman Augustin-Jean Fresnel, the lens that bears his name is a type of composite, compact lens that uses a large aperture and short focal length to produce an optic which magnifies a modest illumination into a monstrous 29,000 candles, visible for nearly 33km (21 miles).

Not all fatalities on this stretch of the coast were due to poor visibility at sea

The cliffs at the Mull of Galloway resonate with the calls of kittiwakes. The name is derived from the bird's call, a shrill "kittee-wa-aaake, kitte-wa-aaake"!

level. On 8 June 1944, pilot Claudius Echallier and engineer Royston Edwin Staniford were delivering a Beaufighter plane from Prestwick, Ayrshire, to Cumbria when, in heavy fog, they clipped the outer boundary wall of the lighthouse, bouncing off the roof of the supplies store and then crashing into the sea. Both men sadly perished and a plaque has been erected at the site to commemorate the crash.

By 1971, electricity had arrived at the station and the light was converted to a sealed beam on a gearless revolving pedestal – not dissimilar to a row of car headlights rotating to create a flash sequence; this arrangement made the light almost fully automatic. Full automation followed 17 years later, in 1988, and today the light is monitored from the Northern Lighthouse Board's headquarters in Edinburgh.

In 2012, the South Rhins Community Development Trust, responsible for the management of visitor attractions at the Mull, made the decision to apply for a community buyout of the site, as the Northern Lighthouse Board were considering dispensing with the buildings, with the exception of the lighthouse tower. The trust was successful in raising the necessary funds and the buyout was completed in 2013.

Today, not only can you climb the lighthouse tower, but you can visit the engine rooms and foghorn, view an engaging exhibition of lighthouse history and stay in one of the three lighthouse keepers' cottages. The surrounding area is officially designated as a Site of Special Scientific Interest (SSSI) in recognition of its importance as a precious maritime habitat.

A foghorn has been in operation at the Mull of Galloway since 1894 and would be used by keepers if visibility dropped below 6.5km (4 miles). It last sounded as an aid to marine navigation in November 1987 but has since undergone restoration and is now the only operational foghorn on mainland Scotland.

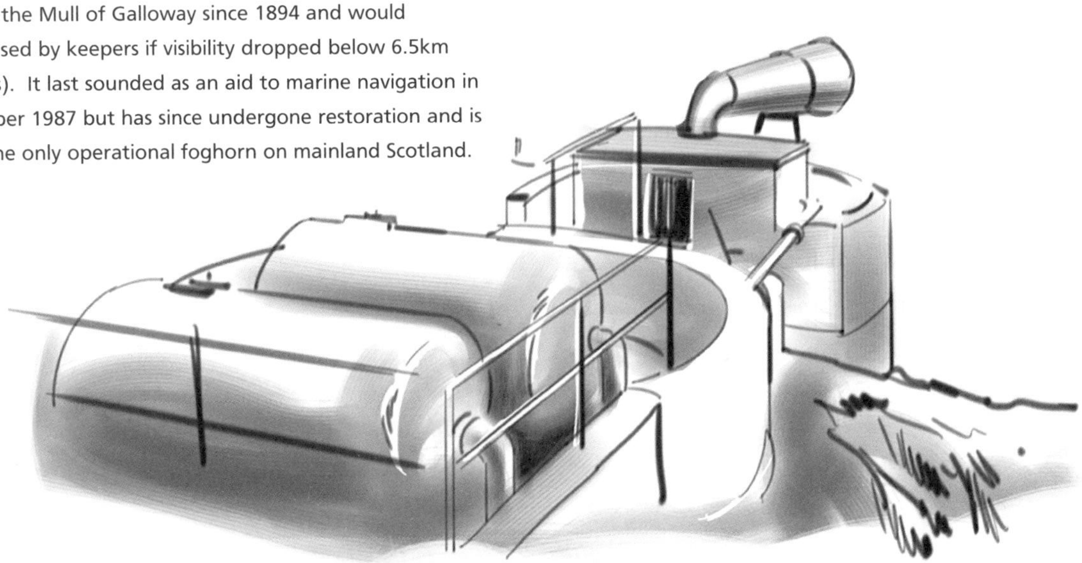

TURNBERRY

LOCATION: 55°19′34″N, 4°50′39″W
OS GRID: NS196072
ELEVATION: 29m (95ft)
CHARACTER: Fl 15s
RANGE: 22km (14 miles)

In 1869, the wonderfully named Receiver of Wreck, a revenue official answerable to parliament and based in Ayr, suggested to the Board of Trade that a light should be erected on the Bristo Rock, a reef responsible for numerous wrecks along the Ayrshire coast. This request was passed on to the Northern Lighthouse Board, and their engineers David and Thomas Stevenson, after due diligence, responded that a better position for a light would be at Turnberry Point at a location where the moat of Turnberry Castle had once been.

The castle, originally the stronghold of the lords of Galloway, had by the 13th century come into the possession of Marjorie, Countess of Carrick. Legend has it that the newly widowed noblewoman held a visiting knight, Robert de Brus, captive until he agreed to marry her. He seemed to acquiesce without too much arm twisting, and she bore them a rather famous son, Robert the Bruce, future king of Scotland. It's not certain that Turnberry was his actual birthplace, but he would certainly have spent his boyhood exploring the castle halls.

Turnberry is a popular destination for golf. Its three courses and associated luxury hotel were bought by the Trump Organization in 2014.

Today, little more than the lower vaults and cellars of the castle remain, although there are also hints of a drawbridge and portcullis. Below, caves leading out into the sea may have served as a harbour. From its surviving footprint, the castle would appear to have been a major fortress.

Construction of the lighthouse commenced in 1871 and was completed two years later. The light was converted to solar power in 2012 and a year later downgraded from a major to a minor light. Previously, in 1992, the attached keeper's accommodation had been sold to the adjoining golf club.

TURNBERRY
LIGHTHOUSE
TURNBERRY POINT
FIRTH OF CLYDE

From the start, Turnberry was a popular golf course and resort, made easily accessible thanks to the arrival of the Maidens and Dunure Light Railway. The golf club was the brainchild of Archibald Kennedy, third Marquess of Ailsa, who held 71 hectares (175 acres) of land at Turnberry. During both world wars the military took possession of the club and there was concern it would not open again following World War II. Instead, the course was redesigned by Mackenzie Ross and reopened to acclaim in 1951. The course has hosted the Open Championship four times, including the famous 1977 event in which Tom Watson beat Jack Nicklaus by a single stroke, a contest that became known as the "duel in the sun". The property has been owned by the Trump Organization since 2014, which now brands the course Trump Turnberry.

Ailsa Craig, or Creag Ealasaid in Scots Gaelic, meaning "fairy rock", is a startling presence on the horizon. This island of volcanic rock has long been quarried to make, of all things, curling stones. Today, it is a bird sanctuary, attracting a large population of gannets and an increasing number of puffins.

CLOCH
LIGHTHOUSE
FIRTH OF CLYDE
INVERCLYDE

CLOCH

LOCATION: 55°56′29″N, 4°52′50″W
OS GRID: NS202757
ELEVATION: 23m (75ft)
CHARACTER: Fl W 3s
RANGE: 26km (16 miles)

Designed by Thomas Smith and his son-in-law Robert Stevenson, Cloch lighthouse was built in 1797 by the contractors Kermack and Gall and the engineer John Clarkson. The lighthouse consists of a short, round tower with corbelled walkways and triangular windows, and is now accompanied by two sets of keepers' houses. The older generation of these is located to the north of the station and used as stores, while the more recent buildings are attached to the tower and have crow-stepped gables.

Cloch was one of the three lighthouses erected to help ships navigate the unpredictable currents at the head of the Firth of Clyde and is situated about 5km (3 miles) to the southwest of the town of Gourock, at the point where the river's westerly flow turns south into the estuary and out to the open sea. Here, its purpose was to warn ships of the existence of the Gantocks, a dangerous reef located directly west of the point. The word *cloch* means "stone" in Gaelic.

The lighthouse first came into operation on 11 August 1797, using a simple oil lantern installed by Smith and Stevenson. An Argand lamp with silver reflector superseded this in 1829, and this in turn was replaced in about 1900 by an acetylene device utilizing dioptric and catadioptric lenses. The lenses, weighing up to 1.5 tons, floated in baths of mercury and were rotated by a clockwork mechanism powered by falling weights, which the keeper needed to hand-wind to the top of the tower each time they fell down. This operation had to be repeated approximately every half hour – the winding alone could take five minutes – and could not be overlooked or the rotation would stop, rendering the light useless. The keeper also had to tend the light, ensuring the burners and fuel supply worked as intended, and keep the lenses and windows pristine, which – given the smoky, sticky residue that the fuel gave off – required constant attention. Between winding the mechanism, tending to the flame and making reports on weather and shipping, the keepers' shifts of four hours left no time for slacking. On the other hand, the busy schedule made the watch pass quickly.

For the first 15 years of its existence, Cloch lighthouse was often blindsided by high ground at Toward Point further down the river. Until the construction of a lighthouse at the Point in 1812, sailors sailing up the Clyde in dark or stormy weather had to gingerly manoeuvre their craft mid-stream around the turn in the river until the light at Cloch came into view. A few degrees off and there was a good chance of running aground. Once the Cloch was in clear view, the vessel could then safely turn to starboard by the lighthouse, toward anchorage off Greenock. Foghorns operated by compressed air were added between 1895 and 1897.

In the 1930s, the Clyde Lighthouses Trust pioneered the use of "talking beacons", which enabled vessels to determine the position of a lighthouse no matter the weather. Cloch lighthouse and Little Cumbrae, to the south, were part of this system. An automatic radio broadcast announced the name and position of the lighthouse and then counted up to 30, thereby enabling the listener to estimate the distance between his position and the fog station. This invention went on to be used by the US Lighthouse Service at many of their 100 stations. Today, the talking beacon is no longer in use at Cloch and the main light has been replaced by an optic mounted on a pole just outside the lantern. The light continues to flash with the same character but is of restricted range.

Cloch lighthouse, as seen from the turn at Gourock.

DUBH ARTACH

LOCATION: 56°07′57″N, 6°38′05″W
OS GRID: NM121029
ELEVATION: 44m (144ft)
CHARACTER: Fl (2) W 30s
RANGE: 37km (23 miles)

Between 1800 and 1854, over 30 ships were wrecked on the skerry known as Dhu Heartach, or St John's Rock. This reef was not alone in presenting a formidable obstacle, for beyond it, whether US-bound or en route to the Baltic ports, vessels navigating the passage between the Rinns of Islay and Skerryvore faced the fearsome prospect of the Torran Rocks. A light on the skerry, it was suggested, would not only improve navigation through these choppy waters, but enable ships to reach safe harbour in the small islands lying between the isle of Colonsay and Oban on the Scottish mainland.

So it was that in June 1865, Thomas Stevenson, father of Robert Louis Stevenson and joint engineer to the Commissioners, surveyed the rock with his brother David and submitted their recommendation for the establishment of a light, noting that it would be a "work of no ordinary magnitude". Projects of this complexity usually take time, but the urgency of the undertaking was quickly underlined by the unprecedented storms that raged through the North Channel on 30 and 31 December 1866, when an astonishing 24 vessels were lost or ran aground in the area bordered by the islands of Tiree, Iona, Colonsay and Islay. Ten months later, the statutory sanction of the Board of Trade for a lighthouse on the rock was signed.

The shore station for the lighthouse was to be located on the tidal island of Erraid in the Outer Hebrides and, on 7 June 1867, the steam tug *Powerful* picked up skilled workmen and masons at Aberdeen and set sail for the rock. Because of the exposed site, initial work would primarily take place between June and October, but even then, progress was often interrupted by storms and gales. Inclement weather aside, the build went smoothly and by November 1871, the structure was already 31m (102ft) above its foundations. A late adjustment meant that the tower was now solid up to the 21st course, rather than the 13th, and accordingly, accessing the front door now entailed a 9m (30ft) climb on an exposed metal-rung ladder – no mean feat in the teeth of a storm!

To deliver wages to a workforce stranded on an isolated rock in the western reaches

DUBH ARTACH
LIGHTHOUSE
TORRAN ROCKS
FIRTH OF LORN

of the Atlantic Ocean took some ingenuity before the advent of wireless transfers. Add to this the further complication that the sums involved excluded transactions in higher denomination bank notes but instead required weighty coins and you really had a problem on your hands. Once a month, a member of the construction crew was required to make the 64km (40-mile) return journey by open boat to Oban to collect the pay. Because of the weight of the silver that he carried back, he needed to hire an additional craft to carry it and the whole round trip took a week!

Eventually, an arrangement was reached with the Royal Bank of Scotland whereby the wages (anywhere up to £1,000, depending on the size of workforce) were put in a box (for security's sake referred to only as "The Box"!) and then fastened under lock, chain and key in a secure location aboard the vessel *Dunvegan Castle*, on which it was conveyed to the men working at the lighthouse. For further insurance, there were only two keys – one held by the bank and the other by the cashier at Erraid.

By 1872, the lantern's mechanism and internal fittings were ready to assemble and, on 1 November 1872, the lighthouse was illuminated for the first time with a fixed white light and an arc of 7 degrees showing red. To distinguish it from Skerryvore's single stroke on the minute, the fog bell sounded 10 seconds of rapid strokes every 30 seconds.

In 1890, the distinctive red band was added to the tower, again to distinguish it from nearby Skerryvore, and in 1964 the lighthouse's name was changed from Dhuheartach to Dubh Artach, or "Black Rock". The lighthouse was automated in 1971 and is now remotely monitored from NLB headquarters in George Street, Edinburgh.

After moving from the original location at Hynish, Tiree, the observatory on the island of Erraid served as the signal tower for Dubh Artach.

SKERRYVORE

LOCATION: 56°19′22″N, 7°06′53″W
OS GRID: NL839262
ELEVATION: 46m (151ft)
CHARACTER: FL W 10s
RANGE: 42km (26 miles)

In June 1838, Alan Stevenson, Engineer in Chief to the Northern Lighthouse Board, and a group of hardy workmen made landing on the Sgeir Mhòr, or Skerry Vhor (meaning "Big Rock"), to commence the immense task of constructing a lighthouse on this isolated and treacherous skerry, located 17km (11 miles) southwest of Tiree in the Hebrides. As the rock remained above the tide at all times, Stevenson devised a punishing schedule of 16- to 17-hour workdays in order to build an elevated wooden cabin to accommodate the workmen while they laboured throughout the coming summers. (Working on the reef when the weather deteriorated in the mid-autumn would be all but impossible.)

Hynish shore station, Isle of Tiree. These buildings served as a smithy and workshops.

By November, storms had undone all the summer's work and little survived but the workings on the rock itself. Stevenson, however, was not a man to be discouraged by a small setback like this and by the late spring of the following year, he and his crew were back again, determined to complete the barracks by summer's end. While they laboured on the rock, a larger group of workmen quarried granite on the Ross of Mull, which was then shaped and dressed on the island of Tiree, ready to be brought to the rock and fitted together like a giant three-dimensional jigsaw.

In April 1840, the construction crew returned and found the restored barracks intact. Now work could begin in earnest and, on 7 July, the Duke of Argyle arrived to lay the foundation stone. Thanks to the exactness of Stevenson's measurements and planning, the masons were able to lay as many as 85 blocks a day. Two years of relentless graft and exactitude followed and, on 25 July 1842, the last stone was laid at a height of 42m (138ft). All in all, approximately 4,300 tons of precision-cut masonry had been laid on this lonely

SKERRYVORE
LIGHTHOUSE
AN SGEIR MHÓR
INNER HEBRIDES

reef, without loss of life or limb, itself an incredible achievement given the safety record of such projects at the time. The last piece of the puzzle now arrived, itself in pieces: the lantern was hoisted up in sections and completed in place.

The beam shone out from Skerryvore lighthouse for the first time on the evening of 1 February 1844, accompanied by its two fog bells sounding one stroke every half minute. (The larger of these bells now resides in St Connan's Kirk, Loch Awe.) The tower, the tallest in Scotland at 46m (151ft), was built to a hyperbolic curve that focused the centre of gravity at the lowest possible point of the structure. This guaranteed stability and endurance against the roaring waves.

Skerryvore provided uninterrupted service until the night of 16 March 1954, when fire broke out on the seventh floor of the tower. The keepers had no time to raise the alarm and had to abandon the lighthouse, but luckily they were rescued the following day when the relief vessel arrived as part of its regular schedule. Extensive damage had been done to both the interior and the structure itself and for the next three years, a lightvessel and temporary lights replaced the main light. By the time Skerryvore was back in action, the light had been converted to electric. In 1972, a helicopter pad with additional fuel storage tanks was constructed on the rocks at the base of the tower and the lighthouse was finally automated in 1994.

The signal tower for Skerryvore, built in 1843 to provide semaphore communication with the lighthouse. Semaphore is a means of sending visual messages using hand-held flags, discs or paddles - a 19th-century version of texting!

ARDNAMURCHAN

LOCATION: 56°43′37″N, 6°13′34″W
OS GRID: NM415674
ELEVATION: 55m (181ft)
CHARACTER: Fl (2) 20s
RANGE: 33km (21 miles)

The Ardnamurchan peninsula is located due west of Fort William in the Scottish Highlands. Along its southern shore lie Loch Sunart and the Sound of Mull, and to the north are the islands of Skye, Muck, Eigg and Rum. It is the most westerly point of the British mainland. The origins of the name Ardnamurchan are contested endlessly, but the two most widely supported versions are: "point of the seals or otters" and "point of the pirates or wreckers". There are still plenty of seals to be seen here; the other candidates for eponymity are more elusive.

The lighthouse was established by Alan Stevenson, son of the pioneering lighthouse builder Robert Stevenson and uncle of author Robert Louis Stevenson. The 35m (115ft) stone tower bestrides the headland, looming high above the waves. Designed in the "Egyptian" style, it has a distinctive profile at the balcony and lantern level. The lighthouse is constructed of blocks of pink granite quarried on the island of Erraid and took three years to complete. During this time, deliveries of fresh food to this isolated site were sporadic at best and scurvy broke out among the construction workers. Fruit and vegetables (and a doctor) had to be hastily sent for!

The oil light was first exhibited on the night of 5 October 1849 and the station was attended to by two keepers on a yearly allowance of £18. It is recorded that

The West Ardnamurchan Community Garden was established in 2010 as an initiative to grow food locally. The self-service shop has an honesty box in place of a cashier.

they kept two cows and about a dozen sheep. There's no mention of fresh fruit or veg, but we can presume they propagated an adequate provision of neeps and tatties.

Throughout January 1852, Scotland was subject to storms of unusual ferocity, with houses washed away in Stranraer and tides said to have risen 5m (16ft) higher than ever

ARDNAMURCHAN
LIGHTHOUSE
LOCHABER
HIGHLANDS

before. On the morning of 22 January, the tempest turned its fury on Ardnamurchan. Lightning struck the tower, exploding window panes and stripping plaster from the interior. The heavy seas destroyed more than 15m (50ft) of boundary wall and 12m (40ft) of road, as well as the keepers' boat.

The station is now automated and the keepers' cottages and other buildings are privately operated as a visitor centre and social enterprise, where guests can discover more about Scottish lighthouses in general and the flora and fauna of Ardnamurchan in particular.

Camas nan Geall (the "Bay of Strangers") is a lovely sandy bay on the southern shores of the Ardnamurchan peninsula.

NEIST POINT
LIGHTHOUSE
GLENDALE
ISLE OF SKYE

NEIST POINT

LOCATION: 57°25′23″N, 6°47′20″W
OS GRID: NG126471
ELEVATION: 43m (141ft)
CHARACTER: Fl 5s
RANGE: 30km (19 miles)

The old crane at the landing point for the lighthouse.

Neist Point lighthouse is situated on the most westerly headland on Skye, braced on top of dramatic cliffs and facing toward the Outer Hebrides. Neist Point is a renowned viewing point for Minke whales, basking sharks, dolphins and porpoises during the summer months. The cliffs are also host to a huge variety of seabirds, including guillemots, razorbills, shags and gannets.

The lighthouse, another of David A Stevenson's carefully designed structures, came into operation in 1909; the fog signal, since retired, was completed the following year. Standing high above the sea, the tower itself rises to a height of 19m (62ft).

Neist Point lighthouse tower and lantern.

On the opposite shore of the headland can be seen the old aerial cableway that was used to haul up supplies delivered by boat. While the lighthouse itself sits on private property, the headland is accessible via a short walk from a small car park at the end of the road. The route takes you down some steep steps, past grazing sheep and along a spectacular route with great views eastward to the cliffs of Waterstein Head and the Hoe.

Along the way you'll find a rocky outcrop called An t-Aigeach (meaning "stallion's head"). Here you can see the similarity between the geology of this part of Scotland and the Giant's Causeway on Ireland's Antrim coast. Indeed, Fingal's Cave on the island of Staffa in the Inner Hebrides and the Antrim causeway are part of the same ancient lava flow, which may at one time have formed a "bridge" between the two sites.

A short stroll northeast from the car park will bring you to the start of the Neist and Milovaig clifftop walk from where the view back toward the lighthouse, especially at sunset, is spectacular.

EILEAN GLAS

LOCATION: 57°51′25″N, 6°38′31″W
OS GRID: NG247947
ELEVATION: 43m (141ft)
CHARACTER: Fl (3) 20s
RANGE: 33km (21 miles)

The tower and foghorn at Eilean Glas.

Eilean Glas lighthouse is located on a tiny peninsula on the eastern tip of Scalpay, connected to Harris by a single-track bridge. It was one of Scotland's first four lighthouses (the others being Kinnaird Head, Mull of Kintyre and North Ronaldsay), and the first to be built in the Outer Hebrides.

In 1787, when construction of the lighthouse was first proposed, Scalpay was owned by a Captain Alex McLeod of Harris. Building a lighthouse would have been a substantial undertaking for the time and there were a number of participants keen to get a slice of whatever financial pie might have been on offer. McLeod engaged his tacksman to source building material and labour while Northern Lighthouse Trustees, who had commissioned the light, insisted their own tradesmen be used.

The keepers' dwellings at Eilean Glas were designed by Robert Stevenson's son Alan in the Egyptian style he later used for the cottages at Ardnamurchan lighthouse.

However, McLeod persevered, engaging his men to build the foundations and start on the tower itself "to avoid delays". By the time the trustees' masons arrived, the walls had already risen to a height of 2m (6ft). No doubt to the chagrin of the locals, the mainlanders took over and set about completing the work to their specifications. Realising that McLeod's men had built the tower 1.25m (4ft) wider than indicated on the plans – whether through ignorance or because it generated more work, we'll never know – it was decided to alter the plans rather than the half-finished tower. Work was finally completed in October 1788 and the lantern fitted the following autumn. By early 1879, the glow of Eilean Glas was visible in the night sky.

In 1824, the original tower was demolished and replaced by the current structure. Nearly 30 years later, in 1852, the light was changed to a revolving lens system. By 1907, a fog signal had been added. In 1978, the lighthouse was automated. Nine years later, the fog signal was discontinued. It still sits in place, "weather-beaten and stiff by long exposure on the Point of Glas".

EILEAN GLAS
LIGHTHOUSE
SCALPAY
OUTER HEBRIDES

FLANNAN ISLES
LIGHTHOUSE
EILEAN MÒR
OUTER HEBRIDES

FLANNAN ISLES

LOCATION: 58°17′18″N, 7°35′24″W
OS GRID: NA725469
ELEVATION: 101m (331ft)
CHARACTER: Fl (2) W 30s
RANGE: 37km (23 miles)

The Flannan Isles (Na h-Eileanan Flannach in Scottish Gaelic) are among the smallest and westernmost of the Hebrides, about 115km (71 miles) off the Scottish mainland and 32km (20 miles) from the Isle of Lewis. These isolated islands are too small to be inhabited. Save for the lighthouse keepers atop the lighthouse on Eilean Mòr, who kept the light beam steady and true between 1899 and its automation in 1971, the Flannan Isles have housed no residents since the early Celtic monks came to these rocks and founded a small community centred on the tiny drystone chapel dedicated to St Flannan. The islands are now a bird sanctuary and exude a bleak beauty during calm weather. During winter storms, these remote isles sit right in the path of the gales blowing off the Atlantic and become wild and unpredictable.

The 23m (75ft) tall Flannan Isles lighthouse was designed by David Alan Stevenson and its construction began in 1896. All the materials had to be hauled up the 45m (148ft) high cliffs directly from the supply boats and a shore station was established at Breasclete on the Isle of Lewis. The lighthouse was first illuminated in December of 1899 and automated in 1971, but its light failed once in a manner that remains a mystery.

The eggs of northern fulmars were harvested by fishermen from the Isle of Lewis until the 20th century. The Flannan Isles have been designated a Site of Special Scientific Interest since 1983.

On the night of 15 December 1900, just 12 months after the lighthouse came into operation, the steamer *Archtor* was sailing into Scotland from Philadelphia when it noted in its log that the lighthouse was not in operation and the station stood in darkness as they passed the islands. In those days there was no radio communication between the keepers on Eilean Mòr and the shore station, and it was three days before the ship docked and the alarm was raised. Due to high seas and gale-force winds, the relief ship, the *Hesperus*, was unable to reach the island until 26 December. When it did so, the light was still unlit, the flag was not flying and there was no sign of life at the landing stage.

A flare was fired from the *Hesperus* but brought no answer, so there was no option but to attempt a landing without help from the island. The relief keeper, Joseph Moore, managed to get ashore and set out to find the three keepers. His report indicated that the doors to the lighthouse were closed, the clocks had ominously stopped, the beds were unmade and the fire unlit. Yet the only thing notably out of place was a chair by the kitchen table, which had been knocked over. A further unusual thing was that two of the keepers' oilskins were missing, but the third set was still in place. The lighthouse keepers' log had no further entries after the day that the *Archtor* had sailed past and a message on a slate dated 15 December 1900 (which would have later been transferred to the log) indicated all was well. No trace of the men could be found.

The disappearance of the three men, coupled with the death of an assistant keeper a few years later, gave the lighthouse on Eilean Mòr a sinister reputation. The popular poem "Flannan Isle" by Wilfrid Wilson Gibson took a number of liberties with the truth and made the story familiar to the wider public, sealing the episode's fate as a suspense mystery worthy of Edgar Allen Poe.

The official explanation is a little less dramatic, putting the tragedy down to the keepers being washed away by a rogue wave as they attempted to secure boxes and mooring ropes in a crevice on the western side of the island. The fact that a large stone block weighing 1 ton was carried across a pathway would seem to back up this modest but measured conclusion.

The drystone chapel of St Flannan, dating to about the eighth century. St Flannan is believed to have been either an abbot from Killaloe, County Clare in Ireland, or the half-brother of St Ronan, who gave his name to the nearby island of North Rona.

SULE SKERRY

LOCATION: 59°05′07″N, 4°24′24″W
OS GRID: HX621245
ELEVATION: 34m (112ft)
CHARACTER: Fl (2) W 15s
RANGE: 39km (24 miles)

Situated in the Atlantic Ocean 64km (40 miles) west of Orkney and 56km (35 miles) north of the Scottish coastline, Sule Skerry has the unenviable distinction of being the most isolated lighthouse in Britain. The island is low lying and, although it stretches to 14ha (35 acres), what little ground there is consists mostly of bare rock and the growth of vegetation is inhibited by the constant sea spray.

Sule Skerry lies in the route of vessels plying through the Pentland Firth on their way either to or from the Icelandic seas. Its sole neighbour, the Sule Stack, lies about 10km (6 miles) to the southwest and though composed of the same rock, a Lewisian gneiss, rises to a height of 36m (118ft), compared to the Skerry's miserly 12m (39ft). The islands are both home to puffins and gannets, with the Stack also playing host to kittiwakes, razorbills and terns, among other species.

In early 1892, the Stevenson brothers, David and Charles, surveyed the island with a view to building a lighthouse on it. While this wasn't some diminutive wave-washed rock, heavy seas and shortage of light made winter work impossible. During

Sule Stack, Sule Skerry's closest neighbour, is a perfect nesting ground for the northern gannet. While there are thousands of these birds, somehow they make room for a variety of other avian friends, including puffins, razorbills, fulmars, kittiwakes and guillemots.

SULE SKERRY
LIGHTHOUSE
SULE SKERRY
THE ORKNEYS

the late spring and summer, however, work could continue at a pace and by the middle of 1893 the 27m (89ft) tower was complete. The beam from Sule Skerry shone for the first time in early 1895 using a powerful hyper-radial lens. This was later replaced with a Dalén gas light with a fourth-order lens, giving it the character it has today.

Due to the remoteness of many lighthouse locations, boats were their only means of supplying food and fuel. The Northern Lighthouse Board have had numerous vessels in their service with names that may be familiar, such as the *Pole Star* (which serviced Sule Skerry from the start), the *Hesperus* (of Flannan Isles fame), the *Pharos* and the *Fingal*, among others. The names, of course, have been re-used over the years. These tenders were tasked with making sure that Scotland's numerous lighthouses were stocked with provisions, fuel and whatever materials might be needed for repairs, visiting once a fortnight and changing keepers in the course of their visit.

The ship would make toward the lighthouse and anchor off a safe distance. Smaller boats or ribs would then be launched and make their way on the landing point. There they would be met by the keepers, who would secure the boats by rope and start reeling in the provisions by pulley. The relief keepers usually went up and back the same way. In the meantime, the keepers had to get the goods into the lighthouse as quickly as possible. On a calm day on Sule Skerry, this was easily done, as tracks had been laid to help move material across the island, but on a blustery winter's evening, loading sacks of provisions must have been hair-raising, to say the least. On numerous occasions Sule Skerry was cut off for weeks by heavy seas, preventing any landing, and the keepers had to make their rations stretch for who knew how long.

Supplies arrive at Skule Skerry by air.

In 1973, a helicopter relief service was introduced to Sule Skerry, and the days of rationing stale biscuits were over. The station was finally automated in December 1982.

DUNNET HEAD
LIGHTHOUSE
EASTER HEAD
CAITHNESS

DUNNET HEAD

LOCATION: 58°40′17″N, 3°22′36″W
OS GRID: ND202767
ELEVATION: 105m (344ft)
CHARACTER: Fl (4) 30s
RANGE: 42km (26 miles)

Razorbills at Dunnet Head.

Perched on the vertiginous clifftop of Easter Head, Dunnet Head lighthouse marks the most northerly point of the Scottish mainland, further north even than John o' Groats. On a clear day, you can see the Old Man of Hoy and the Orkney lighthouses of Torness, Cantick Head, Stroma and Pentland Skerries. You can also see Duncansby Head, Holburn Head and Strathy Point on the mainland. As the crow flies, it's a short 10km (6-mile) hop across the southern shores of the Orkney Islands.

The water that stands in your way is called the Pentland Firth. Historically, it has been better known by the moniker "Hell's Mouth". As the Atlantic passes through this narrow channel toward the North Sea and then ebbs in the opposite direction, a series of eddies, counterflows, races and overfalls are created, resulting in an unpredictable swirl of tide near the Pentland Skerries that can run as fast as ten knots. The currents are so feared and ferocious that they have their own nicknames: the Swilkie, the Bore of Huna, the Wells of Tuftalie, the Duncansby Bore and the Merry Men of May, which have swallowed many a vessel.

The lighthouse was designed by Robert Stevenson and came into service in 1831. In 1852, Dunnet Head was retrofitted with a combination of lenses with reflectors that had been the norm for newly built lighthouses since 1843. A separate fog signal was added in 1899, but erosion of the cliffs necessitated moving it nearer the lighthouse. A modern fog signal was constructed in 1952, but was discontinued in 1987. The station was automated in 1989, but the former keepers' cottages, and the tower itself, are protected with the Historic Scotland grade B listed status.

Dunnet Head and the surrounding cliffs are home to a variety of sea birds, including guillemots, razorbills, fulmars, kittiwakes, cormorants and puffins; while the high cliffs at Easter Head, the northernmost tip of Dunnet Head, often reward patient observers with glimpses of pods of orcas, porpoises and dolphins migrating around the north coast of Scotland. The slipway at Brough to the south was the historic landing place for lighthouse supplies, while the storehouse still stands and the jetty is used these days by canoeists and kayakers.

SWILKIE POINT

LOCATION: 58°41'45"N, 3°07'01"W
OS GRID: ND353792
ELEVATION: 32m (105ft)
CHARACTER: Fl (2) 20s
RANGE: 37km (23 miles)

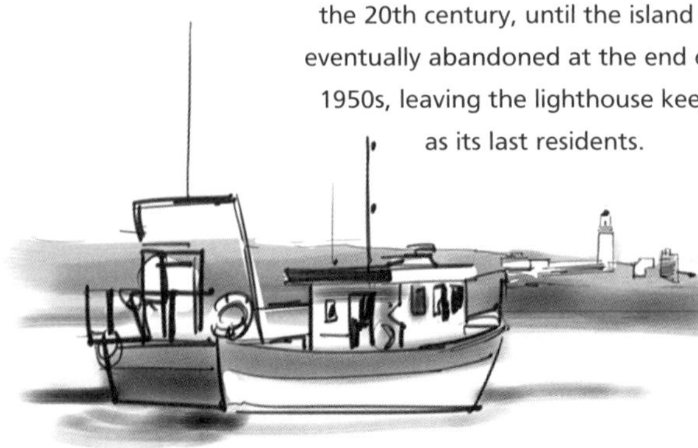

Stroma's population fell sharply through the first half of the 20th century, until the island was eventually abandoned at the end of the 1950s, leaving the lighthouse keepers as its last residents.

The Pentland Firth is the strait that runs between Orkney and the north coast of Scotland. Locally, it has been given the moniker "Hell's Mouth" in reference to the unpredictable swirls of tide, with one of the most powerful tidal currents in the world. Tidal currents of up to 16 knots and waves several metres high have been recorded.

The Swilkie lies off Swilkie Point to the north of the Isle of Stroma, and features in Viking legends. It is a particularly violent tidal race, with numerous whirlpools. The name is said to come from the Old Norse word *svalga*, meaning "the swallower". Legend has it that the whirlpool was created by a sea witch who used it to turn the wheels of her mill, which ground salt to keep the seas salty. Alternatively, it is a giant grinding stone stolen from the Icelandic god Frodi by a jealous sea king called Mysing, who sank under its weight at Stroma and who continues to grind away on the stone, creating the saltiness of the sea.

The lighthouse at Stroma was established in 1896 and was designed by David A Stevenson and his brother Charles. Initially, a Trotter-Lindberg system was used for the light, comprising of a rotating screen which created a light pattern similar to placing a sheet in front of a torch and then removing it. The system used petroleum spirit as its fuel source. To keep it running, a local crofter or fisherman was employed to refuel it. A paraffin lamp later replaced the original.

During World War II, Scotland's lighthouses were extinguished. Many locals regarded them a waymarkers for enemy bombers and the lightkeepers were instructed to cease whitewashing the structures and to let them become stained so they would blend into the background.

By 1972, electricity arrived at the station and Stroma was converted to a sealed beam optic unit mounted on a revolving pedestal. Around this time, a helipad was constructed so the keepers were no longer hostage to the weather for supplies and changeovers.

The automation of the station was effective by 1997, with power provided by batteries that are periodically recharged by a generator. A new optical system with a 250-watt metal halide lamp was installed, which had previously been used in Sule Skerry lighthouse.

SWILKIE POINT
LIGHTHOUSE
STROMA
CAITHNESS

NORTH RONALDSAY
LIGHTHOUSE
DENNIS NESS
ORKNEY

NORTH RONALDSAY

LOCATION: 59°23′22″N, 2°22′53″W
OS GRID: HY784559
ELEVATION: 43m (141ft)
CHARACTER: Fl W 10s
RANGE: 44.5km (28 miles)

The first lighthouse on North Ronaldsay – and the third to be built, after Kinnaird Head and the Mull of Kintyre, by the Commissioners of the Northern Lighthouse Board was constructed by Thomas Smith, aided by his son-in-law Robert Stevenson and the lighthouse designer Ezekiel Walker. The undressed stone structure was positioned at Kirk Taing, the most easterly point of Dennis Head.

The lighthouse first came into operation on 10 October 1789. The illumination was provided by a catadioptric or reflecting system, which used an array of oil burning lamps initially backed by copper or silver-clad parabolic reflectors. These curved, polished surfaces (not dissimilar to the silver reflectors in a car headlight) directed the reflected light in a single direction, unlike a flat mirror which would have scattered it everywhere. Burning oil, of course, creates sooty stains, so the reflectors needed to be regularly cleaned using a soft linen rag and fine powdered chalk.

Although the tower was 21m (70ft) high, the beam was too low because of the lighthouse's location on low-lying land, and it could easily be mistaken for the light of a fellow ship. In 1806, a new lighthouse was established at Start Point on the Isle of Sanday, and the original North Ronaldsay light was considered surplus to requirements. Its lantern and apparatus were removed, and the tower was capped with a great stone ball finial. Whether

The Old Beacon from the shoreline. The 20m (66ft) tower was in active use until Start Point lighthouse on the Isle of Sanday become operational in 1806. In the mid-1800s, the new tower came into operation, restoring a lighthouse to this part of the Scottish coast.

the Commissioners intended to preserve the tower for future use is debatable, but when they sealed the structure from the elements, they unfortunately failed to protect it from the bird life on the island and when the North Ronaldsay Trust embarked on the restoration of the tower in 2008, it took five days alone to dig out a couple of centuries' worth of guano.

To the south, the dangerous 5km (3-miles) wide North Ronaldsay Firth separates North Ronaldsay from its neighbouring isles and, while open sea lies to the island's north, the surrounding waters are full of hidden reefs and dangerous currents. It quickly became apparent that the island did in fact need a lighthouse of its own and plans were soon afoot to replace what had become known as the Old Beacon. This new structure was to be built on higher ground to the north, to warn ships of the hazardous presence of the Reef Duke and Seal Skerry offshore.

The job of designing the new tower fell to Alan Stevenson, the engineer behind Skerryvore and Ardnamurchan. Then, as now, cost was a consideration and Stevenson gave the board a choice of two structures: a brick tower or an iron edifice. The latter must have been proposed in the spirit of the old saying "if you pay peanuts, you get monkeys" – because it's hard to imagine how an iron structure could have lasted more than half a century, grimly clinging to this storm-tossed shore. To emphasize his point, Stevenson warned that in high winds, the movement of the structure would be likely to interfere with the apparatus. The board unsurprisingly chose the brick structure.

The new light was duly established in 1854, standing 42m (138ft) high. In the late 19th century, it must have looked as foreign as an alien space craft on this remote island, with its light flashing every 10 seconds, sending a beam over 43km (27 miles) out to sea. It remains the tallest land-based lighthouse in Britain.

In 1889, the tower was painted with two white bands to make it stand out as a daymark. In 1907, the original apparatus for the light was replaced with incandescent oil vapour burners and a radio beacon was added in 1932. North Ronaldsay lighthouse was finally automated on 30 March 1998.

On North Ronaldsay, a stone wall or dyke encircles the entire island. Its purpose is to keep the sheep off the delicate grassland. Instead, they forage on the seaweed that washes up on the shore!

FAIR ISLE SOUTH

LOCATION: 59°30′51″N, 1°39′12″W
OS GRID: HZ197698
ELEVATION: 33m (108ft)
CHARACTER: FL (4) W 30s
RANGE: 40.5km (25 miles)

Fair Isle, situated north of mainland Scotland, lies midway between Orkney and Shetland. It is Britain's most remote inhabited island. It was purchased by the National Trust for Scotland in 1954 from George Waterson, the founder of the bird observatory on the island.

Despite the island's diminutive size – it's only 5km (3 miles) long and 2km (1.25 miles) wide – its landscape is spectacular, with red sandstone cliffs rising to 100m (328ft) at Sheep Rock in the east and to almost 200m (656ft) along the more rugged west coast. The terrain is one of contrasts, ranging from wild high moorland in the north to cultivated croft land on the south of the island. The island has been occupied since Neolithic times, and between the 9th and 15th century was in Norwegian possession.

There are two lighthouses on the island: Fair Isle North is located at Skroo on the northeastern tip of the island and the Fair Isle South lighthouse is at Skaddan. The North lighthouse tops out at a paltry 14m (45ft), in comparison to its 26m (85ft) high southern neighbour, but with an elevation of 65m (213ft), it's by far the taller of the two. Both lighthouses were built in 1892 and designed by David and Charles Stevenson. To keep costs down, they were designed as mirror images of each other and the machinery and equipment at both lighthouses is almost identical, with the exception of an extra 35 steps in the southern tower.

The well-known Auld Haa Guesthouse on Fair Isle was originally built for the laird of the island in 1700 and has welcomed guests ever since, including Sir Walter Scott in 1814. The guesthouse is now a registered historic building owned by the National Trust for Scotland.

FAIR ISLE SOUTH
LIGHTHOUSE
SKADDEN
FAIR ISLES

With the outbreak of World War II, of all the lighthouses around the Scottish coast, you might have expected that those near industrial centres would have suffered the most. You certainly wouldn't think that isolated Fair Isle would draw the short straw. The island was, of course, regarded as being in a strategically important location – as evidenced by the fact that the RAF built a radar station on the top of Ward Hill nearby.

In the first of two attacks on the South lighthouse in December 1941, Catherine Sutherland, the wife of the assistant lightkeeper, was killed while standing by her pantry window, and her infant daughter was slightly hurt. The family of Principal Lightkeeper Smith were not safe from danger either: his wife and ten-year-old daughter were killed when a second air attack resulted in a direct hit on the main block of dwelling houses at 3.45pm on 21 January 1942. One of the soldiers manning a machine-gun post nearby was also killed. Two bombs were dropped; the first registered a direct hit on the gable end of the main accommodation block and caused extensive damage, with the main block being completely burned out. Roderick Macaulay, the principal lightkeeper at the North lighthouse, trudged 5km (3 miles) through snow to assist in restoring the South light to operational order, and then made his way back through the night to resume his regular watch. He was awarded the British Empire Medal (BEM) for outstanding services.

Because Fair Isle is not connected to the National Grid, it must generate its own electricity. In 1983, the community installed the first commercial wind turbine in the UK and have managed the combined wind-diesel power system ever since. At the same time, both lighthouses installed generators of their own to guarantee enough power to electrify the lights.

On 31 March 1998, Fair Isle South became the final lighthouse in Scotland to be automated and the keepers left the station for the last time.

The walk by Malcolm's Head and Sheep Rock (pictured) takes in some of the most dramatic coastal scenery on Fair Isle and there's a good chance of spotting puffins in the late spring and summer.

SUMBURGH HEAD

LOCATION: 59°51′14″N, 1°16′31″W
OS GRID: HU407078
ELEVATION: 91m (300ft)
CHARACTER: Fl (3) W 30s
RANGE: 42km (26 miles)

The life of a lighthouse keeper involved tenacity, discipline and resolve. We sometimes imagine keepers whiling away the hours whittling wood or building model ships to fold into bottles, but the daily routine of a lighthouse keeper was hard graft. The primary responsibility of keepers and engineers was to ensure the continuous and smooth operation of the vital lights – and in turn to ensure the safe passage of vessels around the coastline.

In the days before electricity (and indeed long after), moving parts were turned by means of clockwork or weights that needed to be wound on a regular basis. A revolving light, for example, was operated by a set of weights that slowly dropped through the centre of the lighthouse, turning the lens at a specific speed and requiring rewinding at regular intervals. Falling asleep on watch was the most serious offence a keeper could commit, as this might mean the revolving machinery would stop or, even worse, the light might go out. There were 15 recorded instances in Scotland of sleeping on the job between 1850 and 1900 – including one instance at Sumburgh in 1871 when the light did go out. The subsequent investigation revealed a pact between the two men not to report each other, which led to the dismissal of the assistant lightkeeper and the permanent demotion of the principal lightkeeper.

The lighthouse at Sumburgh Head sits at the southern end of Shetland, overlooking a turbulent stretch of water called the Sumburgh Roost. The name Sumburgh is thought to be derived from the Old Norse name Dunrøstar høfdi, or Sunn Borg, meaning "the head of the loud tidal race" and referring to the noise created by the racing tides of the Sumburgh Roost.

A Shetland pony with the lighthouse in the distance.

SUMBURGH HEAD
LIGHTHOUSE
SUMBURGH HEAD
SHETLAND

As international trade scaled up toward the end of the 18th century, the volume of shipping plying the route between Norway and Britain increased accordingly. Vessels carrying timber and tobacco sailed eastward past Sumburgh Head and, as the traffic increased, so did the number of shipwrecks and lost lives.

In 1815, Robert Stevenson, engineer to the Northern Lighthouse Board, surveyed the site and deemed it "an eligible situation for a lighthouse". Building commenced in January 1819, with walls constructed to double thickness to keep out the damp. The project did not go without incident and tragically the supply ship the *Freemason* of Lerwick, bound from Peterhead, foundered at Greetness Voe. Only one of the crew survived.

The tower, the oldest on Shetland, was first lit in 1821 and contained 26 parabolic reflectors with lamps, rather than the usual 21. It initially displayed a fixed white light, soon to be replaced by group flashing every 30 seconds.

The station was fully automated in 1991 and the former keepers' cottages and outbuildings, excluding the tower, now comprise the Sumburgh Head Visitor Centre and provide a unique visitor experience to the nature reserve on the island. The Sumburgh Head lighthouse, Visitor Centre and Nature Reserve were officially opened by HRH the Princess Royal in 2014.

Sumburgh lantern and foghorn. Recently restored and repainted, the bright red trumpet, built in 1905, was last sounded in 1987.

MUCKLE FLUGGA

LOCATION: 60°51′20″N, 0°53′09″W
OS GRID: HP606196
ELEVATION: 66m (217ft)
CHARACTER: Fl (2) W 20s
RANGE: 40.5km (25 miles)

On a rocky outcrop off the coast of Unst, at one of the most northerly points of the UK, Muckle Flugga lighthouse clings precariously to its wave-washed perch, seemingly impervious to either tide or time. The name, taken from the Old Norse Mikla Flugey and meaning "large steep-sided island", gives some indication of what the builders of this isolated outpost must have thought when they first surveyed the site. In fact, when David A Stevenson first visited the area, the conditions at Muckle Flugga led him to recommend that the lighthouse should be built at a number of alternative sites, but not here.

The initial impetus for building an aid to navigation this far north came from the Royal Navy's need to protect battleships as they headed off to the Crimean War. Moving quickly, by 11 October 1854 a temporary light had been established in just 26 days. The sturdy wooden structure stood almost 17m (56ft) in height and sat 61m (200ft) above sea level. It was built to resist the worst that the wind and rain along this stretch of coast could throw at it. What hadn't been accounted for, however,

Located further north than any other lighthouse in the UK, Muckle Flugga sits on the edge of the Hermaness National Nature Reserve. Apart from Out Stack, a small rocky outcrop 0.6km (about half a mile) further north, nothing stands between the lighthouse and the North Pole.

were the giant waves that can come crashing right across the island in stormy weather. One night, the surge ripped off the door of the keepers' quarters, flooding the rooms and carrying away six casks of precious fresh water. The waves were powerful enough to sweep away 12m (40ft) of protective wall before the storm abated.

The ferocity of the winter seas and the exposed nature of Muckle Flugga caused many to reconsider the site and, when it came to building a permanent structure at this location, the Commissioners of

MUCKLE FLUGGA
LIGHTHOUSE
MUCKLE FLUGGA
SHETLAND ISLES

the Northern Lighthouse Board voted unanimously to relocate the lighthouse to nearby Lamba Ness. In the end, more pragmatic heads prevailed and it was decided that the lighthouse would be built stronger and taller in its original position. Foundations were chiselled out 3m (10ft) into the rock. Above them, a tower 20m (66ft) in height, with walls 1m (3ft) thick, rose into the winter skies. By December 1857, the lantern had been installed and all was ready for the North Unst lighthouse – as it was then called – to shine forth for the first time on New Year's Day 1858. The robustness and strength of this new structure would be tested over the coming years and, while seas swept away pillars and stone, the lighthouse has stood stalwart against the worst that nature can throw at it.

During World War II, the existing radio beacon was recommissioned on Muckle Flugga and the lightkeeper was continually employed in passing on service messages between the headquarters and the rock, while also carrying out his regular duties in maintaining the light.

Accommodation arrangements were primitive and cramped on the rock. The set-up was summed up by one principal lightkeeper as being like "sleeping in a crow's nest and eating in a cell". With the arrival of electricity, some outbuildings were no longer in operational use, and in the late 1960s these were demolished, and an accommodation block was built within the retaining walls. The lighthouse's name was changed from North Unst to Muckle Flugga in 1964 and it was finally automated in March 1995.

Shorehaven Cottage at the Muckle Flugga shore station in Burrafirth, Unst.

KINNAIRD HEAD

LOCATION: 57°41′53″N, 2°00′16″W
OS GRID: NJ998675
ELEVATION: 25m (82ft)
CHARACTER: Fl W 5s
RANGE: 40.5km (25 miles)

Set into a corner tower within the walls of Lord Saltoun's old castle at Fraserburgh, the original lighthouse at Kinnaird Head (Cinn na h'airde in Gaelic, meaning "the head of the point of land") was the first of the Northern Lighthouse Board's lighthouses to be illuminated, preceding the illumination of the Mull of Kintyre lighthouse by a year and North Ronaldsay and Eilean Glas by two. It is now home to the Museum of Scottish Lighthouses.

The lighthouse, designed by Thomas Smith, father-in-law of Robert Stevenson, first shone on 1 December 1787 and displayed fixed oil lights with reflectors. At the time, it was the most powerful in operation in Britain. The 17 reflectors were arranged in three horizontal tiers, giving a range of more than 19km (12 miles).

Kinnaird Head lighthouse is one of the more distinctive lights along the Scottish coast, but it almost didn't survive in its present form. Fewer than 40 years after it had first been lit, the ever-pragmatic Robert Stevenson campaigned for the tower to be demolished and for a new bespoke structure to take its place. Its survival can perhaps be partly attributed to one of Scotland's greatest writers and romantics, Sir Walter Scott, who accompanied Stevenson on a tour around Scotland's coast aboard the Northern Lighthouse Board's vessel the *Pharos*. Scott would surely have understood the historical significance of the castle and perhaps expressed his concern that the lighthouse shouldn't undermine the more

The main purpose of the Wine Tower at Kinnaird Head was to serve as storerooms for the castle, but it is speculated that it was also used as a secret chapel for the Catholic wife of the Protestant Laird Sir Alexander Fraser.

KINNAIRD HEAD
LIGHTHOUSE
FRASERBURGH
ABERDEENSHIRE

The Museum of Scottish Lighthouses at Kinnaird Head. The museum's collection illustrates the story of the Northern Lighthouse Board, from its creation in 1786 to its operations in the present day.

ancient structure. In the end, the tower was retained, though some nearby buildings were removed so that accommodation could be built for the keepers.

In front and separate from the lighthouse sits the ancient Wine Tower. Despite its name, there is some dispute as to what the structure was originally used for. Some think it may have been a secret Catholic chapel, but it's also been speculated that this building may have been where the laird would imbibe wine with his distinguished guests. Whatever the building's origins, the Wine Tower houses a sinister tale.

Isobel, the daughter of Sir Alexander Fraser, eighth Laird of Philorth, fell in love with a commoner (as you do), a lowly piper from the nearby village. The Laird naturally forbade his daughter from seeing this ne'er-do-well. However, one night he was due to travel to Aberdeen and had barely left town when a storm whipped up, growing so fierce that he had to turn back. When he reached the castle, he found his daughter in a heated embrace with the piper. Furious at her betrayal, Sir Alexander locked Isobel in the upstairs room of the Wine Tower and shackled the piper in a cave beneath the building. As the storm grew more wretched, waves surged into the cave, drowning the piper. Hearing his cries of terror from her prison, Isobel was racked with anguish and in despair she threw herself from the window onto the rocks. Local legend has it that whenever a storm is brewing in Fraserburgh, if you listen carefully you will be able to hear the sound of bagpipes carried on the howling wind. Some even say that poor Isobel can be seen sobbing on the shoreline.

On a more prosaic note, the lighthouse was the first to host a radio beacon in Scotland. Introduced in 1929, the beacon could transmit the lighthouse's identifying Morse signal for direction-finding every two minutes during foggy conditions and also provide a calibration service on request for shipping. The fog signal was discontinued in 1987 and in 1991 the lighthouse was decommissioned, replaced by a new automatic lighthouse, which was established close to the original light.

RATTRAY HEAD

LOCATION: 57°36′37″N, 1°49′00″W
OS GRID: NK110578
ELEVATION: 28m (92ft)
CHARACTER: Fl (3) W 30s
RANGE: 33km (21 miles)

The extensive beach at Rattray Head stretches 27km (17 miles) along the Aberdeenshire coast, bookended by St Combs to the north and Peterhead to the south. The remnants of a number of shipwrecks can still be traced in the sands, possible evidence of owners deliberately beaching their vessels in an early instance of insurance fraud, but also an indication of how treacherous the tides and currents can be in this part of the world.

Arguments about the need for a lighthouse on this particular stretch of coast raged for an unrivalled 45 years. Engineer Alan Stevenson was engaged to verify whether the Rattray Briggs, an offshore reef, could be illuminated from Buchan Ness lighthouse to the south. He determined that it could not, but like the proverbial ping-pong ball, the decision about whether or not to build was bounced back and forth as numerous advocates on both sides insisted on having their say. Two years later, further experiments were carried out at the behest of a Captain Bedford, but again they were unsuccessful. Once again Stevenson called for a lighthouse at Rattray Head, once again procrastination won the day and there the matter rested for a decade.

By November 1874, the Sheriff of Renfrew and Bute had joined the clarion call for a lighthouse. The senior engineer at the time was asked for his opinion and although he was in favour, Trinity House again refused to consider the proposal, suggesting instead that vessels sound the depths and that a bell buoy would be good enough to mark the reef. By this stage, several ship owners

With turquoise waters and unspoiled golden sands, on a balmy summer's day the beach at Rattray Head could be mistaken for somewhere in more southerly climes. During the winter, it's a completely different beast.

RATTRAY HEAD
LIGHTHOUSE
BUCHAN
ABERDEENSHIRE

and the fishermen of Peterhead had joined the fray. You almost have to admire Trinity House for their resolve to be immovable.

As the years continued to pass, by 1890 there was a list the length of your arm of companies and bodies agitating for a lighthouse on this perilous stretch of coast, including harbour trustees, shipping companies, underwriters and fisherman's groups. Eventually, it was decided to bypass Trinity House completely by requesting that the Board of Trade arbitrate in the matter. The Board of Trade duly announced that they had written to Trinity House, informing them that they had sanctioned the erection of a lighthouse and fog signal at Rattray Head as proposed.

Work began in 1892 and the structure, debated for almost a half century, was completed in under two years. The light was finally illuminated for the first time on 14 October 1895. The design is unusual in that it is a rock station (an offshore lighthouse) in two distinct parts. The lower section houses an engine room and fog horn, while the upper structure houses the lightkeepers' room and lantern. The base, which is 16.8m (55ft) in diameter, comprises of almost 1,500 tons of cut and dressed granite sourced from Aberdeen's Rubislaw quarries and rises to a height of 13.4m (44ft), with the entrance doorway set 10m (32ft) above the sand below and reached by an open metal ladder. On top of this sits a smaller white, enamelled brick tower, coped with granite 1m (3ft) thick, topped off with the lightroom, lantern and dome, giving total height of 37m (120ft) above the rock.

As it is situated a short distance offshore, the structure is accessible with care at low tide via a causeway. When the tide rises, the lighthouse once again sits aloof and isolated in the chilly North Sea.

The wreck of the fishing boat Sovereign BF380 at Cairnbulg, between Rattray Head and Fraserburgh.

BELL ROCK

LOCATION: 56°26′04″N, 2°23′14″W
OS GRID: NO762269
ELEVATION: 28m (92ft)
CHARACTER: FL W 5s
RANGE: 33km (21 miles)

A Northern Lighthouse Board helicopter brings supplies to Bell Rock.

Eleven miles offshore from Arbroath on the eastern shores of Scotland, a narrow glittering beam of light sweeps across the leaden horizon and then disappears into the gathering night. At this distance, you can't see the source of light, but out there illuminating safe passage through the treacherous waters that form the gateway to the ports of Edinburgh and Dundee is one of the wonders of the industrial age, the Bell Rock lighthouse.

This slender Georgian sentinel stands on Inchcape reef, a particularly treacherous outcrop of razor-sharp sandstone that is only visible at low tide and extends to almost 457m (1,500ft) in length and 91m (300ft) in width. Prior to the arrival of the lighthouse, Bell Rock heralded the demise of thousands of seafarers as vessels were run aground and wrecked on its perilous rocks.

The name is reputed to have originated in the 14th century, when the Abbot of Aberbrothok, John Gedy, sailed out and erected a device containing a wave-activated warning bell on the rocks. Whether it worked or not is unknown, but legend has it that the bell lasted only a year before a Dutch pirate by the name of Ralph the Rover stole it – only to founder like a pantomime villain on the self-same rocks 12 months later.

By the beginning of the 1800s, the number of ships lost to the rocks had reached alarming rates, with up to six ships perishing each winter. Robert Stevenson suggested the construction of a light on the rocks to the Commissioners of Northern Lighthouse Board in 1799, but due to the cost and difficulty of building on the rock, the response had been lukewarm. Four years later, he had developed a proposal for a tower similar to Smeaton's at Eddystone and once again submitted his proposal. It almost passed muster at parliament, but at the last hurdle, funds were unforthcoming. His scheme, however, had intrigued the Northern Lighthouse Board enough to engage the opinion of the engineer John Rennie, who readily supported Stevenson's plan. It was the loss in 1804 of the warship HMS *York* with all hands that rallied the authorities into action. Because of Stevenson's relative inexperience, Rennie

BELL ROCK
LIGHTHOUSE
ARBROATH
ANGUS

was assigned the senior role of Chief Engineer, while Robert was assigned the title Resident Engineer.

The build of the lighthouse was an extraordinary feat of engineering and imagination. The hours when work could feasibly be carried out on the rock were scarce, to say the least. Except at low tide, the reef was submerged by up to 5m (16ft) of water and work could only proceed during the (relatively) calm months from April to September.

On 17 August 1807, Stevenson and around 35 workmen set sail for the rock and work began in earnest. The first task was to fix the foundation supports for a beacon house, a tall wooden structure that would serve as a store, blacksmith's forge and sleeping quarters, but before this could be finished, disaster struck when the support ship *Smeaton* broke her moorings and drifted away. Stevenson and his workmen were still toiling on the rock and found themselves stranded 17km (11 miles) from shore, with the tide staring to lap about their feet. Just as panic started to set in, a supply ship was spotted on the horizon and came to their rescue. Unsurprisingly, 18 of the men refused to return to work the next day.

Despite setbacks, work progressed, albeit slowly (after two years only three courses of stonework were complete and the tower stood at a majestic 2m (6ft) tall), but bit by bit the huge interlocking granite stones of the lighthouse rose from the reef. Stevenson even had a miniature railroad erected on stilts to help manoeuvre the weighty blocks to their designated position.

By February 1811, work was finally complete and, having consumed almost 2,500 granite blocks, the lighthouse was at last ready to illuminate the chilly charcoal skies.

Bell Rock lighthouse with the workers' accommodation hut built on wooden struts, which also served as a temporary beacon during the build. The accommodation was designed to house 15 workers at the site.

ISLE OF MAY

LOCATION: 56°11′08″N, 2°33′27″W
OS GRID: NT654993
ELEVATION: 73m (240ft)
CHARACTER: Fl (2) W 15s
RANGE: 33km (21 miles)

A lighthouse was first established on the Isle of May in 1636, when a coal-fired beacon was erected by order of King Charles I. Housed at the top of a 12m (39ft) high stone building, the light consisted of a metal brazier which burned coal mined from the nearby Forth coalfields. A pulley system was used to raise the coal to the upper floor, with the light consuming almost 400 tons of the stuff every year. That amounts to over a ton per day! It took three men to maintain, replenish and supervise the fire, which despite the paltry wages of the time, gives an idea of just how expensive maintaining a navigational light like this must have been.

While coal was a preferable fuel to fast-burning wood, there must have been times – especially during damp weather – when the brazier produced more smoke than light. The conditions for those working the lighthouse were less than perfect, too. In January 1791, the keeper George Anderson, his wife, Elisabeth, and five of his six children perished when they suffocated from the fumes given off by a large heap of carelessly disposed ash and clinker, which was set smouldering by stray sparks from the beacon. The quality of the coal-fired light also varied considerably according to the weather conditions, and could easily be mistaken for a fire produced by a house or small industry – as was the case when two ships floundered near Dunbar in December 1810 after confusing the light on the Isle of May with that of a nearby lime kiln.

The May Princess sails from Anstruther to the Isle of May most days from the beginning of April to the end of summer.

The Northern Lighthouse Board purchased the island and the old coal lighthouse in 1814 from the Duke and Duchess of Portland, by which time the beacon had become the last lighthouse to remain in private hands in Scotland. Engineer Robert Stevenson was then tasked with designing

ISLE OF MAY
LIGHTS
FIRTH OF FORTH
FIFE

a suitable lighthouse for the island, and by 1816 the new structure was complete, comprising an ornate gothic tower on top of a castellated stone dwelling, with accommodation for three lightkeepers and their families. In 1836, the lighthouse was upgraded, and a new light and refractor lens were installed. It housed Britain's first dioptric fixed light.

In 1885, a further upgrade was undertaken and the engine house was fitted with two steam-powered generators, giving an output of 8.8 kilowatts. With this latest refurbishment, the range of the light rose to 35km (22 miles), although there were reports of vessels recognizing the light at distances of up to 80km (50 miles) away by dint of the light's flashes illuminating the clouds overhead.

To keep the whole set-up running smoothly still required a lot of personnel. A principal lightkeeper with technical experience served as the engineer-in-charge and was aided by four assistants – two for lightroom duty and two to attend to the engines and boilers. Yet another member of staff was required to attend to the station horse and supervise the conveyance of supplies, including the annual transportation of 150 tons of steam coke from the landing stage to the new steam engines. To accommodate all these people, a new dwelling block was built. About 0.4km (0.25 miles) from the main lighthouse, on the east side of the island, are the tower and buildings of the smaller low light lighthouse. This first came into operation in April 1844 and was used in tandem with the main lighthouse as a range light, so that when both lights were aligned, ships could be sure they were clear of the North Carr Rock, 11km (7 miles) north of the island. When the North Carr lightship was launched in 1887, the low light was no longer needed and was discontinued. It is currently used as an ornithological centre.

In 1924, due to the ruinous cost of the coal, and improvements in oil lighting, the electric light in the main tower was replaced with an incandescent mantle. The Isle of May lighthouse was finally converted to a rock station in 1972, when the keepers and their families moved to live in Granton shore station. Seventeen years later, on 31 March 1989, the last of the keepers left for good and the operation of the light was changed to the use of a simple photoelectric cell, which determines when darkness has fallen, at which point the light is automatically turned on.

The Isle of May is home to Scotland's oldest bird observatory, founded in 1934. During the breeding season, the island is sometimes home to almost 200,000 seabirds, including puffins, razorbills, guillemots, shags, black-legged kittiwakes, fulmars, oystercatchers, eider ducks, and assorted species of tern and gull.

OXCARS
LIGHTHOUSE
FIRTH OF FORTH
FIFE

OXCARS

LOCATION: 56°01′21″N, 3°16′49″W
OS GRID: NT202818
ELEVATION: 16m (53ft)
CHARACTER: Fl (2) W R 7 s
RANGE: 24km (15 miles)

The celebrated Oxcars lighthouse stands resolute on a rock in the middle of the Firth of Forth, located between the islands of Inchcolm and Inchmickery. From here, its light guides vessels safely up the River Forth toward Rosyth, Grangemouth and the oil and gas terminals further on.

The rock, which appears at two thirds ebb, was marked with a cast-iron beacon as early as 1804. This structure was replaced by a stone beacon in 1846. However, it became apparent that a proper light was required for this busy channel and, in 1885, a tower 22m (72ft) tall was built to designs drawn up by Thomas and David Stevenson. The tower was painted white with a red band and housed cramped accommodation for two keepers. Three houses were leased ashore for the keepers' families, with provisions being supplied to the lighthouse via the Inchkeith boatmen. From February 1886, the new Oxcars lighthouse displayed a fixed light with white and red sectors. In 1894, it became the first manned Northern Lighthouse Board lighthouse to be converted to automatic operation.

The lighthouse came about as a result of the Northern Lighthouse Board's decision to establish minor lights in the Highlands and islands as part of a wider policy to encourage the development of the fishing industry. The Board had been impressed

Kayakers exploring the Firth.

with the Swedish Trotter-Lindberg light system, an inexpensive yet effective set-up that burned a petroleum spirit in a specially designed apparatus and only needed to be recharged once a fortnight. A special feature of the apparatus was that an intermittent light was produced by the automatic action of a screen, which revolved by using the hot air produced by the light. One of these lights had already been used in the Thames Estuary and the Board swiftly established two of their own in Scotland, one on Stroma and the other in the Sound of Mull. By 1880, the Clyde Lighthouse Trust had introduced gas-lit buoys and the Northern Lighthouse Board soon followed by placing six in the Forth. This form of semi-automation was a clear signal of the pace at which technology was now changing.

The fuel used for the first light at Oxcars had been oil (probably whale or colza oil), but was changed to compressed gas with the automation of the light in 1894, when a platform was built on the rock to house three containers which could be replenished fortnightly from the works at Granton. The automatic gas light was operated by clockwork wound up every 14 days, when the engineers changed the gas supply. The flame was always alight, but its intensity increased during hours of darkness. This mechanism was replaced in due course with an Aga sun valve.

Today, the lighthouse is operated by the Forth Ports Authority. One of the best ways to get a good look at it (and enjoy a spectacular view of the Firth) is to take one of the sightseeing cruises that depart from Hawes Pier at South Queensferry.

The lighthouse is more imposing and taller than it seems from a distance.

BASS ROCK

LOCATION: 56°04′36″N, 2°38′28″W
OS GRID: NT601872
ELEVATION: 46m (151ft)
CHARACTER: Fl (3) W 20s
RANGE: 17km (11 miles)

About 5km (3 miles) northeast of North Berwick, a steep crag at the southern entrance to the Firth of Forth rises from the surf to a height of some 107m (350ft), with a circumference of almost 2km (1.25 mile). Running from east to west through the rock is a tunnel that is accessible only at low tide. It could almost be the setting of a work of fiction from the pen of Robert Louis Stevenson. Instead, it is the location of a lighthouse designed by his uncle, David A Stevenson, the renowned engineer responsible for over 80 of Scotland's lighthouses.

The isolated Bass Rock was once famed as the site of the hermitage of St Baldred, a sixth-century Christian monk who had been sent by St Mungo to spread Christianity among the Lothians. The ruins of a pre-Reformation church, dedicated to him, can still be found about halfway up the rock.

Sir Robert Lauder is recorded as being the first known owner of the rock. According to legend, the island is said to have been a gift from King Malcolm III of Scotland. The family (Lauder of Bass) were in all likelihood the sponsors of the church, which was

"Solan geese" or gannets.

dedicated to St Baldfred in 1542, as well as responsible for the building of the fortress on the rock.

The Lauders lost the Bass in the 17th century during Cromwell's invasion, and in 1671 the castle became a notorious gaol to which religious and political prisoners were consigned. In 1691, while the jailors were busy with the tricky job of unloading a coal ship, a party of four Jacobite prisoners escaped from their cells and took control of the fortress. Remarkably, with the support of Jacobite sympathizers ashore and aided by supply ships from France, they managed to hold on to the Bass for three years and repulsed all attempts by government

BASS ROCK
LIGHTHOUSE
FIRTH OF FORTH
NORTH BERWICK

forces to retake it. A blockade in 1694 failed to dislodge them and eventually the hold-outs negotiated favourable terms to leave the rock, including freedom, passage to France if they wished and the release from prison of those onshore who had aided them.

The lighthouse on Bass Rock is a 20m (66ft) tall structure built in 1902 utilizing the stone from the demolished 13th-century keep, or governor's house, and other buildings within the castle. Construction came about as a result of the Northern Lighthouse Board's decision that two lights were needed on that stretch of the coast – one at Bass Rock and another at Barns Ness near Dunbar. By 1 November 1902, the building was complete and for the first time the lighthouse beam shone out across the Berwick coast. Since 1988, Bass Rock lighthouse has been unmanned and is now remotely monitored from the Board's headquarters in Edinburgh.

The rock is, of course, also home to thousands of birds. Gannets or "solan geese" as they're known locally have colonized almost all of the island, with the exception of the castle and landing areas. The cliffs also host razorbills, guillemots, cormorants, puffins, eider ducks and a variety of gull species.

In medieval Scotland, a synonym for the impossible was to "mak a brig tae the Bass" (ie build a bridge out to Bass Rock). Long may the lighthouse live in splendid isolation!

Bass Rock, a weathered "plug" of volcanic rock, is home to one of the world's largest colonies of gannets.

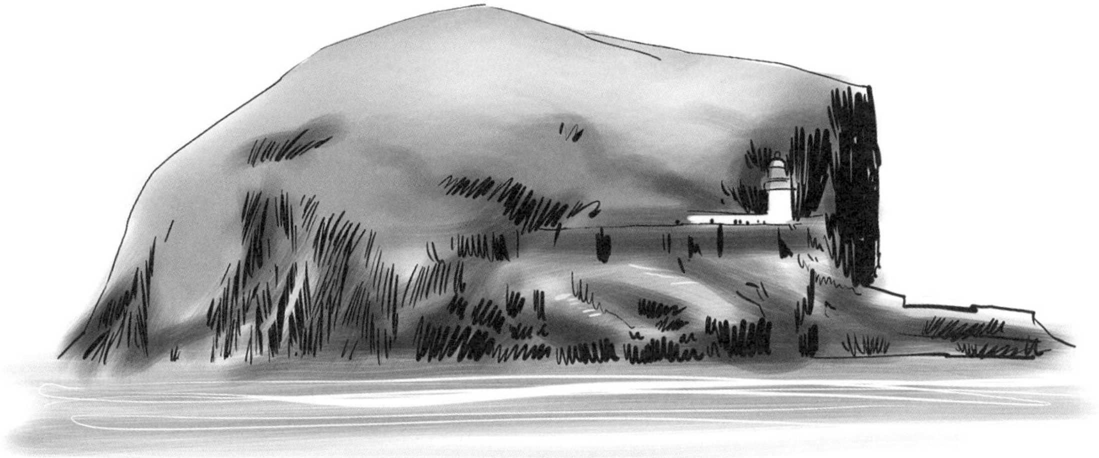

BAMBURGH
LIGHTHOUSE
BLACK ROCKS POINT
NORTHUMBERLAND

BAMBURGH

LOCATION: 55°37′00″N, 1°43′27″W
OS GRID: NU174359
ELEVATION: 12.5m (41ft)
CHARACTER: Oc (2) WRG 8s
RANGE: 26km (16 miles)

The first thing that comes to mind as you walk down the weathered wooden steps toward Bamburgh lighthouse is Munch's painting *The Scream*, or Macaulay Culkin aping it in the movie *Home Alone*. When the lighthouse was built, I'm sure the engineer or architect must have grinned inwardly as they laid out the arrangement of round windows and arched doorways. It's just a pity they didn't turn the lantern enclosure above into a top hat and then tilt it at a jaunty angle.

This, of course, isn't the original lighthouse. That took the form of a 13m (43ft) circular metal-framed tower on support struts about 4m (13ft) high. Its appearance was not unlike the lantern tower of a light vessel, but painted white instead of red. It was built in 1910 to guide shipping passing along the Northumberland coast and vessels in the waters around the Farne Islands, and was the most northerly land-based lighthouse in England. In 1975, use of the tower was discontinued and the new electric light was placed on top of the building we see now, which once housed the acetylene fuel for the original light. Today, Bamburgh lighthouse is monitored and controlled from Trinity House's Planning Centre in Harwich, Essex.

The lighthouse is set amid marram grass on the coast to the north of Bamburgh Castle. The castle itself is a looming and impressively austere presence. It has been fought over by the Danes and the kings of Mercia and Northumbria. It was captured by the Scots and stood as a forbidding deterrent for invading Vikings, but it also played its part in shepherding vessels safely to shore.

By the late 18th century, Bamburgh Castle had fallen in a state of disrepair and was run as a charity school by Dr John Sharp, the Archdeacon of Northumberland. Alongside

The Anglo-Saxon citadel of Bamburgh Castle looking majestic in the early morning sunlight.

the many other charitable projects he funded, the Archdeacon was keen to initiate new support systems for boatmen in the area. He restored the ramparts and walls of the castle to provide a platform for a fog cannon and accommodation for up to 30 shipwrecked sailors, and employed 2 riders to patrol the coastline and keep a lookout for ships in distress in stormy weather. Dr Sharp later used his personal wealth, and funds from Lord Crewe's Charity, which offers support for education and religious bodies, to fund a patrol along the Bamburgh coast for survivors of shipwrecks. In 1789, he commissioned Lionel Lukin to construct an "unimmergible" boat, an unsinkable boat, which was stationed at Bamburgh. Lukin's boat became the first patented lifeboat in the world, and Bamburgh the first lifeboat station. The nearby Bamburgh Dunes are a protected area of coastal sand dunes, which has a rich diversity of flora and fauna. The terrain ranges from open sandy beaches to low ridges dominated by marram and then the more stable grass-anchored dunes. There are plant species such as pyramidal orchid, centaurium, sea sandwort and petalwort, and over 500 species of insects with, of course, the birds who feed off them, such as the grasshopper warbler, sedge warbler, European stonechat, meadow pipit and reed bunting. In winter, short-eared owls and water rails are also found.

I have to admit to having a particular soft spot for this wild marram-dotted seascape. The beaches where I grew up on Ireland's northeast coast resemble this wild Northumberland shore. The brittle winter light and the metallic glint of the wintertime sea are as familiar as the ridges and runnels on the wide sweeping sands.

BLYTH EAST PIER

LOCATION: 55°06′59″N, 1°29′12″W
OS GRID: NZ328803
ELEVATION: 19m (62ft)
CHARACTER: Fl (4) 10s
RANGE: 39km (24 miles)

Blyth dates from the 13th century but didn't really get into its stride until the mid-1800s. By 1827, despite benefiting from a decent port, a rebuilt breakwater and an abundance of raw materials, the town's population barely numbered 2,000. That would change with the arrival of the Blyth and Tyne Railway in 1849, which connected Blyth to the region's thriving collieries.

The town received another boost with the Harbour Act of 1858, which permitted the dredging of harbours to allow larger ships to enter ports. Dredging dramatically increased the amount of coal that could be shipped out of Blyth. In 1855, the town exported 250,000 tons of coal; by 1900, this increased twelvefold to 3 million tons.

Sandpipers on the shoreline.

In 1882, a Bill of Parliament allowing the formation of the Blyth Harbour Commission was given royal assent. This paved the way for finance to be raised to construct the South Harbour, and in 1906 the East Breakwater was extended by 300m (985ft).

As recently as 1961, Blyth could claim to be the busiest port in England, shipping over 6 million tons of coal a year, including that extracted from the six collieries within the town's boundaries. During the late 19th and early 20th centuries, Blyth was also a major centre of the shipbuilding industry.

The town had actually had a lighthouse since 1730, when the harbour was going through the early stages of development and a coal-burning light was built at the waterfront. Nothing of this now survives, but in 1788 the lighthouse now known as Blyth High Light was built to a height of 12m (39ft) and lit by oil lamps. It was originally situated on the shore, but due to various stages of land reclamation it now stands 100m (328ft) inland on Bath Terrace. The tower was heightened over the years as surrounding buildings became taller and blocked its beam; it now stands 18m (59ft)

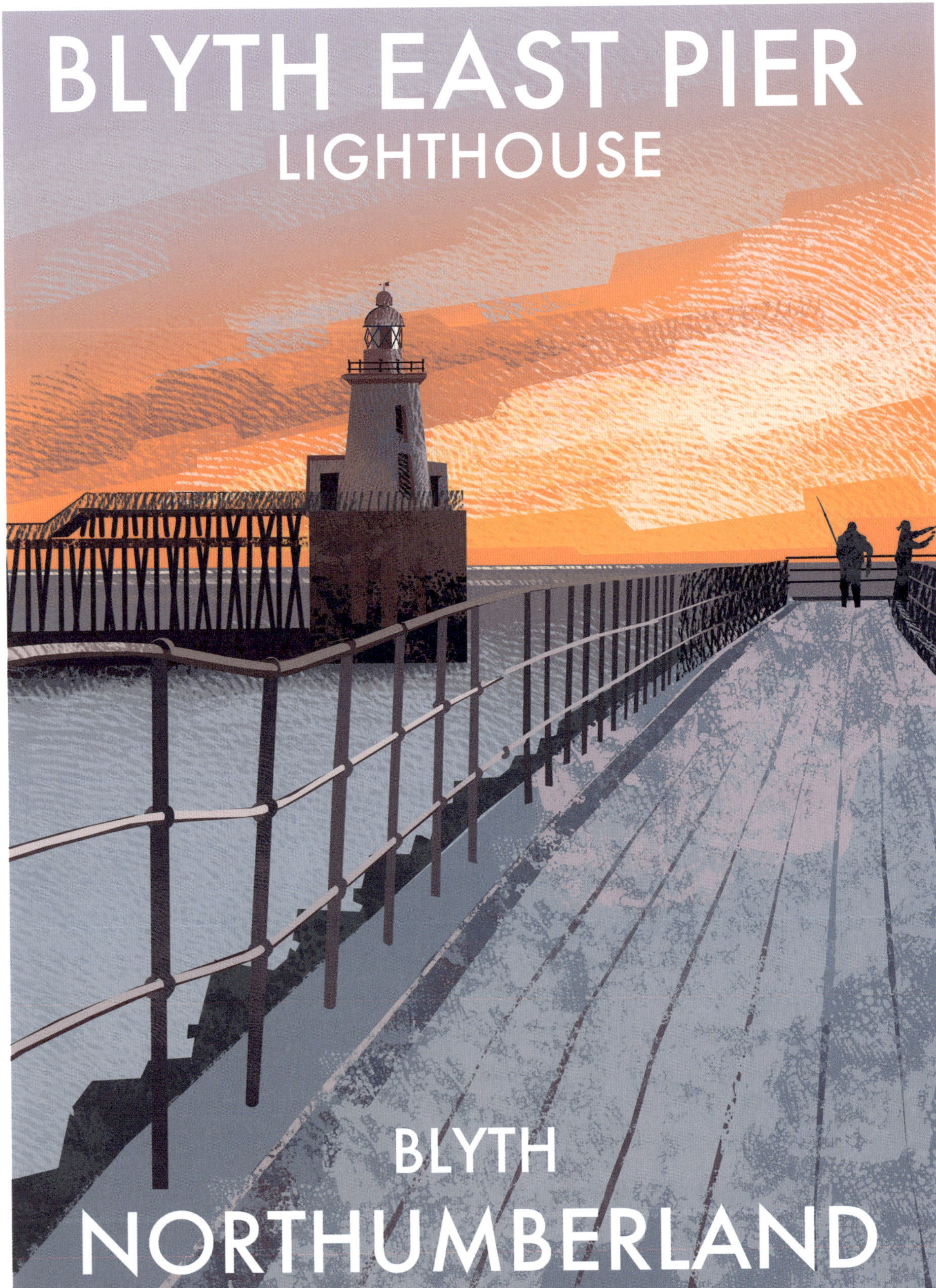
BLYTH EAST PIER
LIGHTHOUSE
BLYTH
NORTHUMBERLAND

tall. Converted to electricity in 1932, the old High Light acted in conjunction with several harbour lights until it was finally retired in 1984. It now serves as a daymark.

Blyth's only surviving operational lighthouse, the East Pier light or Harbour light, was opened in 1907. When debuted, the new light had a third-order rotating prismatic lens driven by a clockwork mechanism, giving a flashing white light every 20 seconds with a range of 34km (21 miles). Below it a red light with a similar character had a range of 27km (17 miles). When the lighthouse was electrified in the mid-20th century, the characteristic was changed to the present four white flashes every ten seconds.

More than a century after its debut, Blyth Pier lighthouse was looking the worse for wear, and in 2016 a major restoration of the building was undertaken. Because scaffolding couldn't be used, all the work was carried out by a six-person team abseiling down the sides of the tower. The project took just under 2 weeks and the lighthouse emerged corrosion-free and looking as smart as it did when it was first unveiled over 100 years ago.

The South Pier overlooking the lighthouse is a popular spot for sea angling and the waters below offer cod and whiting in winter, plaice and other flatfish in spring, and coalfish all year round.

At the boatyard, Blyth, Northumberland.

INNER FARNE
ISLAND LIGHTHOUSE
FARNE ISLAND
NORTHUMBERLAND

INNER FARNE ISLAND

LOCATION: 55°36′55″N, 1°39′21″W
OS GRID: NU217358
ELEVATION: 27m (89ft)
CHARACTER: Fl (2) WR 15s
RANGE: 19km (12 miles)

The pele tower on Inner Farne, built around 1500 and restored using old material from Durham Cathedral. Originally serving a defensive function, it now accommodates National Trust bird wardens on the island.

Following the restoration of Charles II in 1660, Sir John Clayton proposed to build lighthouses at four different sites along the east coast: the Farne Islands off Northumberland, Flamborough Head in Yorkshire, Foulness at Cromer and Corton near Lowestoft. None of these schemes ever came to fruition. Clayton managed to build a tower on Inner Farne, in 1673, but the project foundered and this stretch of the coast remained unlit for a further 50 years.

In 1776, Trinity House licensed Captain John Blackett to build two coal-fired lighthouses at his own expense on Inner Farne and Staple, one of the smaller Farne Islands. Blackett in turn would be permitted to collect dues on passing shipping. The two lighthouses were duly lit on 1 December 1778. Pinnacle lighthouse, as the tower on Staple was known, was destroyed by a storm six years later and it was decided to locate its replacement on nearby Brownsman Island.

The beacons were much appreciated by mariners negotiating the hazardous coast, but coal fires could be inconsistent and were often obscured by smoke. By 1809 both towers were in an advanced state of decay and so arrangements were made for Trinity House to take over their operation.

In 1811, the present Farne lighthouse was built to a design by Daniel Alexander, which consisted of a circular white tower 13m (43ft) in height and keepers' cottages, all of which was surrounded by a stone retaining wall. The lantern room was installed with reflectors and Argand lamps and ringed by a gallery with narrow railings. At the same time, a smaller light tower was constructed on the northwest point of the island, 150m (492ft) from the main light. This additional tower displayed a fixed white light that the keeper could monitor through a small aperture at the back of the tower. The final part of the 1811 development was a new oil-powered lighthouse on Brownsman island, which was moved to Longstone island.

In 1910, the smaller light on Inner Farne was obsolete and the main light was converted to automatic operation with an acetylene light controlled by a sun valve, which shut off the gas supply during daylight hours. This remained in operation until the station switched to solar power in 1996.

LONGSTONE
LIGHTHOUSE
OUTER FARNE ISLAND
NORTHUMBERLAND

LONGSTONE

LOCATION: 55°38′38″N, 1°36′39″W
OS GRID: NU245390
ELEVATION: 23m (75ft)
CHARACTER: Fl 20s
RANGE: 33km (21 miles)

In 1806, Trinity House began to replace its beacons with oil-fired lights. Around this time, it was decided that the lighthouse on Brownsman Island was no longer fit for purpose and a plan was drawn up to build a new lighthouse on the farthest of the outlying islands, Longstone. This new building was designed and built by Joseph Nelson. It consists of a red and white painted circular tower constructed of rough stone, with iron railings around the lantern gallery. The light was originally powered by Argand lamps, with 12 burners, parabolic reflectors and a catadioptric optical apparatus.

Once Longstone lighthouse became operational in 1826, William Darling was appointed its first keeper and moved there with his family from the decommissioned Brownsman Island lighthouse. Longstone was a bleak and remote location where fierce storms could whip up waves so enormous they would engulf the living quarters and drive the keeper and his family to seek safety in the upper levels of the tower.

On 5 September 1838, the SS *Forfarshire* was on its way from Hull to Dundee, carrying some 60 passengers and crew, when its boilers failed and the paddle steamer began to drift helplessly. Making for the Farne Islands and with his ship now powered only by a makeshift sail, the captain is believed to have mistaken the light of Longstone for that of Inner Farne lighthouse. However, before he could change course, the *Forfarshire* struck Big Harcar Rock, over 1km (0.6 miles) from Longstone. Within 15 minutes the creaking hull had split in two and the rear of the vessel was swept away into the roaring sea, while the front remained wedged on the rocks.

A sightseeing vessel anchored off Inner Farne Island, with Prior Castells tower in the background.

The wreck was spotted by William Darling's 22-year-old daughter, Grace, from her home in the lighthouse, but it was early morning before there was enough light to see that there were still survivors clinging to Big Harcar Rock. Reasoning that the sea was too rough to call out the lifeboat from North Sunderland, Grace and William decided to row out themselves to bring in however many souls they could fit into their small rowing boat. Grace sculled the boat backward and forward to avoid crashing on the rocks, while her father checked the injured and, assisted by other survivors, managed to get the least able on board first.

It soon became apparent that they would need to make two trips. At the lighthouse, Grace remained with her mother to attend to the casualties, while William and two crew members rowed back to get the remaining survivors. By 9am the rescue was complete and nine survivors were now safely recovering at the lighthouse. Nine other people had survived the night too by jumping into a lifeboat before the stern of the ship sank. Their boat had been swept away by the current at first but was rescued that same night by a sloop.

A shag struts his stuff.

Grace's story was printed far and wide and she became feted as a heroine. She and her father, William, were awarded the Gold Medal for Bravery by the Royal Humane Society and a Silver Medal for Gallantry by the RNLI. Tragically, just four years later Grace succumbed to tuberculosis and died in her father's arms on 20 October 1842. Her funeral four days later was attended by hundreds who travelled from all over the country to pay their respects.

COQUET

LOCATION: 55°20′02″N, 1°32′23″W
OS GRID: NU293045
ELEVATION: 25m (82ft)
CHARACTER: Fl (3) WR 20s
RANGE: 35km (22 miles)

Situated off the Northumberland coast, the island of Coquet (pronounced "co-ket" as in "go get") housed a small but vibrant religious community as early as AD 684. Today Coquet's only residents are of the avian kind and it is now a dynamic seabird sanctuary, hosting masses of nesting puffins and common, Sandwich and Arctic terns, and it is notable as the home of the UK's only breeding colony of roseate terns.

The former keepers' buildings in the compound are now used by RSPB wardens who keep watch during the breeding season. Because of its importance for roseate terns, the island is off limits to the general public. Interestingly, though the roseate tern is a fairly tame and willing charge of the RSPB, its cousin, the common tern, is extremely territorial and will dive-bomb intruders, nipping their scalps or dropping a well-aimed wedge of guano on their heads. When my brother was engaged by the Commissioners of Irish Lights to maintain the lighthouse at Rockabill off the north Dublin coast – another tern colony – staff were advised to wear helmets at all times!

Tour boat at Coquet lighthouse.

Following the act of 1836 that empowered Trinity House to purchase the remaining English and Welsh lighthouses in private hands, aids to navigation in the area were reviewed and Coquet lighthouse was built in 1841. The lighthouse, a white square tower of sandstone with walls more than 1m (3ft) thick and surmounted by a turreted parapet, was designed by the renowned engineer James Walker. The structure is built on the remains of the Benedictine monastery that occupied the island until the dissolution of the monasteries under Henry VIII, and the light is housed in a circular lantern room complete with a conical roof and domed ventilator.

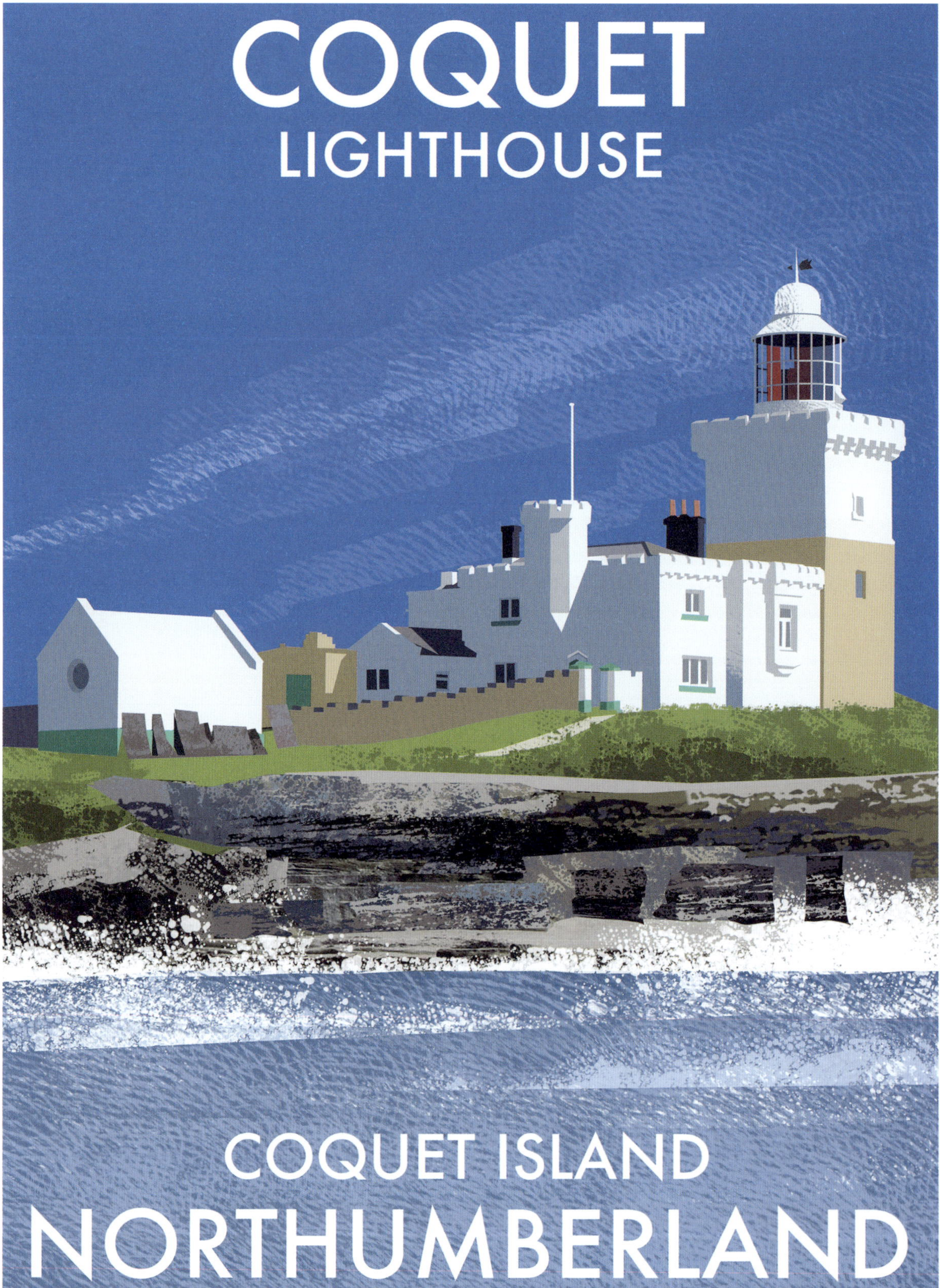
COQUET
LIGHTHOUSE
COQUET ISLAND
NORTHUMBERLAND

The first keeper appointed to Coquet lighthouse was William Darling, elder brother of famed rescue heroine Grace Darling (see page 217 [Longstone]). He was the second of her brothers to become a Trinity House lightkeeper.

The light was a first-order fixed dioptric lens initially fuelled by oil. Red sectors were added in 1854 to warn of rocks at Hauxley Point to the south and the Boulmer rocks to the north. The configuration was altered 16 years later when a separate sector light was installed, pointing south from a lower window in the tower. In 1891, the lamps were updated again, with the main lamp's character changed to occulting, flashing for 2.5 seconds every minute. Electrification arrived in 1976, automation in 1990 and solar power in 2008. The original optic is now on public display, along with the old occulting apparatus, at Souter lighthouse, down the coast near South Shields.

St MARY'S
LIGHTHOUSE
WHITLEY BAY
NORTH TYNESIDE

ST MARY'S

LOCATION: 55°04′19″N, 1°26′59″W
OS GRID: NZ352754
ELEVATION: 46m (151ft)
DEACTIVATED: 1984

This concrete pillar was built on the rocks to the east of St Mary's at the start of World War I. It served as a rangefinder to calibrate the guns at nearby Tynemouth Castle.

St Mary's, a tidal island located off Curry's Point to the north of Whitley Bay, is accessible at low tide by a causeway. During medieval times it was known as Bates or Bait Island and was occupied by a small chapel dedicated to St Helen. Inside the chapel was the Lady Light, also known as St Katherine's Light. The light was later incorrectly ascribed to St Mary, which is how the island came by its current name. Legend has it that the light was used in the seaward window to warn mariners of the rocks. However, all traces of St Helen's Chapel were destroyed during construction of the lighthouse between 1896 and 1898.

St Mary's lighthouse was commissioned by Trinity House to replace the light on the headland at Tynemouth Castle, which had become obscured by smoke from local industry. The 45m (148ft) tower was constructed using a quarter of a million bricks by the John Livingston Miller company of Tynemouth and finished in cement render. The keepers' cottages were constructed of stone and connected to the tower by a covered passageway.

The lighthouse was fitted with a first-order "bivalve" rotating optic similar to the one provided the previous year for Lundy North lighthouse. It displayed a group-flashing characteristic, flashing twice every 20 seconds. St Mary's was the last Trinity House station to be lit by oil, being powered by paraffin until electrification in 1977. Just seven years later the lighthouse was decommissioned and started a new life as a museum and visitor centre. This iconic landmark received a Grade II listing in 2012.

Since 1974, St Mary's has been designated as a conservation area. On the seaward side of the island a viewing area and hide overlook the outer rocks, where in winter grey seals haul themselves out to rest in the pale sunshine having made their way from Lindisfarne and the Farne Islands to the north, following the autumn's birthing season. The island is also a haven for birdlife with redshanks, curlews, oystercatchers, dunlins, sanderlings and various species of plover and gull sighted all year round and then joined in winter by visitors from Scandinavia and Russia. Many of these are passage migrants, such as redwings, fieldfares and pink-footed geese, glimpsed as they fly inland toward more sheltered farmlands and freshwater ponds.

HERD GROYNE
LIGHTHOUSE
SOUTH SHIELDS
TYNE & WEAR

HERD GROYNE

LOCATION: 55°00′28″N, 1°25′29″W
OS GRID: NZ369683
ELEVATION: 13m (43ft)
CHARACTER: Oc WRG 10s
RANGE: 39km (24 miles)

Facing Herd Groyne across the Tyne, the Collingwood monument is dedicated to Admiral Lord Cuthbert Collingwood, Nelson's second in command at Trafalgar.

At the mouth of the River Tyne are three functioning lighthouses guiding vessels toward docks and berths further upriver at North Shields and Newcastle. Tynemouth lighthouse is right at the end of the pier to the north of the channel, while South Shields lighthouse faces it across the river entrance.

Inside the maw of the estuary and protecting Littlehaven Beach from the wash of passing river traffic stands the Herd Groyne. A groyne is a low wall built out from the shore into the sea, generally running perpendicular to the shore. When the Herd Groyne was built between 1861 and 1867, it originally projected straight out into the channel. However, as the South Pier wall was being constructed and the rubble base laid, it became apparent that a combination of the new works and currents at the estuary was causing sand to disperse into the river mouth. To improve the flow of the river, the groyne was altered, taking a curve to the east to assume its present position.

Balanced at the end of the wall and gazing out to sea like an abandoned spacecraft from an H G Wells novel stands the elegant russet structure of the Herd Groyne lighthouse. This diminutive iron clad structure was completed well before either of the piers which enclose it. Building these piers was a Herculean task. The North Pier, begun in 1854, swallowed over 3,000 tons of stone alone and, barely 2 years after completion in 1895, was almost completely destroyed when a ferocious storm left the Tynemouth lighthouse at its end far out to sea. The South Pier, protected from the northerly gales to some extent, emerged in better condition and repairs were quickly carried out.

Herd Groyne lighthouse was first exhibited on 30 October 1882 and displays an occulting light showing for a duration of 8 seconds at 2-second intervals to seaward. The display also includes red and green sectors. To landward, a fixed light for ships leaving harbour is shown. The lighthouse is also one of just a few left in this country to have an operational fog bell, which strikes every 5 seconds in reduced visibility.

OLD HIGH LIGHT, NORTH SHIELDS

LOCATION: 55°00′33″N, 1°26′13″W
OS GRID: NZ361684
DEACTIVATED: 1810

Generations of Geordies have earned their keep along the River Tyne, working at one of the many busy shipyards, docks and fisheries that have sprung up on its shores down the centuries. The North Shields Fish Quay dates from as early as 1225, when Prior Germanus from Tynemouth Priory established a village of shielings (traditional basic huts) where the Pow Burn meets the Tyne. Soon there were smoke houses, a brewery, mills and, inevitably, complaints from merchants upriver in Newcastle – that trade other than the loading and unloading of salt and fish at North Shields should be prevented by legislation. The Fish Quay, originally known as Low Lights, sat at the centre of North Shields and as the area developed it became the obvious place to position navigational lights to help guide traffic upriver of Herd Groyne and also for those returning to sea.

Buoys on the waterfront at North Shields.

In 1536, Henry VIII authorized the Guild of the Blessed Trinity (now Trinity House of Newcastle) to build a pair of lights at North Shields. Following the dissolution of the monasteries between 1536 and 1541, materials were confiscated from Blackfriars Monastery in Newcastle and used to build the towers. This original pair of lights remained in use until they were eventually replaced by the Old High and Low Lights that can still be seen today. The former, situated on Beacon Street, is a handsome ogee-roofed square tower, topped by a small lantern and crowned with a ball finial. The Low Light to the southeast was situated within Clifford's Fort, part of a network of coastal defences built in 1672 to repel attack by the Dutch. It was housed in a three-storey brick building with the light displaying from its gable wall. The building now serves as a community centre, museum and café.

The two structures served as leading lights for vessels coming upriver; lining the shining dots one above the other would set course for the correct channel. Powered by candles, the lights weren't particularly

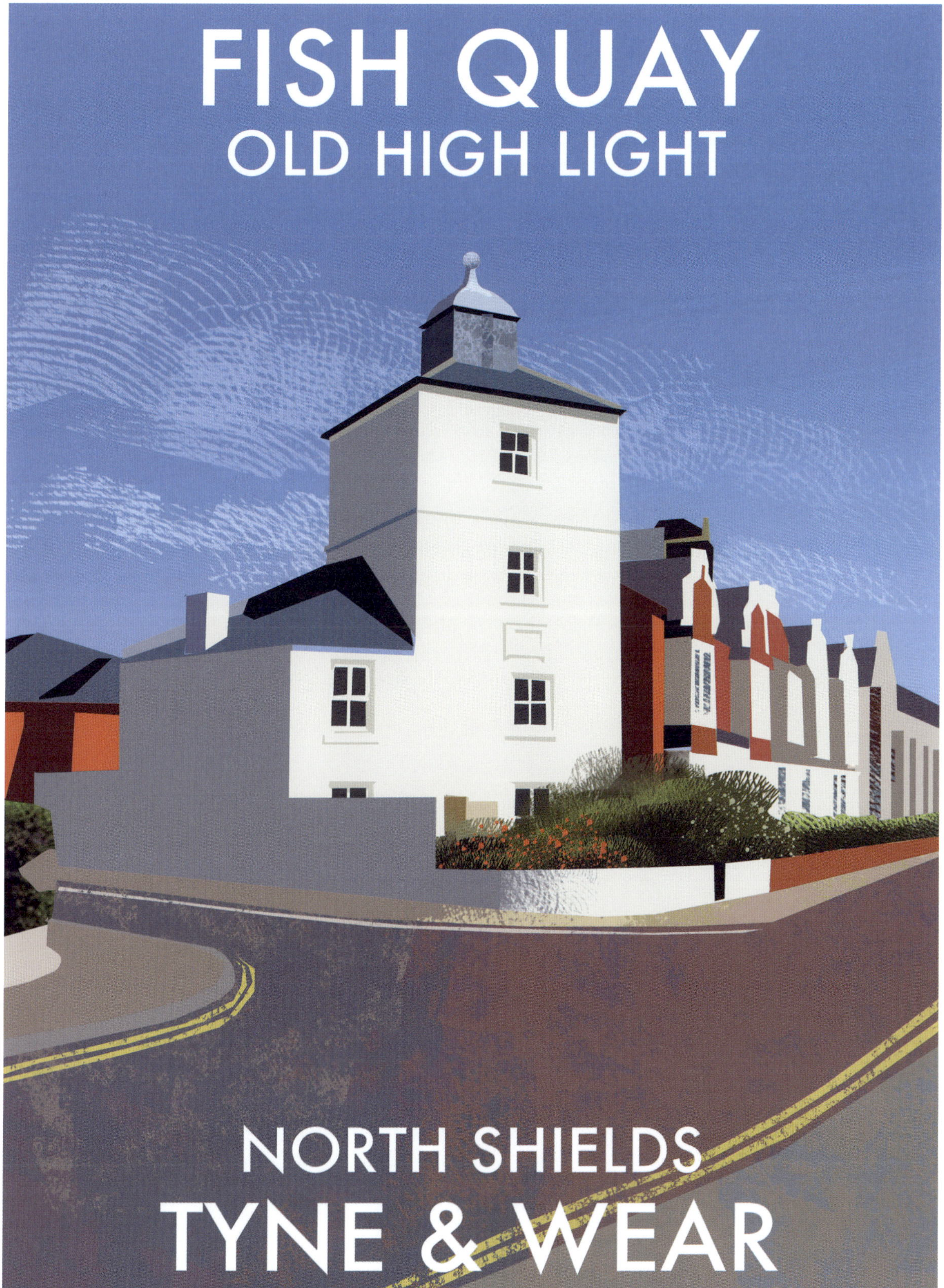
FISH QUAY
OLD HIGH LIGHT
NORTH SHIELDS
TYNE & WEAR

bright, but in a world where there was little else by way of public lighting, they were sufficient. In any event, by 1773, they had been upgraded to oil lamps, shining a little more brightly in the dark.

As the deep navigable channel of the river gradually changed course over time, the High Light became surplus to requirements and a new Low Light was built to a design by John Stokoe. Consisting of a six-storey, ashlar-rendered tower with a small lantern on the roof, the lighthouse displayed a fixed white light powered by oil and visible for 21km (13 miles). In 1808, the new High Light was built at Dockwray Square. This four-storey tower housed a fixed white light visible for 26km (16 miles).

The lights served a fishing industry whose scale can only be imagined today. Come August, North Shields would see the arrival of the herring girls. These girls often came from the Scottish isles, although some were local, and from early summer to late autumn they would follow the fishing fleet down the east coast, stopping at ports to clean and cure the catch. The quays were busy day and night and boats rushed to get to sea to secure their favoured location. The numbers of herring girls were at their height at the start of the 20th century and scale of the fishing industry in the northeast is a fraction now of what it was in its heyday, the North Shields Fish Quay remains an important and thriving fishing community.

The new High and Low Lights remained in use until 1999 when they were retired, though they still serve as daymarks for vessels entering the Tyne.

The new High Light at North Shields.

ROKER

LOCATION: 54°55′17″N, 1°21′09″W
OS GRID: NZ416587
ELEVATION: 25m (82ft)
CHARACTER: Fl W 20s
RANGE: 43km (27 miles)

By the late 19th century, Sunderland was a thriving centre of shipbuilding and commerce that had outgrown its diminutive north and south piers. Plans were put in place to create a new enclosed outer harbour, which would be protected by two elegant, curved breakwaters projecting from the northern and southern shores.

The task of designing and implementing this ambitious plan was entrusted to Henry Hay Wake, who had been appointed Chief Engineer to the River Wear Commission at the age of only 25. He didn't disappoint and by 14 September 1885 the foundation stone was ready to be laid. In the manner of so many Victorian engineering projects, the job almost wasn't worth doing if it wasn't gargantuan and this duo of piers certainly fitted the bill. The two breakwaters were designed to swallow over 700m (nearly half a mile) of granite-faced blocks and required the use of the aptly named Goliath and Titan cranes to first load and then position the boulder-sized blocks in place.

Although the construction of both piers began at the same time, priority was given to the new north, or Roker, pier. In the end, World War I intervened and prevented the completion of the south pier. While the intention had been to have two matching lighthouses either side of the harbour entrance, Roker's twin was never built.

The lighthouse at the end of the new north pier was completed in 1903 and was believed to be the most powerful port lighthouse in Britain. Known as the Roker Pier lighthouse, the 23m (75ft) tower is composed of naturally coloured red and white Aberdeen granite, which gives it its distinctive striped bands. It is topped

Fishing off Roker Pier. Common catches include pollock and coalfish.

ROKER PIER
LIGHTHOUSE
SUNDERLAND
TYNE & WEAR

by a gallery and gleaming white lantern featuring a black domed roof.

The lantern was fitted with a third-order rotating catadioptric optic and displayed a single flash every five seconds. At first, the lighthouse was illuminated with town gas, but the supply at the end of the pier was unreliable and this fuel system was eventually replaced by an incandescent petroleum vapour mantle lamp. This increased the effective intensity of the light and gave it a range of 28 km (17 miles). A compressed air fog siren was also fitted, sounding a 2-second blast every 20 seconds in foggy weather.

The lamp was semi-automated in 1936 and fully automated 36 years later, when it was fitted with a back-to-back array of sealed beam units mounted on a rotating pedestal. This gave the light an extended range of 43km (27 miles). It was again upgraded in 2007, and in 2012 a programme of extensive refurbishment got underway. The lighthouse, a Grade II listed structure, had fallen into disrepair after decades of neglect and the pier needed some serious attention too. With funding from the Heritage Lottery Fund, Sunderland City Council undertook to restore them both to their former glory.

In November 2016, a storm delayed works when gale-force winds and huge waves washed away the railings and attached coping stones at the pier's end. Work resumed and today a new entrance at the mouth of the pier allows safe access into the underground tunnel that was once used by the lighthouse keepers to access the lighthouse in stormy weather.

The entrance portal to Roker tunnel and lighthouse. A tunnel used in its construction still runs the length of Roker Pier and was later used by the keeper to reach the lighthouse in bad weather. You can now take a tour through the tunnel and up to the lighthouse lantern.

SOUTER

LOCATION: 54°58′14″N, 1°21′52″W
OS GRID: NZ407641
ELEVATION: 23m (75ft)
CHARACTER: Fl R 5s
RANGE: 48km (30 miles)

For much of the 19th century, the rocky coastline between the rivers Tyne and Wear was notorious as a graveyard for shipping. In the 1860s, more than 160 vessels were wrecked after running aground on the notorious submerged rocks known as the Whitburn Steel between the villages of Marsden and Whitburn.

The sharp spike in shipwrecks fed the rumour mill and there were accusations of locals luring ships onto the rocks with lanterns in order to plunder their cargoes. When the schooner *Test* foundered in November 1865, the captain testified that he had been navigating toward what he took to be the lights at the mouth of the River Tyne when it suddenly became apparent that his boat was about to run aground. Luckily, all the crew were rescued by the Whitburn lifeboat, but the ship and cargo were lost. On another occasion, two Sunderland sea pilots also testified to seeing a pair of revolving lights off Whitburn late at night.

As the testimonies gathered, suspicion fell on the local fishermen. They in turn were adamant that it was another group who stood to profit from wrecking, stating that "it is a fact that nearly all the vessels which come on shore here are worn-out old colliers, which to the owners are better lost than otherwise, and the 'false-lights', so-called, an excuse for the captains". The truth of the matter was never resolved, but when Souter lighthouse eventually cast its beam across these dark waters, rumours of clandestine lights on lonely cliff paths vanished like smoke as surely as if an illicit candle had been snuffed out.

Thanks to the amount of shipping lost in the previous decade, Trinity House moved

The foghorn at Souter lighthouse.

SOUTER
LIGHTHOUSE
MARSDEN
TYNE & WEAR

A Severn-class all-weather lifeboat belonging to Tynemouth RNLI passes along the coastline at Marsden. The station's crews have been awarded 22 medals for gallantry.

with some urgency to establish a light on this stretch of coastline. While the site at Souter Point had been favoured initially, the higher cliffs at Lizard Point made this their preferred location. However, as a lighthouse had recently been established at Lizard Point in Cornwall, the decision was made to nevertheless use the name of nearby Souter Point. The lighthouse was designed by Trinity House's Chief Engineer, James Douglas and built by local builder, Robert Allison. The 23m (75ft) circular tower was initially painted white; the red band was added in 1924 to improve its visibility as a daymark.

When it was first illuminated in 1871, Souter lighthouse was regarded as a marvel of its age. It was the only lighthouse at that time to have been designed and built to be powered by electricity – making this cutting-edge technology. The light was generated by a carbon arc lamp and was described as one of the most powerful lights in existence. However, although today we are used to the idea of electricity producing a directional beam far more powerful than any created by burning a fossil fuel, early electric bulbs produced a relatively weak light. This was why the lighting apparatus was changed to oil when the lighthouse was modernized in 1915. In June 1952, advances in electric bulbs meant that the lighting could be changed back from mantle burners to electricity.

In 1987, Trinity House announced their decision to decommission the lighthouse and the light was switched off for the last time in November 1988, and the keepers were withdrawn. The lighthouse and cottages were subsequently purchased by the National Trust and developed into a visitor centre with a shop and café.

WHITBY

LOCATION: 54°28′40″N, 0°34′06″W
OS GRID: NZ9288310093
ELEVATION: 73m (240ft)
CHARACTER: Fl WR 5s
RANGE: 33km (21 miles)

There are a number of lighthouses in the historic town of Whitby – two on the piers of the town's harbour and the third situated southeast of the town, on Ling Hill. This last and largest of the lighthouses is known as Whitby High lighthouse and goes by the local moniker the "Hawkser Highlight". It has guarded the coast since 1858.

Whitby High lighthouse is the remaining half of two towers once known as the twin lights of Whitby South and North, which used to serve as a fixed pair of lights to warn of the dangers of nearby Whitby Rock, a local shipping hazard. Each was initially equipped with paraffin lamps and single-storey keepers' cottages. The lower of these lights (the North light) was displayed from a 20m (66ft) octagonal tower, but it was deactivated in 1890 and the building was subsequently demolished. At this time, the South lighthouse was upgraded with an 8-wick oil burner and an occulting mechanism, which gave a flashing signal once every 30 seconds.

A red sector was added to the light to cover the Whitby Rock. The red sector is an ingenious device whereby any boats that are at sea and facing the light, inside the line of the bell buoy, know to keep an eye out should the lighthouse beam show red as they approach from the south toward the harbour. Move a couple of metres and it turns white. Red spells danger, so as long as the light remains white, you're on a safe approach. The system is much the same for all lighthouses that display a red sector, and this system of guiding lights became the basis of the approach lights used today to guide aeroplanes in to land at airports.

Tumbling steps and helter-skelter rooftops beckoning the visitor into the handsome town of Whitby.

WHITBY HIGH
LIGHTHOUSE
WHITBY
NORTH YORKSHIRE

One of the more famous ships to run into trouble at Whitby was the hospital ship *Rohilla*. It was originally built as a steamer for the run to India but was called up for duty at the start of World War I. On 30 October 1914, while en route from the Firth of Forth to Dunkirk to evacuate wounded soldiers, it ran aground at Saltwick Nab, a reef about 1.6km (1 mile) east of Whitby. The lighthouse was unlit due to the war and Captain Neilson claimed that his boat struck a mine before grounding. In the event, the *Rohilla* crashed onto the reef and soon broke its back. Six lifeboats were launched and, in spite of ferocious weather, rescue attempts persisted around the clock for the next three days. In total, of the 229 on board, 146 were rescued – including Mary Kezia Roberts, who had only 2 years previously survived the sinking of the *Titanic*!

When the North light was demolished, the site was retained and in 1901 a new fog signal station was debuted, featuring a pair of Raleigh trumpets powered by compressed air. These gigantic metal horns still adorn the building, which is now a private residence. The fog signal – referred to locally as the "Hawkser Bull" – continued in use until 1987, the equipment having been updated in 1955. Whitby lighthouse was automated in 1992 and the lighthouse is now monitored and controlled from Trinity House's Planning Centre in Harwich, Essex.

The East and West Piers at Whitby.

FLAMBOROUGH HEAD

LOCATION: 54°06′59″N, 0°04′57″W
OS GRID: TA254708
ELEVATION: 65m (213ft)
CHARACTER: Fl (4) 15s
RANGE: 33km (21 miles)

The name Flamborough was originally believed to mean "the place of the flame", but is now thought to derive from the Saxon term *flaen*, meaning dart, which the shape of the headland resembles. The oldest of the two lighthouses to stand sentinel on the cliffs here was erected in about 1669. This chalk tower remains one of the earliest known lighthouse buildings still in existence in the UK and was established by Sir John Clayton, with a patent from Charles II. Sir John planned to build two more lighthouses nearby as part of a series of lighthouses located along the east coast and aimed to make a fortune from tolling ships rounding Flamborough Head. However, the deal he struck was fundamentally flawed, with dues only paid voluntarily, and he was soon declared bankrupt. The other two towers were never built and the evidence suggests that even the single tower he managed to raise in this location was never kindled.

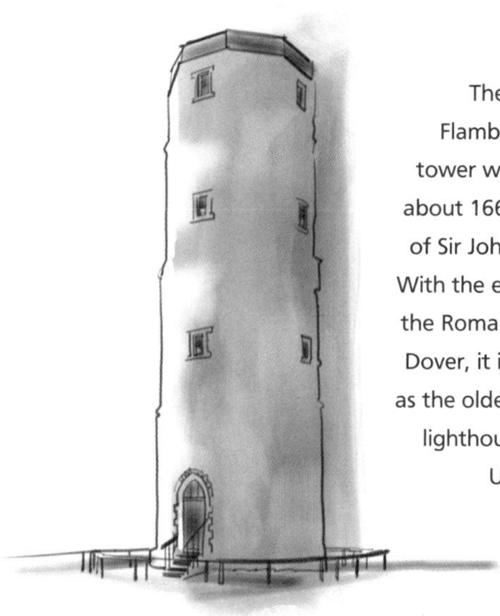

The old Flamborough tower was built in about 1669 by order of Sir John Clayton. With the exception of the Roman Pharos at Dover, it is regarded as the oldest standing lighthouse in the UK.

The second lighthouse at Flamborough Head was similarly intended to mark the headland for vessels heading for Scarborough and Bridlington, but it wasn't built until some 130 years later. It was designed in 1806 by the Trinity House architect Samuel Wyatt and was constructed without the use of scaffolding in nine months by John Matson of Bridlington at a cost of £8,000. This new lighthouse has a brick tower 25.5m (84ft) tall, with a lantern and gallery.

The lighting apparatus was designed by George Robinson, an optics specialist and the Chief Inspector of Lighthouses at

FLAMBOROUGH HEAD
LIGHTHOUSE
FLAMBOROUGH
EAST YORKSHIRE

Trinity House. It consisted of a rotating vertical shaft with a 3-sided frame onto which 21 parabolic reflectors were fixed – 7 on each of the 3 sides. On one side, the reflectors were covered by red glass, giving a distinctive light characteristic of two white flashes followed by a red flash. "Two whites to one red / Indicates Flambro' Head" was an easy prompt to help you remember what you were looking for and the system was subsequently taken up at other lighthouses along the coast.

In 1872, a new paraffin lamp was installed, making Flamborough Head the first lighthouse to use this fuel. Although the chemical engineer James Young had discovered how to distil paraffin from coal and oil shales and patented the process some 20 years earlier, it had only been mass produced in the previous 5 years. In the wake of the success of Flamborough Head, Trinity House upgraded all their lighthouses to paraffin. In 1925, the lantern was modified to house a new 4.5m (15ft) lens and today a first-order catadioptric optic displays 4 white flashes every 15 seconds.

A fog signal station was built close to the cliff edge at Flamborough in 1859. At first, an 18-pound gun was used, sounding once every 15 minutes, but in 1878, explosive rockets replaced the cannon. These were fired every ten minutes, reaching 180m (600ft) into the fog-shrouded sky. In 1908, a fog siren was installed, sounding one long and one short blast every 90 seconds. Sixteen years later, this was replaced by a pair of diaphones and in 1975 an electric fog signal was installed.

In 1940, the lighthouse was electrified and it was finally automated over 55 years later, with the keepers leaving the site on 8 May 1996. Today, the lighthouse is controlled from Trinity House's Planning Centre in Harwich, Essex.

Near to Flamborough Head, North Landing is a lovely little cove with cafés and pubs a short walk away.

WITHERNSEA

LOCATION: 53°43′51″N, 0°01′43″E
OS GRID: TA339279
ELEVATION: 39m (128ft)
DEACTIVATED: 1976

Built between 1892 and 1894, Withernsea lighthouse is one of the very few lighthouses to be situated inland, nearly a quarter of a mile from the shoreline. It was positioned well back to counter fears of coastal erosion. The climb to the top of the tower entails a challenging 144 steps, but you are rewarded with spectacular views over Withernsea and the Holderness coastline.

At the time that the lighthouse was built, the houses that now surround it didn't exist. They were all built when the promenade was later extended along the sea front.

When first put into operation, Withernsea used an eight-wick paraffin lamp. Though these methods of illumination seem puny to us today, you have to remember that the early lighthouses operated at a time when visible lights of any sort were a rarity at night. Today, harbour lights at busy ports have often become redundant, not because of GPS but because there is so much background light that the lighthouse becomes almost invisible. The paraffin lamp was magnified and focused by a catadioptric optic which concentrated the light into a beam.

A twin-hulled fishing boat being hauled up the beach by tractor.

The light was occulting, which meant it was quickly eclipsed by a clockwork shield three times in succession every minute. In 1936, mains electricity came to the lighthouse and the paraffin lamp was replaced by a 1,500-watt lamp set within a third-order revolving Fresnel lens. This was turned by a clockwork mechanism. The lens itself weighed in at two tons and floated on a mercury bath that weighed half as much again. The density of mercury meant that despite its weight the lens array could be easily turned on its mounting. This was achieved by winding up a clockwork

WITHERNSEA
LIGHTHOUSE
WITHERNSEA
EAST YORKSHIRE

mechanism that dropped a weight through the centre of the tower, in turn rotating the light. It needed to be rewound 30 to 40 minutes later, ensuring the keeper on duty was never idle.

For most of its life, Withernsea was operated as a "man-and-wife station", run by a couple who were accommodated in the adjacent cottage, but after 82 years of service the lighthouse was decommissioned on 1 July 1976 and now functions as a museum. The lighthouse keepers' cottages at the base feature RNLI and HM Coastguard exhibits, with models and old photographs. These record the history of local shipwrecks and of the Withernsea lifeboat crews who saved some 87 lives between 1862 and 1913.

Withernsea Bay has groynes like this one all along the shore from the north to the south of the town. These timber structures are essential in helping to keep the sand from moving further down the coast.

SPURN
LIGHTHOUSE
SPURN POINT, KILNSEA
EAST YORKSHIRE

SPURN

LOCATION: 53°34′44″N, 0°07′06″E
OS GRID: TA403112
ELEVATION: 39m (128ft)
DEACTIVATED: 1985

Spurn point is a low sandy spit of dunes and marram grass that extends about 4km into the mouth of the river Humber. Like all sandbars along this coast, it is hostage to the tide and storm, and over the last three hundred years it has moved westward and increased in length. The present lighthouse is the last in a series of lights that have endeavoured to make navigating the shifting channels of the coast a little safer.

The first light on the point is reputed to have been erected by a hermit called William Reedbarrow in the mid thirteenth century, but no remains of his structure survive. Three centuries later in 1674 a London merchant, Justinian Angell, gained permission to build a pair of coal burning lights on the point. These were regularly washed away by the tides and had to be rebuilt. That the point today has moved 3km south of the site of these structures gives some indication of the permeability of this stretch of coastline.

By the mid eighteenth century, the bar had grown almost 2 km to the south, and the lights were now regarded as dangerously misleading. An Act of Parliament resulted in the decision to commission John Smeaton to build a pair of swape towers, where the coal fire was lit in a metal basket or brazier and swung out over the edge of the tower on a wooden swape or wooden swivelled lever. Eventually the brickwork on the upper tower started to crack and in 1892 it was replaced by the present 39-metre lighthouse. Its main light had a range of 31 km with separate sector lights, two of which marked particular shoals or sandbanks, while another indicated the main channel along the Humber. Due to improvements in navigation, the light was discontinued in 1985.

In December 2013, a huge storm charged into the North Sea sending a tidal surge barrelling down the east coast of Britain. When it finally reached Spurn, the thin neck of land simply snapped in two. The road running down to the tip of the point, which had weathered many a storm since its construction at the outbreak of the First World War, was destroyed in less than an hour. Erosion at the landward end of the spit has resulted in the point becoming a tidal island and access now is by foot only at recommended crossing times.

SIR PETER SCOTT
EAST LIGHTHOUSE
SUTTON BRIDGE
EAST ANGLIA

EAST SUTTON (SIR PETER SCOTT LIGHTHOUSE)

Although native to North America, snow geese sometimes overwinter in the UK.

LOCATION: 52°48′30″N, 0°12′41″E
OS GRID: TF491257
ELEVATION: 18m (59ft)
NEVER ILLUMINATED

In 1826 the River Nene was re aligned into a new channel which became the Nene Outfall. This was intended to drain the low lying inland Lincolnshire fens. The East Sutton Lighthouse was built along with its counterpart, the West Sutton Lighthouse on the opposite bank. Both were intended to mark this new Channel which opened five years later in 1831. Neither lighthouse was ever lit.

The conservationist Sir Peter Scott took up residence from 1933 to 1939, making various wildlife studies and paintings during his time here. Regarded as one of the most influential environmentalists of the twentieth century, Scott was the son of the famous "Scott of the Antarctic " and the sculptor, Kathleen Scott. During the 1930s the lighthouse was surrounded by tides on three sides, making it the perfect place to keep wildfowl. It would be Scott's home and studio until the outbreak of the Second World War. From the lighthouse isolated out in the tidal marshes, Scott could observe the wading birds, and it was these that inspired his first book, 'Morning Flight', which contains many paintings completed during his time at Sutton Bridge.

Starting at East Sutton lighthouse, the Peter Scott Walk takes you along the River Nene toward the Wash and the Great Ouse, finishing at King's Lynn Ferry.

The 18m tapered tower is topped by an octagonal lantern with unusually, round windows. A single chimney peeps out over the copper clad roof. The tower was built as a stand alone building, but over the years, various additions have been added to it as accommodation.

Towards end of the Second World War with rationing still in place, the sea walls were moved half a mile seaward to reclaim land which was now needed for additional food production, leaving both towers a short distance inland.

The lighthouse marks the beginning of a number of family-friendly walking routes along the banks of the salt marshes with dramatic views over the Fenland landscape.

CROMER
LIGHTHOUSE
CROMER
NORFOLK

CROMER

LOCATION: 52°55′29″N, 1°19′00″E
OS GRID: TG230415
ELEVATION: 84m (276ft)
CHARACTER: Fl 5s
RANGE: 39km (24 miles)

This stretch of the north Norfolk coast has always been a rich gathering ground for sea-going vessels. These range from the old Dutch fishing boats – doggers – which gave their name to the Dogger Bank (known to all from the shipping forecast), to the crabbers catching the crustaceans that the town is famous for, to, of course, the coal barques that plied these coastal waters on their way down from the northeast to London and the ports of the south.

In medieval times, churches and ecclesiastical centres on the coast shone candles from sea-facing windows as a guide to whatever vessels might be out in the night. While the dim light of a tallow candle might seem a little inadequate, in the black of night on a wind-tossed sea, it would have been a welcome and essential part of finding the way home.

Cromer was one of the sites chosen by Sir John Clayton as part of his plan to build and run a series of lighthouses down the east coast. In 1669, Sir John and his business partner, George Blake, were awarded a 60-year patent, the caveat being that the tolls were to be paid by passing ships on a voluntary basis. This minor detail would prove the scheme's downfall. The tower was built, but while it may have displayed a light briefly, hampered by Trinity House's objections to the project and, crucially, the ship owners' unwillingness to pay their dues, the scheme was quickly abandoned. On Admiralty charts, however, the lighthouse was considered useful as a daymark and indicated as "a lighthouse but no fire kept in it" until it collapsed in about 1700, a casualty of coastal erosion.

In 1720, a fresh patent was issued by King George I to Nathaniel Life, the new owner of the land at Foulness, and to his partner, Edward Bowell. The dues were set at a farthing per ton of general cargo and

Pulling in the boats at Cromer beach.

Cromer Pier.

a halfpenny per chaldron (an archaic and much debated measurement of weight, equal to approximately 2,690 kg or 5,940 lb) of Newcastle coal. Trinity House supported the project on condition that the lease revert to them at its expiration 60 years hence and the light was first illuminated on 29 September that year. The tower was an octagonal affair, three storeys high and built of brick. It was crowned by a glazed lantern that housed a coal fire. The lease, due to run out in 1780, was for some reason extended for a further 42 years.

When several ships sank in a storm off the East Anglian coast on 31 October 1789, pressure was put on lighthouse owners to improve their lights. Cromer's lights were duly updated to 15 Argand lamps and reflectors, mounted on a 3-sided revolving frame. The apparatus was driven by clockwork, making a full revolution every three minutes, and it had to be wound every five and a half hours. It wasn't loved by boatmen, who described the frequent and rapid flash of the light as a will-o'-the-wisp.

In 1822, the lease was finally up and Trinity House took over the lighthouse. The first keepers to be installed were two young women who received a wage and certain "perquisites", or expenses as these would be referred to today. Although not much more than a mile walk from Cromer along the clifftops, the journey to the lighthouse wasn't an easy trek and the two ladies seem to have been smart enough to demand some extra incentives to take up the position! Unfortunately, due to erosion, the lighthouse's location was precarious and in 1799, 1825 and 1852, large parts of the cliff slipped down into the sea, with the building finally being destroyed by a landslip in 1866.

The current lighthouse is set half of a mile from the cliff edge, though erosion continues to narrow that gap. It came into operation in 1833 and is constructed of masonry, with the octagonal tower standing 18m (59ft) tall. When built, the tower was topped by a much larger lantern than at present, but with full electrification in 1958, the array of reflectors was removed, a new optic installed and the old lantern was replaced with the current, much smaller one. In June 1990, Cromer lighthouse was converted to automatic operation and it is still owned by Trinity House today. While the tower is not open to the public, the area around the lighthouse is accessible and the keeper's cottage beside the tower is let out as a holiday apartment.

HAPPISBURGH

LOCATION: 52°49′13″N, 1°32′13″E
OS GRID: TG384306
ELEVATION: 41m (135ft)
CHARACTER: Fl (3) 30s
RANGE: 26km (16 miles)

Happisburgh lighthouse is the oldest working lighthouse in East Anglia, and the only independently run lighthouse in Great Britain.

It is the surviving big brother of a pair of lights built by Trinity House following an unprecedented storm in 1789 that saw almost 70 sailing ships founder off the Norfolk coast with the loss of over 600 lives. A paucity of navigational aids along the crucial stretch of coastline between Cromer and Winterton motivated the speedy building of a low light on the cliff edge near Cart Gap, with the 26m (85ft) high light situated a quarter of a mile further inland. The duo, replacing the old Caister lights, operated as a pair of leading lights so that when a vessel lined both lights up, one above the other, it was set for safe passage around the southern end of the treacherous offshore Haisborough Sands and into the benign waters known as the Would.

The two lights debuted in January 1791, just two years after the storm that prompted their construction. In 1863, a new lantern room was fitted with diamond-shaped panes first trialled by the Scottish lighthouse engineer Alan Stevenson. These larger glass slabs set within a pattern of diagonal astragals gave a better view of the light to vessels from all directions. Due to erosion of the cliffs, the days of the low light were numbered; it was discontinued in 1883, to be replaced by a lightship placed on the Haisborough Sands, and the tower was demolished soon after.

With the high tower reduced to a lonely sentinel on the clifftop, there was concern it might be mistaken for Winterton during

The coastal village of Happisburgh was once some distance inland, but the sea has claimed several hundred metres of territory and numerous houses over the last four or five centuries. Coastal defences slow the process of erosion, but they are counteracted by the effects of climate change.

HAPPISBURGH
LIGHTHOUSE
HAPPISBURGH
NORFOLK

Refreshments at the Hill House pub after a walk to the lighthouse.

daylight hours and so it was decided to dress it in its now familiar colour scheme of red and white bands. The light was also changed to occulting, with the light shining for 25 seconds followed by a break of 5 seconds. With the introduction of acetylene in 1929, the light could be operated automatically and so the keepers' cottages were sold off. With the arrival of electricity in 1947, the light was again changed, this time to its current character of three white flashes every 30 seconds.

In 1988, Trinity House listed Happisburgh as one of five lighthouses slated for retirement. A voluntary organization, the Friends of Happisburgh Lighthouse, was formed and successfully petitioned for a stay of execution. The next task was to establish the now renamed Happisburgh Lighthouse Trust as a local lighthouse authority. With that achieved, Happisburgh now shines as an independently run lighthouse, maintained and operated entirely by voluntary contributions.

LOWESTOFT
LIGHTHOUSE
LOWESTOFT
SUFFOLK

LOWESTOFT

LOCATION: 52°29′13″N, 1°45′21″E
OS GRID: TM551943
ELEVATION: 37m (121ft)
CHARACTER: Fl 15s
RANGE: 42km (26 miles)

Along the eastern coastline of 17th-century England, a sizeable trading route developed as the coal seams of Newcastle were exploited and the coal shipped down from the north to the burgeoning capital. While the seas were not as wild and unpredictable as those of the southwest, there were no shortage of obstacles waiting to catch out the unwary mariner. Prime among these were the shifting sandbanks found along the Norfolk and Suffolk coasts. Many ships, both from the local mackerel fleets and from the flotilla of coal barques, foundered and were lost. In the pitch dark of night, hugging the coast and keeping a wary eye out for signs of life and light must therefore have been a reassuring, if dangerous, gambit for steering to port. Beaching on a sandbank in the gloom of night could spell disaster even in benign weather.

In 1609, Trinity House proposed to build two lighthouses on the coast at Lowestoft. These were to consist of two wooden towers that would act as leading lights, guiding vessels through an inshore passage known as the Stamford Channel. This watercourse, like many on the east coast, has been displaced by tide and time, but was once an important route. The Brethren of Trinity House stated that the lights were "for the direction of ships which crept by night in the dangerous passage betwixt Lowestoft and Winterton".

The two lighthouses were subsequently built on the low-lying foreshore known as Lowestoft Ness and were illuminated by candles. However, they were rebuilt in 1628 and then again in 1676, when the rear light

The Neptune (or Triton) statue on The Esplanade, Lowestoft by John Thomas (1813-1862).

was moved up the cliff face so it could be seen by boats approaching from a distance. This new high lighthouse was a more permanent fixture, built of brick and stone. To ensure the light could be seen far out to sea, it was illuminated by a coal brazier. One of the defining features of the east coast, then as now, is its impermanence, and by 1706 the shifting shoreline meant that the low light was discontinued. For the next 25 years, mariners were forced to navigate the Stamford Channel in darkness. By 1730, a new low light was re-established, this time lit with whale oil. It was a wooden tower designed to be easily moved as the shoreline retreated or the channel changed course.

In 1777, the coal fire in the high light was replaced by a lofty new glass lantern and in it was an experimental type of light known as a "sparkle light". Imagine, if you will, a disco ball, which rather than being round is in the shape of a cylinder. Covered in 4,000 small square mirrors, this glittering tube was surrounded by a circle of oil lamps and reflected the light so efficiently, it could be seen 32km (20 miles) away. It must have been quite a sight! Technology was moving apace at this juncture, however, and it was soon replaced by even more efficient, if less romantic, Argand lamps combined with silvered parabolic reflectors.

When the decision was taken in 1870 to electrify the Lowestoft high light, a new station was built to house the new equipment as the old station was considered inadequate. However, electricity was still in its infancy while paraffin oil was readily available and economical, so a last-minute change of heart ensured that the station would not see the use of electric light for almost a century. The lighthouse was now fitted with a revolving lens, changing the light to occulting and flashing at half minute intervals.

By the early 1920s, the Stamford Channel was just a memory and the low light, having no further purpose, was finally decommissioned. The high light was automated in 1975 and further modernized in early 1997. Lowestoft lighthouse is now managed by Trinity House's Planning Centre in Harwich, Essex.

The Mincarlo, a sidewinder fishing trawler moored on Heritage Quay, is a floating museum that offers an insight into commercial fishing back in its heyday.

SOUTHWOLD

LOCATION: 52°19′38″N, 1°40′53″E
OS GRID: TM5094276284
ELEVATION: 37m (121ft)
CHARACTER: Fl W 10s
RANGE: 44.5km (28 miles)

Southwold lighthouse stands midway between the towns of Lowestoft and Orford. It is set back from the beachfront and located smack-bang in the middle of a residential area, the site chosen by Trinity House having been described by the Victorian press as "very advantageous [. . .] the smoke from the town will not obscure the light and its nearness to the cliff must make it very prominent all along the coast". Coastal erosion had presented a serious threat to the three local lighthouses at Orford Ness, with the Orford low light being destroyed the tail end of the 18th century by storms for the fifth time, so there was some urgency to complete a tower at Southwold as a coastal mark for passing shipping and for service vessels entering Southwold harbour. In fact, such was the urgency to light this part of the coast that a temporary light was displayed from a purpose-built wooden structure while the task of constructing the tower got underway.

Beach huts at Southwold are said to be in such demand that they can sell for the price of a small house.

Building work began in 1887 under the supervision of Sir James Douglass, Engineer in Chief to Trinity House, a task taking three long years to complete. And what a task it was. Some 1,500,000 half-bricks were used to construct the tower, which had to be transported to the site via Halesworth on the Southwold railroad. Having arrived at the railroad station, they were then transferred to the horse-drawn wagons belonging to a local coal merchant, Thomas Moy & Co, who then brought them in relays to the site. Ten months later, the 8-ton lantern house arrived in two sections. Again, Mr Moy and his team carted these to the site. Despite his good working relationship with Trinity House, Mr Moy may well have been relieved that in

SOUTHWOLD
LIGHTHOUSE
SOUTHWOLD
SUFFOLK

future he would only be hauling coal to the lighthouse for the keeper's use. The age of oil illumination had arrived and the era of lighthouses going through up to a ton of coal every three days were gone for good.

When finished, the lighthouse stood at 31m (102ft) tall, standing 37m (121ft) above sea level, and two keepers' cottages were built next to the tower. To reach the lantern room meant climbing 113 steps via two winding staircases. Inside, the first-order fixed Fresnel lens that was fitted had originally been built for Happisburgh low lighthouse, but was re-used when this was demolished in 1883.

The light was kindled by Trinity House on 3 September 1890, but only six days later there was a fire in the lantern that destroyed the burner. This was due to the inexperience of the keepers! After additional training, they were deemed capable of managing the intricacies of the six-wick Argand oil burner. In 1906, this was replaced by a Matthews incandescent oil burner. Seventeen years later, a Hood 100mm (4in) petroleum vapour burner was installed, which remained until the station was electrified and automated in 1938. During World War II, the lighthouse was used by the military for spotting enemy aircraft. It was also lit for convoy purposes under instruction from the Admiralty.

In December 2012, the character and range of Southwold lighthouse were changed, with the range of the main light increased from 32km to 45km (20 to 28 miles) in advance of the decommissioning of Orfordness lighthouse. Two red sectors mark shoals to the north and Sizewell Bank to the south. These have a range of 27km (17 miles). The white and red group flash 4 times every 20 seconds.

Simple seaside pleasures - buckets, spades and an ice cream.

ORFORDNESS
LIGHTHOUSE
ORFORD NESS
SUFFOLK

ORFORDNESS

LOCATION: 52°05′02″N, 1°34′27″E
OS GRID: TM449488
DEMOLISHED: 2020

Orford Ness is a 16km (10-mile) long shingle spit that runs parallel to the Suffolk coast. It is separated from Orford by the River Alde and stretches almost from the town of Aldeburgh, at its northern end, down to Shingle Street in the south. The spit is almost entirely composed of flint deposited by waves through the process of longshore drift. Orfordness lighthouse used to sit near the spit's centre, approximately south-southwest of the town of Orford and at its promontory or "ness", until the building was demolished in August 2020 because of the erosion of the shoreline.

Until 1993, the peninsula remained under the jurisdiction of the Ministry of Defence, who conducted secret tests on the site during both world wars and the Cold War. The spit's time as a military dominion actually began 80 years earlier, when the War Office purchased part of the Ness to serve as a base for the newly formed Royal Flying Corps (RFC). It was later to become the location of the Orfordness Beacon, also known as the Black Beacon, an early experiment in radio navigation, and in the 1930s it hosted the first experiments in what would later become known as radar.

The area has a slightly eerie quality. On the one hand, it could be the setting for a spaghetti western, but there's also a sense of unease about the wild, bare

The so-called "pagodas" at Orford Ness, which were in fact laboratories. Tests on a high-explosive initiator, to be used for nuclear bombs, were carried out at Orford Ness and, for safety reasons, the tests were observed remotely from these huge labs.

landscape, probably fuelled for myself by a fondness for science fiction movies and TV series such as *Quatermass* and *The Damned*. The remains of the Black Beacon, the two "pagoda" test labs and the bomb ballistics building, all now viewing points, collectively contribute to an atmosphere of disconcerting ambivalence.

Probably because of its secretive military history, a number of doubtful stories have circulated about the peninsula, including one which speculates that during World War II, a Nazi landing force disembarked near Shingle Street but was thwarted in an explosive counterattack. This most likely arose from beach barrage flame tests carried out by the British military which, if seen from a distance, could well have resembled a major battle.

There have also been many UFO stories associated with the area, including mysterious lights reported during the well-known Rendlesham Forest incident, which earned the location the sobriquet of "Britain's Area 51". Lights of a different kind were first seen on the Ness in 1637 and were formed by a simple pair of wooden poles with a candle suspended from each to act as leading lights. They were replaced in 1720 by two brick towers. However, despite being sturdier, the lower light was soon washed away in a storm. This was

In the Middle Ages, Orford was an important port and its castle still stands witness to its historic status. The village offers the only access point to the nature reserves of Orford Ness and Havergate Island.

replaced by a series of structures that all suffered much the same fate due to either the whim of tempests or shoreline erosion.

In 1792, the then landowner, Lord Braybrooke, decided to build a new, more robust tower further inland. This structure became the new high light, while the old high light now served as the lower light in this arrangement. They were both fitted with the latest Argand lamps and reflectors, giving a much-improved light.

In 1836, an Act of Parliament gave Trinity House the power to buy out private lighthouse operators and they purchased the two towers at Orford Ness, paying Lord Braybrooke the sum of £13,414.00 – the equivalent of almost £2 million today – for the pair. In 1888, major upgrades were carried out at the high lighthouse, in which red and green sectors were added and the beam changed to occulting. The previous year, the lower light had again become a victim of coastal erosion and the decision was now made not to repair it and it was taken out of use.

The year 1914 saw a new revolving lens fitted to Orfordness lighthouse, producing a flash every five seconds and giving an extended range of 46km (29 miles). Electrified in 1959, in 1964 Orfordness became the first lighthouse to be remotely monitored by Trinity House from their Headquarters in Harwich and the keepers were withdrawn the following year.

Because of sustained erosion on the peninsula, the decision was eventually made to decommission the lighthouse in 2013 and the process of removing equipment began. The building was then purchased by the Orfordness Lighthouse Trust, whose aim was to preserve it as long as was feasibly possible. Unfortunately, time and tide wait for no man and further encroachments by the sea sealed the fate of the lighthouse. By July 2020 demolition work had begun and a month later the lighthouse was no more. The trust plans to rebuild the top third of the lighthouse as a memorial on land situated on the other side of the Ness, facing the quay at Orford.

HARWICH HIGH LIGHT

LOCATION: 51°56′40″N, 1°17′19″E
OS GRID: TM261324
DECOMMISSIONED: 1917

If you are at all interested in navigation, the history of safety at sea or are simply curious to see some of Britain's more unusual lighthouses, a trip to Harwich is a must. The town is where Trinity House's monitoring operations are based and from where they supply and maintain over 450 buoys, including cardinal, lateral and a variety of other types. They also inspect those maintained by port and harbour authorities around the country, and those belonging to utility companies and oil, gas and wind farm operators. The town has a small maritime museum housed in the old Low Light, while between Harwich and Dovercourt, there are four rather unusual lighthouses, all within a stone's throw of each other.

In 1665, two lights were displayed in Harwich to assist navigation into the River Stour. One installed on top of the old town gate was consisted a coal-fed brazier. The other was a much simpler affair: a basic 7m (23ft) tall wooden-frame tower with a candle displayed from its top. The patent for both lights had been granted to Sir William Batten of the Royal Navy and supported by the Brethren of Trinity House (of which Batten was a member). It secured a fortune for its owner. Not only would vessels bound for Harwich and the nearby ports have to pay dues, but also those simply passing along the coast. However, the lights were soon decried as inadequate and pressure was put on the Commissioners to ensure they were improved. When General Francis Slater Rebow (who was distantly related to Batten) was granted a patent in 1816, it was on the proviso that two new towers be built, the equipment improved and that he contribute a percentage of his profits toward the upkeep of the church and street lighting in the area.

Trinity House HQ at Harwich. The yellow Special Mark buoys are used to denote a special area or feature whose nature may not be apparent from reference to a chart or other nautical publication.

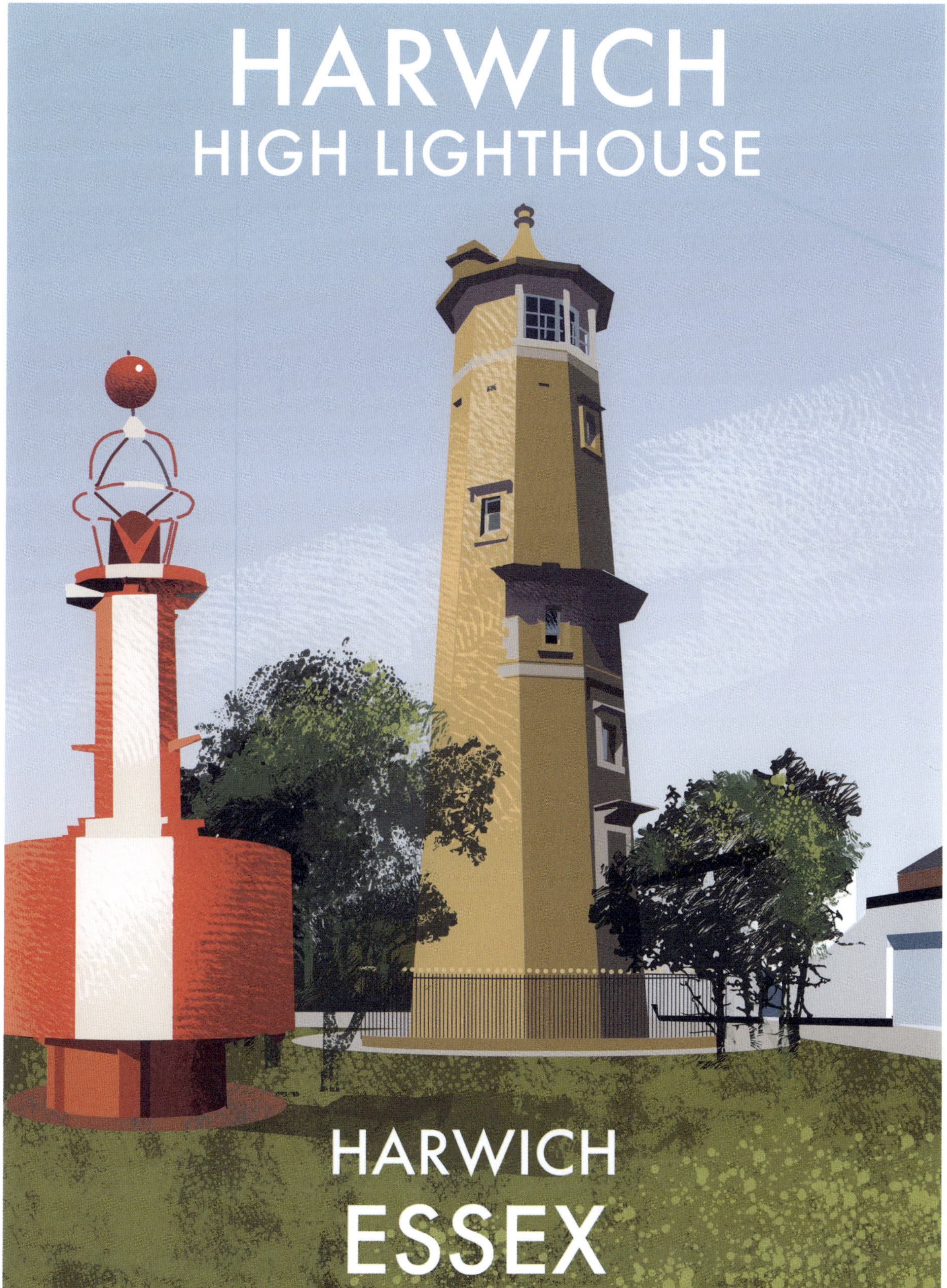
HARWICH
HIGH LIGHTHOUSE
HARWICH
ESSEX

By 1818, the two towers were complete and the lights illuminated using oil lamps and reflectors: nine in the high lighthouse, three in the low. The lights were displayed at the same height as the old ones but realigned by 3m (10ft) to the southwest, as the river channel had also migrated in that direction. The high light, which had initially displayed from a window halfway up the tower, quickly proved inadequate, and the light was moved to the top of the tower and the apparatus increased to ten burners, giving it an improved range of 21km (13 miles). The low light was designed as a ten-sided brick structure by John Rennie and stands 16.5m tall (54ft). The canopy was added in the late 19th century to provide shelter for walkers on the seafront. The lighthouse now houses the Maritime Museum.

In 1836, Trinity House eventually bought out the lease for the lights from General Rebow. However, the continued movement of shingle off Landguard Point had caused the river channel to migrate further and by 1863 Trinity house came to the conclusion that the lighthouses should be deactivated. By this stage, the towers had earned themselves the moniker of "the misleading lights of Harwich"!

The two lights at Harwich were swiftly replaced by two equally intriguing structures at Dovercourt. What could, on a foggy morning, easily be mistaken for some retro alien spacecraft, are in fact two prefabricated leading or range lights, originally designed so that they could be moved if the course of the channel shifted. They are connected by a causeway that can only be accessed (with care!) at low tide. An external ladder leads to the first floor, which housed the living quarters. From there, the lantern can be reached by way of an internal ladder. The lights were originally powered by gas, giving the high light a range of 17km (11 miles) and the low light a range of 14km (9 miles). Accommodation for the keepers was spartan, consisting of a small living room, a stove for cooking, toilets and a bunk bedroom. The lights were eventually retired in 1917 and Trinity House sold the structures six years later to Harwich Town Council, with the proviso that they would be demolished should they decay to such an extent that they became unsafe.

BLACKWALL

LOCATION: 51°30′28″N, 0°00′30″E
OS GRID: TQ394806
DEACTIVATED

In the early days of lighthouses, a hodgepodge of systems for providing shore lights and markers existed around Britain's shores, with no real regulation or oversight. Private franchisees and operators ran lighthouses that were often inefficient, poorly lit or sometimes simply not lit at all, due to cost-cutting or negligence. In the 1830s, the keeper of Lowestoft lighthouse, after lighting the lamp, would regularly lock up the building and head into town to ply his second trade as a waiter in nearby hostelries for five shillings a night. More worrying still was that, on occasion, keepers subcontracted their duties to others to make a little extra income. In one case, a keeper hired an elderly woman who lived quite a distance from the lighthouse. In bad weather, when the light was most needed, she simply stayed at home. The situation was only brought to a head when a ship struck the rocks below the tower, with the loss of a costly cargo and all lives on board.

When Trinity House was established, one of the tenets of the new body was that there would be consistency and regulation applied to the operation of its lighthouses. To this end, it was decided that a place of training should be provided. Located deep within the Docklands at the confluence of the Thames and Bow Creek, Trinity Buoy Wharf at Blackwall was chosen as the site for a training facility and experimental lighthouse. The original lighthouse was designed by the Chief Engineer of Trinity House, James Walker, in 1852; it was later demolished in the late 1920s. A second lighthouse was built between 1864 and 1866 by James Douglass. The building, which survives today and is sometimes

The decommissioned lightvessel No 93, moored at Trinity Buoy Wharf, was previously in service on the Humber. It was retired in 2003 and sold the following year. Its position is a nod to the wharf's former role as the place where Trinity House once manufactured and maintained the buoys and lightships used around the coasts of Kent, Essex and Suffolk.

BLACKWALL
LIGHTHOUSE
TRINITY BUOY WHARF
LONDON

known as Bow Creek lighthouse, was designed as a site for testing various new advances in illumination technology but was never used as a working lighthouse. At one time even Michael Faraday, one of the most important scientists of his age, carried out experiments here. Indeed, the only invention by Faraday to be patented – a type of chimney to stop lamp gases combusting – was produced in the workshops of Blackwall.

The lantern at the top of the lighthouse had originally been exhibited at the Paris Exposition of 1867, where it had been used by Trinity House to demonstrate an improved system of electric lighthouse lighting designed by Professor Frederick Hale Holmes. Over the years, the lantern was used by Trinity House to test a variety of lighting systems using new and improved lenses, new fuel types and the wondrous possibilities of electricity as this technology developed, with the results being visible at Charlton across the river.

The site was also used as a maintenance depot and storage facility for warehousing buoys and other marine equipment. It included workshops for testing, overhauling and the repair of lightships. By 1910, the wharf was kept so busy maintaining buoys and lightships from Suffolk to Kent that it employed almost 150 people, from platers to riveters, carpenters to tinsmiths. However, the wharf had outlived its usefulness by 1988 and its future looked uncertain. The London Docklands Development Corporation stepped in and set up the Trinity Buoy Wharf Trust, with a 125-year lease. In 1998, Urban Space Holdings Ltd were granted a long lease for the site, which has now been developed as a centre for arts and culture. Inside the lighthouse is Jem Finer's *Longplayer* installation, a continuous piece of music that has been running since 31 December 1999 and is programmed to keep playing until 2999.

The lighthouse remains the central attraction at Trinity Buoy Wharf but there are a number of other interesting features, including an old Trinity lightship that has been turned into a music recording studio, stacked shipping containers that have been painted and made into a studio and office complex called Container City, and an authentic chrome American diner called Fatboy's.

NORTH FORELAND

LOCATION: 51°22′30″N, 1°26′42″E
OS GRID: TR398696
ELEVATION: 57m (187ft)
CHARACTER: Fl (5) WR 20s
RANGE: 35km (22 miles)

The North Foreland lighthouse gazes across the North Sea from atop a sheer cliff on the Isle of Thanet – which is actually a peninsula, not an island, although it was one in the past. As recently as Roman times it was separated from the mainland by the Wantsum Channel, but the channel slowly silted up during the Middle Ages, thereby creating the peninsula. Legend has it that snakes cannot live on the isle and that the remedy for any den of serpents you may chance across in your home is simply to sprinkle some soil from Thanet on the creatures and that will be the end of them!

Reports of a beacon on the promontory date back to 1499, but the first reliable record of lights on this coast is from 1636, when Charles I granted a letters-patent to Sir John Maldrum to operate and maintain the lighthouses that appear to have been already extant on the North and South Forelands.

Joss Bay beach.

By all accounts, the original lighthouse at North Foreland appears to have consisted of a simple timber lath and plaster house, on the top of which a light was illuminated in a large glass lantern to serve as a beacon for shipping. Surprisingly, the house survived intact until 1683 when, perhaps unsurprisingly, it accidentally burned down. It was replaced by a coal-fired beacon, which was suspended from a jib set into the cliff face. By the close of the century, an octagonal structure of flint with an iron brazier of burning coal had replaced the jib and this was kept blazing throughout the night. The light is reported to have gone through a ton of coal about every three days!

In 1719, ownership of both the North and South Foreland lights was bequeathed to the Trustees of Greenwich Hospital, with the proviso that whatever profits the lights made were to be put toward the upkeep of

NORTH FORELAND
LIGHTHOUSE
ISLE OF THANET
KENT

a hospital for seamen. The fire was enclosed in a glass lantern but the build-up of soot on the panes and the gentle blaze that this often created made it hard to see the light, and within a decade it was moved out into the open again. In 1793 or thereabouts, work began on extending the height of the lighthouse by two storeys and the coal fire was replaced by 18 oil lamps housed within a new optical system designed by Thomas Rogers.

In 1832, the lighthouse was purchased by Trinity House and in 1858 a spacious new lantern room was added to the tower. From it, a new first-order catadioptric optic using a multi-wick burner illuminated the coast. Shortly thereafter a red sector was added to the beam shining northwards. A programme of general refurbishment was implemented and two keepers' cottages were built next to the lighthouse. The tower itself was gutted and a new cantilevered stone staircase was installed. The whole station was painted white.

Updates and improvements to the lighting apparatus continued as technology progressed: a pair of eight-wick Trinity House pattern burners were installed in 1894, then a triple mantle burner in 1904 and a Hood 100mm (4-in) petroleum vapour burner in 1923.

In 1998, North Foreland became the last Trinity House lighthouse to be automated. To mark the occasion, Prince Philip, Duke of Edinburgh, presided over a special ceremony in his capacity as Master of Trinity House. The lighthouse is now managed from Trinity House's Planning Centre in Harwich, Essex.

North Foreland at dusk.

PRINCE OF WALES PIER, DOVER

LOCATION: 51°06′51″N, 1°19′23″E
OS GRID: TR326402
ELEVATION: 23m (75ft)
CHARACTER: Fl GW 1.5s
RANGE: 7.5km (4.5 miles)

Following the Roman invasion of Britain in AD 43, Dover was chosen as the base for the Roman fleet as it afforded the shortest crossing to the continental mainland and had a good natural harbour. The Pharos that can still be seen in the grounds of Dover Castle was probably one of a pair that guided ships into harbour. Today, Dover has four operational lighthouses to protect the vessels entering Britain's busiest port.

Operationally, Dover is separated into two docks. The Eastern Docks serve cross-channel ferries, while the Western Docks include a cruise terminal, a marina for yachts and a cargo facility. Admiralty Pier lighthouse, built in 1908, sits on the western arm of the harbour and takes the form of a lattice tower fitted with port control entry lights. The cast-iron tower replaced an earlier light built in 1876.

The Southern Breakwater was constructed between 1907 and 1909 from gigantic granite-faced concrete blocks and was designed to protect the harbour, providing a refuge for the British fleet. Together, the Admiralty Pier and the Eastern Breakwater, enclose a harbour area of over 283ha (700 acres), with two entrances of 204m (670ft) to the east and 225m (740ft) to the west. Armed with two 15.2cm (6-in) breech-loading Mk VII guns, the breakwater formed part of Britain's defence during both world wars. On the Southern Breakwater, two lighthouses sit at either end. The West Head lighthouse is, as advertised, at the western end, while Knuckle lighthouse guards the eastern approach. Both are fabricated of cast iron.

Security personnel at Dover Port.

Construction of the Prince of Wales Pier Lighthouse was started in 1892 and finished ten years later. It is the only Dover Harbour lighthouse to be made of stone. When it was built, a cast-iron pier connected the

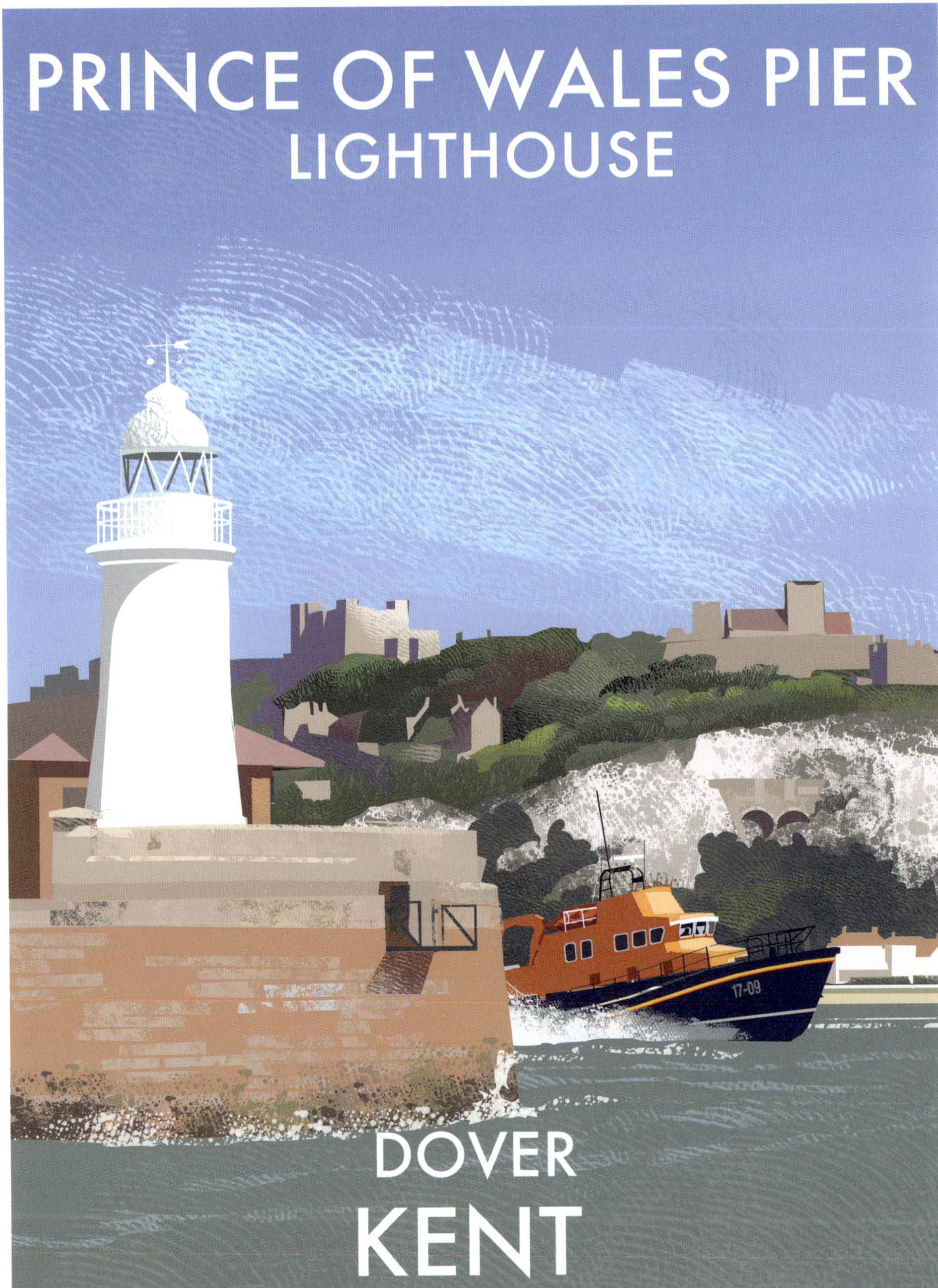
PRINCE OF WALES PIER
LIGHTHOUSE
17-09
DOVER
KENT

stone causeway it sits on with the land, allowing ships to berth alongside it. The pier was named after Edward VII, who, as Prince of Wales, laid the foundation stone in 1892. A railroad track was built on the pier in 1905, as it was envisaged that the site would become an embarkation point for large Atlantic liners. Trade flourished for a mere two years, during which time a café was built at the base of the lighthouse.

The Lighthouse Café, or the "nearest café to France" as it was known, had an enviable view of all the comings and goings in the busy harbour, and on a clear day you could see right across the water to the French coast, just over 32km (20 miles) away. Mounted on the side of the café was the figurehead from the wooden barque *Rouseau*, which plied the waters between England and the West Indies (Rousseau – with an extra "s"– being the capital of the West Indian island of Dominica).

During the great storm of 1987, when almost 15 million trees were blown down, the MV *Seafreight Highway* was blown into the café and lighthouse, leaving the upper section of the structure wrenched half a metre (approx. 2ft) out of line with its base. The café was also fatally damaged and, although repairs to the lighthouse were quickly underway, the café would soon be demolished. To repair the lighthouse itself, the structure needed to be dismantled. All the blocks were marked and cleaned. The copper dome was repaired and the iron base refurbished. The lens was damaged beyond repair, but luckily there was a spare in the Harbour Boards storerooms. With the lighthouse back in action, a smaller café called the Fo'c'stle was unveiled, this time giving a little space to the tower so that people could walk around and admire it.

In 2015, the Port of Dover closed the Prince of Wales pier to the general public as part of their redevelopment of the Western Docks. A fantastic new marina has been built alongside the pier, but the lighthouse sadly remains out of bounds.

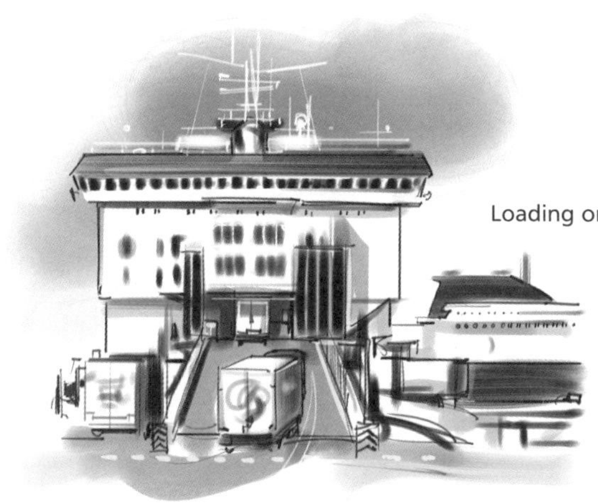

Loading onto a ferry at Dover.

DOVER CASTLE
PHAROS
DOVER
KENT

DOVER CASTLE PHAROS

LOCATION: 51°07′42″N, 1°19′23″E
OS GRID: TR326418

After the Roman invasion of Britain in AD 43, Dover, being the shortest crossing to the continental mainland and having a good natural harbour, was chosen as the base for the Roman fleet. The Pharos was probably one of a pair (the other would have been situated on the Western Heights opposite), which together guided vessels toward the entrance to the harbour in the Dour Estuary below. It is one of only three Roman-era lighthouses still standing. The other two are at A Caruña in Spain (the oldest lighthouse in use) and Leptis Magna in Libya.

The Pharos was designed to communicate not only with the second lighthouse but with one on Cap Gris-Nez on the French coast. A coal-burning brazier flared from the top floor of the tower. We know from similar structures dating from the Middle Ages that these beacons could consume up to 200 tons of coal a year, so the task of supplying the tower with fuel would have been immense.

The octagonal tower is sited on the highest part of Castle Hill, later becoming enclosed within the outer curtain wall of the medieval castle. The tower stands 16m (53ft) high and is 12m (39ft) wide at the base, although the original Roman fabric survives only to a height of 13m (43ft). The higher parts of the wall were added

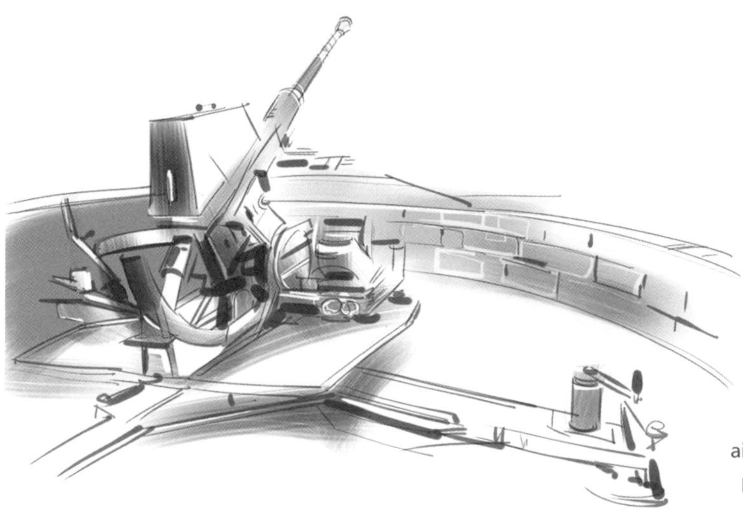

Bofors anti-aircraft guns at Dover Castle.

later to act as a belfry for the Anglo-Saxon church of St Mary in Castro, which was built beside the Pharos. This probably ensured the tower's survival and prevented it from being used as a source of stone for other buildings in the castle grounds.

In the first half of the 15th century, Humphrey, Duke of Gloucester, had the top section of the belfry rebuilt and the five upper windows, brought from Folkestone, were inserted.

After Henry VIII's dissolution of the monasteries between 1536 and 1541, three of the bells were sold and the belfry converted into a gunpowder store. In the early 18th century, the tower started to fall into disrepair and remained neglected until excavations in 1915 revealed its ragstone plinth. At this point the Pharos was re-evaluated and appreciated for the unique structure that it is.

Dover Castle, resplendent in the early morning sun.

FOLKESTONE PIER
LIGHTHOUSE
WEATHER IS A
THIRD TO
PLACE AND TIME
FOLKESTONE
KENT

FOLKESTONE PIER

LOCATION: 51°04′34″N, 1°11′41″E
OS GRID: TR238356
ELEVATION: 14m (45ft)
CHARACTER: Fl (2) 10s
RANGE: 19km (12 miles)

Ships and boats have been landing on Folkestone's shores since Roman times, but the ever-migrating shingle made grounding heavy vessels next to impossible and loading and unloading cargo a chore. In the 1540s, with war threatening to break out between France and England, Henry VIII had planned to turn Folkestone into a major embarkation point for troops and supplies, and he dispatched surveyors to scope out the potential of the site. Detailed plans were duly produced, but by then Henry's focus had shifted to nearby Dover and the Folkestone harbour project would be shelved for almost three centuries.

In 1807, with the new French threat of an imperialist Napoleon Bonaparte looming, parliament passed an act to provide anchorage at Folkestone for warships and support vessels. Within three years the town's West Pier was complete. By 1820, the harbour enclosed an area of almost 6ha (15 acres), but this early venture was not a success. With sand and silt constantly choking the entrance, fewer and fewer vessels put into the harbour and it fell into dereliction. The facility was eventually put up for sale and the South Eastern Railway, spying an opportunity, stepped in and immediately undertook an aggressive dredging operation to unchoke the harbour. With a new railroad line reaching Folkestone in 1843, and the harbour branch line established soon afterwards, the town now became

The Folkestone Mermaid by Cornelia Parker. Although inspired by Copenhagen's Little Mermaid, the artist chose a Folkestone resident as her model. Her aim was not to replicate the Copenhagen mermaid, but to find "a real person, a free spirit". The sculpture achieves that superbly.

The Leas Lift funicular railway was built in 1885 to take passengers between the seafront and the promenade. The Grade II listed facility has been closed to the public since 2017, but a campaign to raise funds for its restoration is underway.

the company's principal packet station for continental traffic.

This new development fared much better than the original enterprise. By 1849, almost 60,000 passengers were using the harbour each year, and over the next 50 years Folkestone became a fashionable coastal resort. With success came further development, and toward the end of the century the pier was extended into deeper water to provide berthing for steamers. It was with this extension that the Folkestone lighthouse we see today came into being. There had been an earlier lighthouse, an ornate white wooden structure called the Horn Tower, at the end of the old harbour pier since 1848. This ultimately made way for a gun emplacement during the Second World War.

Completed in 1904, the new 9m (28ft) tall sandstone lighthouse had a light showing two white flashes every 10 seconds and visible for 19km (12 miles). As part of the redevelopment of the pier as a leisure destination, the tower was fully refurbished in 2011 and now forms part of a particularly attractive champagne bar, mainly open at weekends. On the lighthouse wall, an inscription from a poem by Ian Hamilton Finlay reading "Weather is a third to place and time" reminds us how important the interaction of these three variables is to all of us – but particularly to those who work at sea.

DUNGENESS
LIGHTHOUSE
DUNGENESS
KENT

DUNGENESS

LOCATION: 50°54′48″N, 0°58′33″E
OS GRID: TR093169
ELEVATION: 40m (131ft)
CHARACTER: Fl 10s
RANGE: 39km (24 miles)

Dungeness lies at the most southerly corner of Kent and boasts one of the largest expanses of shingle in Europe. This enormous tract of pebbles and sand has posed a hazard to shipping for centuries. The constant movement and migration of the shingle on the east of the spit in particular has affected the fate of the lighthouses here too, as with the passing years they have found themselves at various times sitting further and further from the water. Over the centuries, there have been eight lighthouses built at Dungeness, consisting of five main high lights and three low lights; the fifth of the high lights is the current operational tower.

Prior to 1615 the first light on this shore was a simple coal-fired brazier whose illumination served to warn sailors of the danger posed by the spit. This was superseded by a more permanent structure in 1615, but within 20 short years the migration of the shingle left it high and dry and far from shore. In 1635, it had to be replaced by a new lighthouse nearer to the water's edge. Known as Lamplough's Tower, this structure remained in use for over 100 years; however, its fate was to mirror that of all its successors. Gradually, the spit of sand and gravel drifted along the shore and eventually the lighthouse found itself beached far from the sea. The third lighthouse raised on the shore, Samuel Wyatt's tower of 1792, also got a good run for its money, lasting just over a century before it too was deemed to sit too far from the tides.

Derek Jarman's wonderful house and garden at Dungeness, now preserved for the nation.

Because of the continuous build-up of shingle between the beach and the high lighthouse, ships passing Dungeness Point often missed sight of the lighthouse, with some running aground. To remedy this, an additional smaller low light was built near

Old boats dragged up
on the shingle.

the shoreline. The first low lighthouse was built in 1884 with a range of about 16km (10 miles) compared to 27km (17 miles) for the high lighthouse. By 1932, this structure was no longer fit for use and was replaced by a new light. In 1959, this was demolished to make way for the current high lighthouse.

As the shingle bank continued to grow in size and left the lighthouse further adrift, work began on the fourth high lighthouse in 1901, which was operational between 1904 and 1960, before being superseded by the fifth lighthouse. With further movement of the sands hastening the shoreline's retreat, and with the construction of the new nuclear power station obscuring the beam from certain quarters, the fifth Dungeness lighthouse was to be situated about 0.8km (half a mile) away from its predecessor.

A lighthouse like it hadn't been built in the country for over 50 years and it almost seemed to belong to a bygone era, but when it was unveiled on 20 November 1961, the new tower turned out to be a very welcome marriage of bold new architecture while also acknowledging the legacy of its older brothers. It is built from precast concrete rings 1.5m (5ft) high, 15cm (6in) thick and 3.6m (12ft) in diameter, which are stacked one above the other to form the tower's distinctive black and white bands.

It was the first lighthouse to be illuminated with a flashing xenon arc lamp. However, despite the brave new sheen of its modern light technology, it was soon retro-fitted with sealed beam units when the xenon arc lights were deemed unsuitable. Just below the lantern floor housing the main light, sector lights are displayed from windows. Since 1962, the tower has been floodlit from the seaward side to aid visual identification and to reduce the mortality rate of passing birds, which had been prone to hitting the tower at night during the migrating season.

Trials had been carried out at the 1904 Dungeness tower of a triple-frequency electric fog signal in the 1950s. These employed Tannoy speakers built into curved concrete. It proved such a success that Tannoy systems were subsequently fitted at over a dozen stations around the country. For the new tower at Dungeness, an array of 60 such emitters were incorporated into the design of the lighthouse tower, and remained in use until 2000, at which point they were replaced by an electronic signal installed at the base of the tower.

Dungeness lighthouse was converted to automatic operation in 1991 and is now managed by Trinity House's Planning Centre in Harwich, Essex. Today, it is classified as a Grade II* listed building.

OLD LIGHTHOUSE, DUNGENESS

LOCATION: 50°54'50"N, 0°58'11"E
OS GRID: TR088168
ELEVATION: 46m (151ft)
DECOMMISSIONED: 1960

A marsh harrier at Dungeness. The birds are slightly larger than buzzards and breed in reed beds and farmland. They feed on small birds, mammals and reptiles.

With its deceptive shifting banks of sand and shingle, Dungeness Point has a long and formidable reputation as a graveyard for shipping. The 16th century saw a huge increase in shipping on England's south coast and the subsequent rise in shipwrecks and maritime mishaps cost thousands in lost revenue, quite apart from the cost in lives. During one particularly ill-tempered winter, it was said that over 1,000 seamen lost their lives along this coast during a single ferocious storm.

The first light on this coastline was a simple coal-fired brazier operated by William Lamplough, a Clerk of the Royal Kitchen, who by all accounts was so efficient at collecting dues that the ship owners attempted to have his patent withdrawn, while complaining that the light shown was miserly. However, parliament was having none of it, although Lamplough was warned to improve the illumination or face their ire. As the sands shifted and sea receded, the complaints grew, asserting that the light was too far from shore. In 1615, the tower was pulled down and a larger edifice known as Lamplough's Tower was built nearer the point.

By 1668, the lighthouse was again embroiled in a dispute over the quality of illumination. However, the lighthouse was bringing in healthy profits and the owner saw no reason to waste good money on unnecessary improvements, so Dungeness continued to be dimly lit by coal for the next 70 years. While the owner might have resisted change, he couldn't resist the ever-changing movement of the shingle, and by the closing decades of the 18th century, a new lighthouse was being demanded of Trinity House.

In 1792, Samuel Wyatt, consultant engineer to Trinity House, built a 35m (115ft) tall tower similar to Smeaton's Eddystone, with 18 oil lamps in place

OLD DUNGENESS
LIGHTHOUSE
DUNGENESS
KENT

of coal. By 1818, it was using parabolic reflectors. In 1862, when electricity was barely regarded as a potential power source rather than a scientific curiosity, the third Dungeness lighthouse was at the forefront of introducing this utility to power its light. The pioneering technology unfortunately didn't live up to expectations and was soon replaced by a huge oil lamp of 850 candle power surrounded by glass prisms, which increased the illuminating power by a hundredfold. Accommodation for the keepers was built in a circular form around the base of Wyatt's tower and remains in situ, although the tower itself was demolished in 1904.

The shifting shingle saw construction start on the fourth lighthouse in 1901, which was opened by the Prince of Wales on 31 March 1904. This fourth tower rose to 46m (150ft), making it one of the tallest in the country. The lantern room housed a massive revolving catadioptric lens, flashing every ten seconds. Weighing two tons, the whole assembly floated smoothly on a bed of mercury.

By the turn of the 20th century, it was again apparent that the lighthouse was not adequate and the tower that is operational today was constructed 50m (164ft) from what is now known as the "Old Lighthouse". While no longer illuminated, the fourth tower still stands and is open to the public as a visitor attraction. After it was decommissioned it was painted black so as not to confuse it with the present operational tower. It is no longer owned by Trinity House and is open to the public.

A precursor of radar, acoustic mirrors or "listening ears" were designed to provide early warning of incoming enemy aircraft. They were built on the northeast and south coasts of England between 1916 and the 1930s.

BEACHY HEAD
LIGHTHOUSE
BEACHY HEAD
EAST SUSSEX

BEACHY HEAD

LOCATION: 50°44′02″N, 0°14′29″E
OS GRID: TV583951
ELEVATION: 31m (102ft)
CHARACTER: Fl (2) 20s
RANGE: 30km (19 miles)

It is thought that as early as 1670 a coal-fired beacon burned on the cliffs near Beachy Head to guide vessels past this tricky part of the coastline. By 1832, the original Belle Tout lighthouse had replaced these temporary structures and was beaming out a far more consistent and predictable light to mariners offshore. Consistent also was the gradual erosion of the cliff. This and the fact that the lighthouse was often obscured by fog led to the decision in the late 19th century that it might be prudent to start the planning process of building a new lighthouse, this time near the base of the cliffs.

Black-headed gulls.

At the turn of the 20th century, under the direction of Sir Thomas Matthews, work began on the new Beachy Head lighthouse, which took two years to complete. A cofferdam was built around the site to protect the groundworks from encroaching tides during construction. It was also necessary to install a cableway to move materials via large winched buckets from the top of the cliff to the works below. All in all, 3,660 tons of granite were laboriously moved into position using this device.

In 1902, when the lighthouse was first illuminated, Beachy Head was equipped with a first-order revolving catadioptric optic. The lighthouse also had an explosive fog signal. During foggy weather, this would have sounded every five minutes. The procedure was that one of the keepers would attach a small charge and detonator to each arm of a jib, which swung out over the galley. When ready, the charge was detonated using an electric firing mechanism from the relative safety of the lantern housing. Between cleaning out the previous charge and priming its replacement, this left little time for the keeper to relax and enjoy the lack of view.

When the lighthouse was complete, it remained in its bare granite state for many years. Eventually, it was decided that for the sake of better visibility against the cliff, a broad black horizontal stripe should be added to it. In 1951, this was changed to the present jaunty red and white stripes. In 2011, Trinity House announced that they intended to let the paint peel and the lighthouse revert to its nude state, citing the not unreasonable explanation that mariners these days navigate primarily by GPS – which is colour blind – and also the cost of repainting: £27,000! Happily, a successful fundraising campaign by the Save Our Stripes group has ensured that the iconic red and white stripes will remain for the foreseeable future.

The lighthouse was manned for just over 80 years and was served by 3 keepers, in the way that other rock stations were. While just a stone's throw from the mainland, it took until 1975 for electricity to reach the lighthouse. During that time all the processes on board – from cooking to heating to lighting not just the lantern, but their own accommodation – relied on solid fuels in the form of either coal or paraffin oil. Men had landed on the moon 6 years earlier and now suddenly it was as though the 20th century had just arrived in this small corner of the world as well. As is often the case, with incipient change came further, more accelerated transformation, and in just short of a decade, the lighthouse had been automated and the keepers retired. The lighthouse was converted to solar-power operation in 2011 and the fog signal discontinued.

A tour boat passing the lighthouse.

BELLE TOUT

LOCATION: 50°44′18″N, 0°12′53″E
OS GRID: TV563955
DECOMMISSIONED: 1902

The origin of the name Beachy Head is often attributed to a corruption of the medieval French name Beaucheif, meaning "beautiful headland", which is believed to have morphed over time into "Belle Tout" or "beautiful everything". However, unlike Beachy Head, the name Belle Tout has no French etymology. It derives from a Neolithic fort dedicated to the Celtic sun god Bael and means "Bael's lookout". The location itself has a history of smuggling and piracy. Because of high taxes imposed on imports, a profitable trade in contraband grew up in the area and the game of cat and mouse with the authorities could often involve entire communities.

The area was also a graveyard for shipping, and numerous petitions were raised by ship owners in an attempt to have the cliffs lit. It is often the case that a singular calamity concentrates the mind where countless previous attempts were unsuccessful. The sinking of the East Indiaman *The Thames* at the turn of the 18th century was one such event, but whether it was loss of life or loss of revenue that ultimately motivated change remains a mystery. The first Belle Tout lighthouse was a simple wooden structure but it fulfilled its purpose and started service on 1 October 1828.

While the contemporary but temporary timber Belle Tout shone across the cliffs, construction of a more permanent lighthouse was underway. Granite quarried from as far away as Aberdeen was brought to the site and the first courses laid some 34m (112ft) from the edge of the cliff. The light was first exhibited in October of 1834 but was often shrouded in sea mist and was never regarded as being fully effective. Erosion of the cliff face forced a rethink of the lighthouse's future, and although the cost of closing Belle Tout would not have been welcomed by Trinity House, it was seen as an opportunity to build a more

Beware, cliff edge!

BELLE TOUT
LIGHTHOUSE
BEACHY HEAD
EAST SUSSEX

effective replacement lighthouse at the base of the cliff.

The decommissioned Belle Tout lighthouse was occupied for some years as a family home, but by the advent of World War II it had been abandoned. The derelict building was occasionally used for anti-aircraft target practice by the Canadian Air Force and by 1943 daylight could be seen through the shattered 2m (6ft) thick walls. The building was eventually taken over by the local council and, in 1956, it was leased out to the Cullinan family, who undertook numerous renovation programmes.

By 1986, the gap between building and cliff edge had narrowed to only 16m (53ft), equivalent to a rate of cliff retreat of 11cm (4in) per year. Eleven years later, cliff erosion was seriously threatening the foundations of the building and measures had to be taken to stop it from falling into the sea. In the morning sunshine of 17 March 1999, 93-year-old Joy Cullinan flipped the switch on a system of hydraulic jacks, which slowly pushed the building along four steel-topped concrete beams to move it incrementally away from the cliff edge. The operation progressed at a snail's pace of about 20cm (8in) per hour. By the evening of Thursday, 18 March, Belle Tout reached its final position.

"Built in 1832 and decommissioned in 1902, a teashop, a home, part-destroyed during the second world war and lovingly rebuilt in the 50s. Owned and filmed by the BBC, moved due to erosion – and now, beautifully restored and renovated" goes the online publicity for its latest incarnation as a luxury bed and breakfast. While "Belle Tout" may have been misunderstood by generations who've imagined its name derives from the French, I think even Bael might agree that's as good a description as any.

Up with the skylark! The skylark prefers open countryside. Usually inconspicuous on the ground, it is easy to see or hear this little brown bird in flight. In fact, the bird's flight song can often be heard when it's flying nearly half a mile above you and is hardly visible.

St CATHERINE'S
LIGHTHOUSE
NITON
ISLE OF WIGHT

ST CATHERINE'S

LOCATION: 50°34′32″N, 1°17′52″W
OS GRID: SZ498753
ELEVATION: 41m (135ft)
CHARACTER: Fl 5s
RANGE: 46km (29 miles)

On the morning of 11 October 1836, the merchant ship *Clarendon* was sailing from the West Indies past the Isle of Wight on her way to Southampton, carrying an exotic cargo of sugar, rum and molasses, when she found herself in the teeth of a ferocious storm. Attempting to seek safe passage through huge seas, the ship struck the rocks at Blackgang Chine off St Catherine's Point and hit the beach broadside, rolling onto her side. On board were 11 passengers and a crew of 17.

John Wheeler, a local fisherman, tied a rope around his waist, threw himself into the surf and managed to rescue three crew members. Within minutes, the power of the waves had broken the ship to pieces, leaving a mass of shattered timbers, cargo and bodies. The dead eventually washed up on shore – with one exception. The body of a Miss Gourlay, daughter of Captain Gourlay R.N., was carried out into the Channel and later came to rest in the shallow waters at the bottom of her father's garden in Southsea. As the latest tragedy in over 60 ships to be lost in Chale Bay between 1746 and 1808, the wreck of the *Clarendon* focused the minds of Trinity House on the need to improve the aids to navigation in the area.

As early as 1323, a beacon was lit at St Catherine's, reportedly at the request of the Pope and as part of an endowment. This endowment was met by Walter de Godyton, who erected a small chapel and entrusted the priest to say prayers for his family and tend to the coal light, which warned ships of this perilous coastline. The chapel formed part of St Catherine's Oratory and its octagonal stone tower still stands to this day.

The Buddle Inn, located on the walk to St Catherine's lighthouse.

In 1838, the present lighthouse, designed by James Walker, was constructed as a 40m (131ft) ashlar stone tower with 94 steps leading up to the lantern. The light was an oil-fuelled lamp, with 4 concentric wicks, set into a first-order fixed lens and surmounted by 250 mirrors. The amount of spilled incidental light bouncing around in the lantern room must have been blinding for any keepers who went near it for routine maintenance! The light was first illuminated on 1 March 1840, but it soon became apparent that the beam was too high and frequently obscured by fog. It was decided to reduce the height of the tower by 13m (43ft) and at the same time the light was upgraded.

The smaller tower to the front was built in 1932 and housed the fog signal. The original signal house had been built on the cliff edge and required an additional keeper to operate it. When that structure was undermined by cliff erosion, the decision was made to keep the two operations closer together. Since both towers are similar in style, they're known locally as the Cow and Calf. During World War II, the lighthouse was an important landmark for shipping and aircraft, but on 1 June 1943 the engine house was bombed and the three lighthouse keepers sheltering in it were sadly killed. In 1987, the fog signal was retired altogether and replaced by a more pedestrian if more efficient radio transmitter.

St Catherine's was one of the first Trinity House lighthouses to be converted to electricity when electric arc lamps were fitted in 1888. Today, the lighthouse has a range of 46km (29 miles) and is the third-most powerful of all the lights maintained by Trinity House. St Catherine's lighthouse was automated in 1997, with the keepers leaving the lighthouse on 30 July.

THE NEEDLES

LOCATION: 50°39′44″N, 1°35′31″W
OS GRID: SZ290848
ELEVATION: 24m (79ft)
CHARACTER Oc (2) WRG 20s
RANGE: 32km (20 miles)

The setting of the Needles lighthouse on the Isle of Wight could hardly be more dramatic. Standing in the lee of the outermost of a line of towering chalk stacks, it effects a lonesome but defiant profile in the teeth of the prevailing westerly winds. Positioned at the western approach to the Isle of Wight, the narrow peninsula that comprises the Needles lies close to the notorious submerged Goose Rock and the shingle at Scratchell's Bay, a shifting bank of pebbles that occasionally rises out of the sea. Even the canniest of sailors have at times misjudged safe passage and come a cropper while approaching the Solent.

The 9-inch guns on display at the Old Battery.

In the late 18th century, Richard Jupp designed a lighthouse that was situated high above the Needles, but which proved to be an abject failure when it was lit in 1786. The light was often shrouded in fog and effectively disappeared when most needed. Plans were put into action to replace it with a light nearer sea level, and in 1853 James Walker was commissioned to draw up designs for a lighthouse to be located at the outermost of the chalk "needles". This was finally completed in 1859 at a cost of £20,000.

As the tower was composed of granite block, the construction process was challenging, to say the least. The initial digging of the chalk base to prepare for foundations took over two months, during which time the workmen were permanently up to their calves in seawater. Eventually, the granite base began to rise and during 1858 the various courses of the 33m (108ft) tall tower were dovetailed together. On 22 May of the following year, the lighthouse was exhibited for the first time.

Engineers used dynamite to create a platform in the chalk stack and to

THE NEEDLES
LIGHTHOUSE
THE NEEDLES
ISLE OF WIGHT

provide space for an enormous water tank, coal store and cellars. Thanks to this arrangement, the lighthouse could still be manned even when the weather was too bad for supplies to be sent out. Its base was stepped like those of other wave-washed towers to break up the force of the tides slamming into it and to discourage seas from sweeping up the tower.

The Needles initially displayed a fixed red light with a white sector signalling safe approach running south of Durlestone Head and past the southwest Shingles and Dolphin Bank. A narrow white sector was added to indicate the northeast approach past Warden Ledge and, later, a green sector was added and the light made occulting.

For years the lighthouse was just bare granite, but in 1886 it was painted with a broad black horizontal stripe around the middle, and the metalwork of the lantern was also painted black, with dark curtains hung within the glass when the lamp was not in use. The purpose here was to make the tower stand out against the white cliffs during daylight hours.

In line with all rock stations, the Needles was manned by three keepers. Usually this consisted of a principal keeper and assistant keeper and often a supernumerary, who was not yet a permanent employee and was serving, if you like, a form of probation or apprenticeship. Conditions were spartan and in severe weather keepers could be cut off for weeks at a time. Before the advent of TV, which usually came late to the lighthouses because of the lack of mains power, hobbies of one sort or another were essential, though not all keepers fitted wooden schooners into old whiskey bottles! Reading, writing, painting, even knitting helped to while away the long hours when duties had been seen to, but you needed to be comfortable in your own company above all.

Along the final stretch of the walk to the Needles, approaching Freshwater Bay.

In 1987, change arrived in the shape of a helipad on the top of the tower, and in 1994 the Needles lighthouse was automated and the keepers left the tower for the last time. The original optic composed of coloured glass indicating the green and red sectors was retained after automation, but with the addition of a three-position lamp changer with two 1,500W main lamps and a 24V battery-powered emergency lamp.

HURST POINT

LOCATION: 50°42′29″N, 1°33′1″W
OS GRID: SZ3184589911
ELEVATION: 23m (75ft)
CHARACTER: Fl (4) WRW 15s
RANGE: 24km (15 miles)

The original lighthouse at Hurst Point was situated at Hurst Spit, to the southwest of the old Hurst Castle. Wrecks were a frequent occurrence on the busy waterways of the Solent and despite the attempts of earlier beacons to provide some guidance, a formal petition was raised by interested shipmasters and merchants that Trinity House undertake to erect lights to ensure safe passage around the Isle of Wight.

Once a patent was granted in January 1782, Richard Jupp was commissioned as architect and Joseph Huddard employed to supervise the project. Construction began alongside those of the lighthouses at St Catherine's and on the clifftop above the Needles. The red-brick tower was lit for the first time on 29 September 1786. However, soon complaints were being made about how the light was obscured from certain directions. To counter this, another higher light was constructed on the spit about 15m (49ft) east of the first lighthouse, and the light of 1786 was renamed the "low light". Between the two, they acted as a pair of leading lights: when one light appeared exactly behind the other, the ship's captain knew he was heading into the safe channel.

In 1911, the effect of the shifting shingle bank on the navigable channel led to the construction of a new metal low light further west. This last iron-clad light was built on steel gantry so it could be moved laterally if the shingle bar migrated with the tides, and it was originally painted red. Yet, it never had to be moved, and when it was eventually decommissioned, it was painted grey to blend into the background and not resemble a navigational mark.

The original lighthouse of 1786 was finally demolished when it became necessary to extend Hurst Castle and, at this stage, a new low light was built on the rear wall of the castle wing. A timber staircase from

A life buoy and
the lighthouse beyond.

HURST POINT
LIGHTHOUSE
KEYHAVEN
HAMPSHIRE

outside the wing gave Trinity House staff access to the light, so they didn't need to pass through the castle to gain entry to the lighthouse. In 1867, to further confound the reader, the original high light was demolished and the tower you see today replaced it. By this point, there had been five lights – two of which are gone, while three remain. Two of those three are small low lights attached to the castle wall, and the third is our shining, bleached white 26m (85ft) lighthouse tower. The 1890s saw this fitted with the latest technology of a first-order Fresnel lens using a Douglass-designed six-wick lamp. The mechanism served the lighthouse well, but by 1923 acetylene technology in conjunction with a sun valve had progressed to the point where the light could now be automated.

It wasn't until 1997 that the lighthouse was converted to electricity. With increased traffic in the shipping lanes, a high-intensity projector designed to be seen day and night was installed in the high lighthouse, adjustable in case of further shifts in the sandbanks and using white, red and green light to indicate the narrow passage between the Needles and the Shingles Bank. The main navigation light still uses an unusual first-order lens, which is separated into sectors with different focal lengths and a red sector provided by shades inside the lantern. The lighthouse is now managed by Trinity House's Planning Centre in Harwich, Essex.

Hurst Castle artillery fort was established by Henry VIII.

ANVIL POINT

LOCATION: 50°35′31″N, 1°57′37″W
OS GRID: SZ029769
ELEVATION: 45m (148ft)
CHARACTER: Fl 10s
RANGE: 17km (11 miles)

Lying on the Isle of Purbeck peninsula, Anvil Point is toward the eastern end of the world famous Jurassic Coast, which stretches eastward from Exmouth in Devon to Studland Bay in Dorset. There is a long tradition of quarrying stone on the coast near Anvil Point, especially at Dancing Ledge and the Tilly Whim caves. Using only hand tools, quarrymen undertook the dangerous task of mining workable blocks of stone horizontally out of the cliff face. Generally, the stone was also worked in the quarry to create cut stone blocks or finished items such as sills or troughs. The "whim" from the Tilly Whim name referred to a special type of wooden crane used to lower the finished stonework from the quarry ledges onto boats at the jetty below. From here they were taken to the stone yards on Swanage Quay or transferred to larger sailing ketches anchored offshore.

A restored capstan at Purbeck limestone quarry overlooking Anvil Point lighthouse.

During the Napoleonic wars, fortifications along the entire south coast were built using Purbeck stone. However, once the threat of invasion receded the demand for stone slumped and the quarries closed. Today, the caves serve as roosts for bats, while the cliffs and ledges provide nesting grounds for a variety of seabirds. The area surrounding Tilly Whim is also a popular vantage point for observing marine life, including grey seals and dolphins.

Chances are that the stone from which Anvil Point lighthouse is made came from one of the Purbeck quarries. The building materials are certainly local. The station was built in 1881 and opened by the then President of the Board of Trade, Joseph Chamberlain, father of the future prime minister Neville Chamberlain. Anvil Point is the next marker for vessels that have

ANVIL POINT
LIGHTHOUSE
SWANAGE
DORSET

safely navigated offshore of Portland Bill and hope to negotiate their way into the Solent, while avoiding the hazards of St Aldhelm's Head and Durlston Head.

The diminutive tower, with its lantern, stands a mere 12m (39ft) in height, with two mirror-image keepers' cottages linked to it by a corridor. The original Fresnel lens was illuminated by a paraffin vapour burner, but was replaced when the light was connected to the electric grid in 1960. The old lens is now on display at the Science Museum in South Kensington, London.

The lighthouse's first fog signal consisted of a small cannon that issued a loud blast every 5 minutes. This was replaced in 1971 by a much less romantic-sounding automatic Tannoy system, but even this was discontinued in 1988 when a VHF radio signal operating in partnership with the Needles at the Isle of Wight was installed. Three years later, Anvil Point was fully automated and it is now controlled remotely.

Rock climbers near St Aldhelm's Head.

PORTLAND BILL
LIGHTHOUSE
PORTLAND
DORSET

Beach huts near the lighthouse.

PORTLAND BILL

LOCATION: 50°30′51″N, 2°27′23″W
OS GRID: SY677684
ELEVATION: 43m (141ft)
CHARACTER: Fl (4) 20s
RANGE: 33km (21 miles)

At the most southerly point in Dorset, on the island after which it is named, Portland Bill lighthouse, built in 1906, stewards vessels en route for Portland and Weymouth and acts as a waymark for ships navigating the English Channel. With the notorious Shambles sandbank just offshore, navigating this passage has always been a challenge, and the strong currents that comprise the Portland Race continue to make the task of steering a course toward Portland Harbour or Weymouth a dangerous undertaking.

Because of the urgency of providing safe navigation to port, over the centuries there have been three lighthouses built at Portland. Ever since Roman times, beacons have been lit on Branscombe Hill above the Bill and on Verne Hill, but a shortage of fuel meant that the beacons were not lit regularly over the coming centuries. Later, two stone windmill towers near Wakeham provided only unsatisfactory navigation marks.

In 1669, Sir John Clayton received a patent to build a lighthouse on the island, but partly due to the high cost of construction in such a remote, exposed location – and as the patent was also subject to the condition that any shipping tolls would be voluntary – the scheme eventually came to nothing. The headland remained in darkness for almost a half century before Captain William Holman, a veteran of the colonial wars in Newfoundland, rallied the support of the ship owners and the corporations of Weymouth to put serious pressure on Trinity House to establish a lighthouse. Initially, the Brethren were unconvinced that lights were necessary and saw no need to burden the maritime trade with the cost of the building and upkeep of a lighthouse on this stretch of coast. However, Trinity House eventually accepted that the Portland Race posed a grave risk to shipping passing around Portland Bill and a patent was obtained from George I. They then subcontracted a 61-year lease to a private landlord, with the proviso that two lighthouses with enclosed lanterns and coal fires be built.

The Old High lighthouse stood on the hilltop and the Old Low lighthouse on lower ground near the cliff. Although they

The obelisk was built as a daymark in 1844 to warn ships off the coast of Portland Bill.

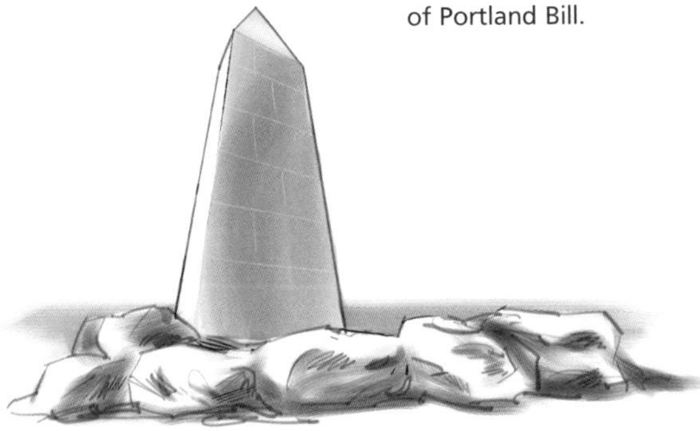

had been privately built, Trinity House took over responsibility for the lights in 1752 on finding them poorly maintained.

In 1789, William Johns of Weymouth was tasked with building a new tower at the Low lighthouse. The resulting tower stood 19m (62ft) high and had an internal spiral staircase that led through four storeys of accommodation and storage to the diamond-glazed lantern room, where an arrangement of six Argand lamps were focused through the lens into a series of intense fixed beams reaching 29km (18 miles) out to sea. The foundations of the new tower were sited to the east of the demolished old tower, providing a navigational marker for ships using the channel and bringing vessels clear of the Shambles.

At this point in time, a 7m (23ft) tall white stone obelisk was built at the southern tip of Portland, beyond the lighthouse, to act as a daymark warning of a low shelf of rock extending some 30m (98ft) south into the sea. The obelisk can still be seen today.

In 1903, Trinity House obtained a plot of land at Bill Point near the Old Low lighthouse. Given the advances in technology, their intention was to combine the operations of the two existing lights in one modern lighthouse. Work began immediately and by the year's end the foundations had been laid. Rising to a height of 41m (135ft), the sandstone tower and lantern room were completed by late 1905 and Portland Bill's new first-order revolving optic was illuminated on 11 January 1906. The lighthouse also displayed a red sector from a lower window to mark the notorious Shambles sandbank.

The Old Low and High lighthouses were duly decommissioned and in 1907 they were both put up for auction as desirable residences requiring little by way of conversion or upgrading. The public were quick to see their potential and the two properties were quickly snapped up.

In 2015, Trinity House renovated the visitor centre at Portland Bill and in addition to viewing an engaging exhibit on lighthouses and the keepers who manned them, you can now climb the 153 steps to the top of the lighthouse, where you will have a spectacular view over the Channel and surrounding area.

OLD HIGH LIGHT, PORTLAND BILL

LOCATION: 50°31′20″N, 2°27′23″W
OS GRID: SY677692
ELEVATION: 12m (39ft)
DEACTIVATED: 1906

Over the centuries, many vessels were shipwrecked in the area of Portland Bill and Chesil Beach. In 1716, after years of local petitions to Trinity House, George I granted the patent for two lighthouses to be erected on Portland Bill. The Old High Light was built at Branscombe Hill, while the other, the Old Low lighthouse, was situated on lower land. Designed as leading lights to guide ships between the Portland Race and the Shambles sandbank, they shone out for the first time on 29 September 1716. Initially, both were fire lights.

Very soon after their construction, disquiet started to spread that the lighthouse fires were not always lit. When, in 1752, overseers from Trinity House sailed to Portland to inspect the lights, they reported that, "It was nigh two hours after sunset before any light appeared in either of the lighthouses." With the termination of the lease, the lights reverted to Trinity House.

In 1788, Trinity House commissioned the installation of Argand lamps at the Old High lighthouse, making it the first lighthouse in

The Low Tower at Portland Bill.

PORTLAND BILL
OLD HIGH LIGHT
ISLE OF PORTLAND
DORSET

Britain be fitted with this new technology, which consisted of a wick enclosed in a glass tube and which gave a clean, intense light roughly ten times brighter than that of the earlier apparatus. The lamps were designed by Thomas Rogers.

In 1824, the High Light was further improved by Trinity House: a three-sided revolving apparatus was installed (with Argand lamps and reflectors), with "each face exhibiting its greatest light every two minutes"; however, in 1835, Portland High was again made a fixed light (matching the Low Light, which had remained fixed throughout) after the construction of Start Point lighthouse, which had revolving Fresnel lenses.

Both Portland lighthouses were rebuilt in 1869 and provided with first-order fixed optics designed and built by James Chance. At the turn of the 20th century, Trinity House decided to build a new lighthouse at Bill Point to replace both the existing lighthouses. The new lighthouse was completed in 1905, and the original two lighthouses were then auctioned off. In 1923, the Old High Light was purchased by the palaeobotanist, pioneer of birth control and Portland Museum founder Marie Stopes to use as her summer residence.

During World War II, the local branch of the Royal Observer Corps (ROC) used the lighthouse tower as a lookout post to identify aircraft approaching the UK. The lighthouse was run as a restaurant during the 1960s but fell into disrepair over the following decade, until it and its cottages were refurbished in 1981. With a total of four cottages within the lighthouse grounds, both the Branscombe Lodge Cottage and Stopes Cottage are now available as holiday lets.

The National Coastwatch Institution (NCI) lookout station. The station is equipped with radar, Automatic Identification System (AIS) for identifying shipping, a weather monitoring system, CCTV and – just as important as all the technology – high powered binoculars. The lookout is run entirely on public donations.

START POINT
LIGHTHOUSE
START POINT
DEVON

START POINT

LOCATION: 50°13′21″N, 3°38′32″W
OS GRID: SX829371
ELEVATION: 62m (203ft)
CHARACTER: Fl (3) 10s
RANGE: 33km (21 miles)

Start Point is the southern point of Start Bay, with Warren Point in the north. The bay stretches for 24km (15 miles) along the Devon coast and includes sandy beaches as well as rocky outcrops such as Start Point itself. The point is one of the most exposed peninsulas on the English coast, running sharply for almost a mile out into the sea. The name "Start" derives from the Anglo-Saxon word *steort*, meaning tail. (This word also appears in the names of birds with distinctive tails, such as the redstart.) The rugged topography of the headland is echoed in the dangerous reefs lying just under the surface of the water, including the famed Blackstone Rock. These reefs and the strong tidal race around the tip of the headland make Start Point a very dangerous spot for shipping.

Just off the point and stretching in a northeasterly direction lies the Skerries Bank, a body mainly composed of sand and shell and running underwater for almost 7km (4 miles). At low tide the bank is barely 2m (6ft) below the surface and forms a barrier to the movement of sediments, forcing the energy of the waves into the southern part of the bay, toward south Slapton Sands, Beesands and Hallsands. As is often the case, what is good for one is a disaster for others and in this instance the unsettled currents make for rich fishing grounds, but create a sizeable hazard to shipping.

The lighthouse was designed by James Walker in 1836 in the gothic style popular at the time and incorporates crenellated battlements below the lantern room. The station sits hunkered down at the end of a winding and exposed road hewn from the rocky headland. Such was the isolation of the location that the building materials used to construct the tower were brought to the site by sea, rather than overland, despite the difficulty of hoisting 18 courses of granite blocks off the waiting ketches and up the cliffside.

Two white lights were originally exhibited. The revolving white light in the main lantern room had a range of 40km (25 miles) and was intended to shepherd passing traffic, while the fixed light, displayed from a window 7m (23ft) below marked the Skerries Bank; a fixed red subsidiary light still marks this hazard and has a range of 19km (12 miles). The optic used, a form of dioptric mechanism, was the first of its kind used by Trinity House and displayed a group flashing light three times every ten seconds.

However, the light was found to be deficient in foggy conditions and a bell was installed in the 1860s, for which the machinery was housed in a small building set into the cliff. There, it was operated by a weight that fell in a tube running down the sheer cliff face. Fifteen years later, this was replaced by a siren. In 1989, the cliff under the fog signal house shifted and the building collapsed. Repairs were hastily undertaken and the southernmost keeper's house was demolished and a new retaining wall completed.

The tower originally housed two keepers and their families on the first floor, but over time the internal space was redesigned and the living quarters improved. By 1844, a separate flat-roofed dwelling had been added, but as the principal keeper expressed a preference for living in the tower, this was given to his assistant. As part of a general updating of the station in 1871, the three-storey building you now see was completed and two of the stone floors in the tower were removed.

The lighthouse was automated in 1993 and the keepers withdrawn. A caretaker still lives on site and the lighthouse is open for limited tours during the year. The cottages are available to rent.

One of numerous wreck remains along this part of the South Devon coast.

CASQUETS

LOCATION: 49°43′19″N, 2°22′37″W
ELEVATION: 37m (121ft)
CHARACTER: Fl (5) 30s
RANGE: 33km (21 miles)

The Casquets are a group of rocks 13km (8 miles) northwest of Alderney and 37km (23 miles) from Guernsey and are part of an underwater sandstone ridge. Other parts to emerge above the water include the islets of Burhou and Ortac. Exposed to the full force of the Atlantic, little grows on them and they present a significant danger to shipping in the area.

In the 16th century, the Casquets were a peripheral fragment of the estate of Thomas Le Corq, but in 1722 the ship owners plying these waters petitioned Le Corq to build a lighthouse on the island and offered him a half penny per ton on all vessels passing the light. With the blessing of Trinity House, work began on building a distinctive arrangement of three towers lit by coal fires. These became known as St Peter, St Thomas and the Dungeon. The layout was designed to ensure that the lights would not look like those in nearby France.

By 1724, the station was complete, and the coal-fired beacons were successfully warning ships off the rocks. In 1770, the lights were improved to oil-burning lamps, and 13 years later the terms of the lease

The helipad at Casquets.

reverted the lighthouse to Trinity House, who set about a number of upgrades, including converting the lights to house metal reflectors and Argand lamps. Later, a revolving apparatus was fitted to the light in each tower. This had a clockwork mechanism which was wound up every hour and a half, and gave 1 flash every 15 seconds.

A severe storm in October 1823 left the towers badly damaged and the lanterns destroyed, and the opportunity was taken to increase the height of the towers by a further 9m (30ft). In 1877, the north-west tower was again raised, and, on

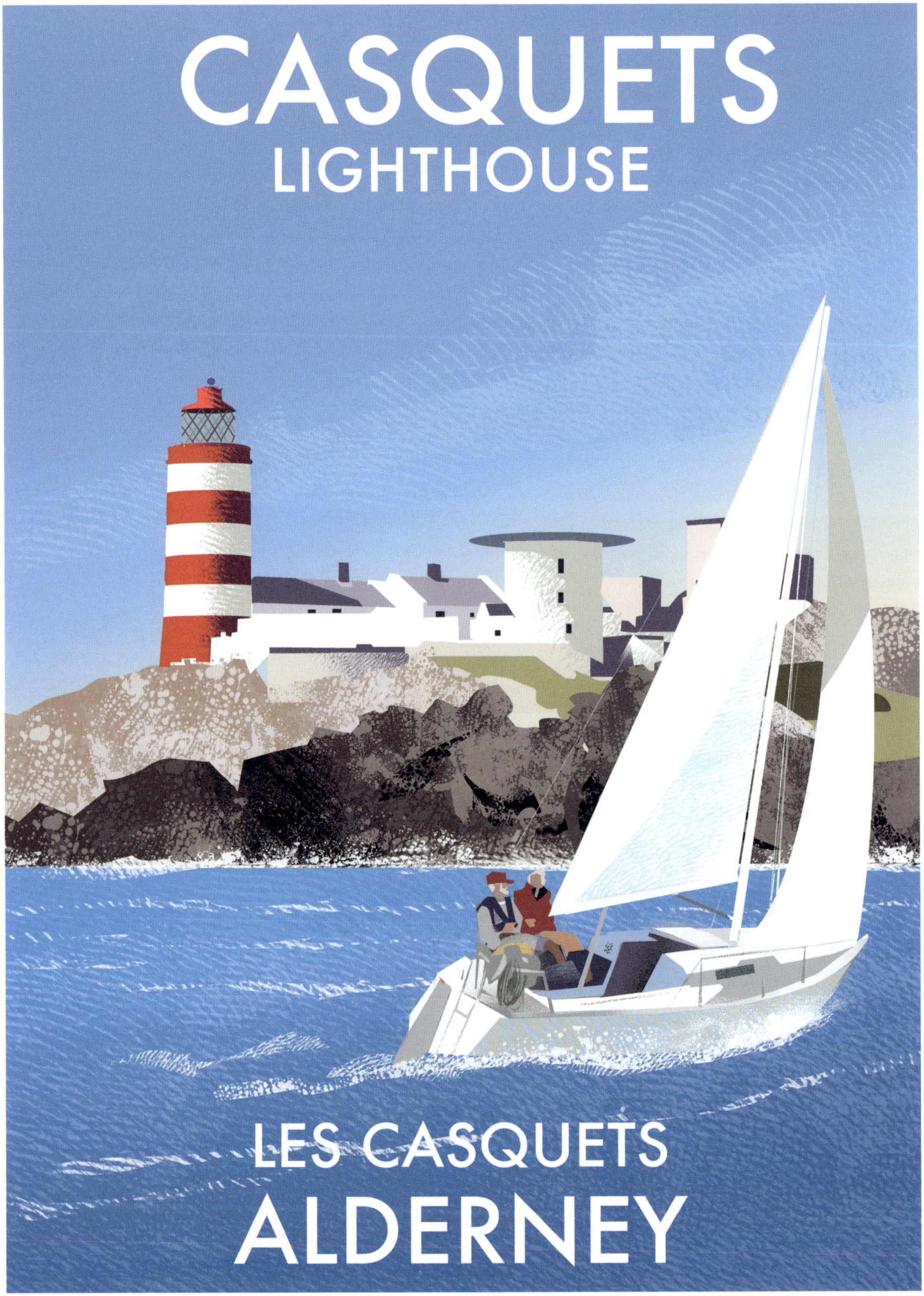
CASQUETS
LIGHTHOUSE
LES CASQUETS
ALDERNEY

this occasion, the other two towers were discontinued.

While the addition of lights to the Casquets has undoubtedly saved untold lives over the centuries, it hasn't been without incident or drama in the intervening years. Probably the most tragic, if not the worst, accident happened on 30 March 1899, when the London & South Western Railway (LSWR) company passenger steamer *Stella* was on her way from Southampton to Guernsey and Jersey, and ran full speed in thick fog onto the Casquets reef where she sank within minutes with the loss of over 112 lives. For the convenience of holidaymakers, LSWR had arranged for the *Stella* to make an extra daytime trip to and from the Channel Islands, and a large number of passengers from London were tempted to take up the opportunity for a daytrip by the low fare of 24s 6d return and the convenience of a special train from Waterloo to the ship's side in the dock at Southampton. For many, the lure of a cheap day away proved a fateful mistake.

Just over 40 years later, a drama of a different stripe unfolded, when commandos of the small-scale raiding forces made two raids on the lighthouse, following the German occupation of the Channel Islands in 1940. The first raid, Operation Dryad, led by Major Gus March Phillips, took place on 2 to 3 September 1942 and the seven German keepers, some still in their pyjamas, were spirited back to England where they were interned as prisoners of war. Later in the war, a number of additional raids on the lighthouse were attempted, including one in 1943 that involved the actor Douglas Fairbanks Jr.

For many years, it was believed that HMS *Victory* was wrecked in 1744 on the Casquets. The Alderney lightkeeper at that time was even court-martialled for his failure to keep the lantern lit when the ship sank. However, when the wreck of HMS *Victory* was eventually discovered in 2008, it was located more than 110 km (68 miles) from the Casquets.

In 1955, the station was electrified and while all three towers survive, only the northwest tower displays a light. The east tower is used to house fog signal equipment and the other tower acts as a helipad. The lighthouse complex was automated in 1990 and is managed by the Trinity House Operations Control Centre in Harwich Essex.

MANNEZ
LIGHTHOUSE
NORTH POINT
ALDERNEY

ALDERNEY (MANNEZ)

Oystercatchers by the shore.

LOCATION: 49°43′45″N, 2°09′51″W
OS GRID: N/A
ELEVATION: 37m (121ft)
CHARACTER: Fl (4) 15s
RANGE: 22km (14 miles)

Alderney lighthouse (also known as Mannez or Quesnard lighthouse) is a granite tower situated on Quesnard Point on the northeast coast of the island. It was constructed to protect shipping from the dangerous waters of the Alderney Race, a notorious strait between the island and Cap de la Hague in Normandy. This channel boasts the strongest tidal surge in Europe, which results from the body of the Atlantic pushing into the Gulf of Saint-Malo and then squeezing between Alderney and the Cap. The waves burst through at high tide and then retreat just as fast as the tide recedes. The unevenness of the seabed only makes these waters more treacherous, both by adding to the unpredictability of the current and by throwing up hazardous offshore rocks within a few miles of the lighthouse.

The passing centuries have seen countless wrecks off this most northerly of the Channel Islands. One of the most notable, discovered in 1977 by a local fisherman provides insight into the armed vessels that plied these waters in the 16th century. The ship dates from the Elizabethan period and would seem to have originated in London, and may have played a part in the religious wars of this time. Numerous muskets and swords were found on the seabed alongside "fire pots", a type of Elizabethan hand grenade contained in a ceramic pot. Many of the artefacts retrieved from the wreck are on display at the Alderney Museum.

Another more recent wreck was the SS *Liverpool*, a four-masted iron sailing ship which hit rocks off the small tidal islands of Les Homeaux Florains in 1902 while carrying 60,000 tons of cargo. This disaster led directly to the building of the lighthouse.

The lighthouse itself is 32m (105ft) tall and is painted white with a central black band to make it stand out as a daymark. The tower was completed in 1912 under the guidance of local businessman William Baron. The former keepers' dwellings adjoin the tower, as do the service rooms. There was a resident lightkeeper here until 1997, but in October of that year the station was finally automated. Its first-order, four-panel catadioptric lens was replaced by four LED lanterns 20 years later.

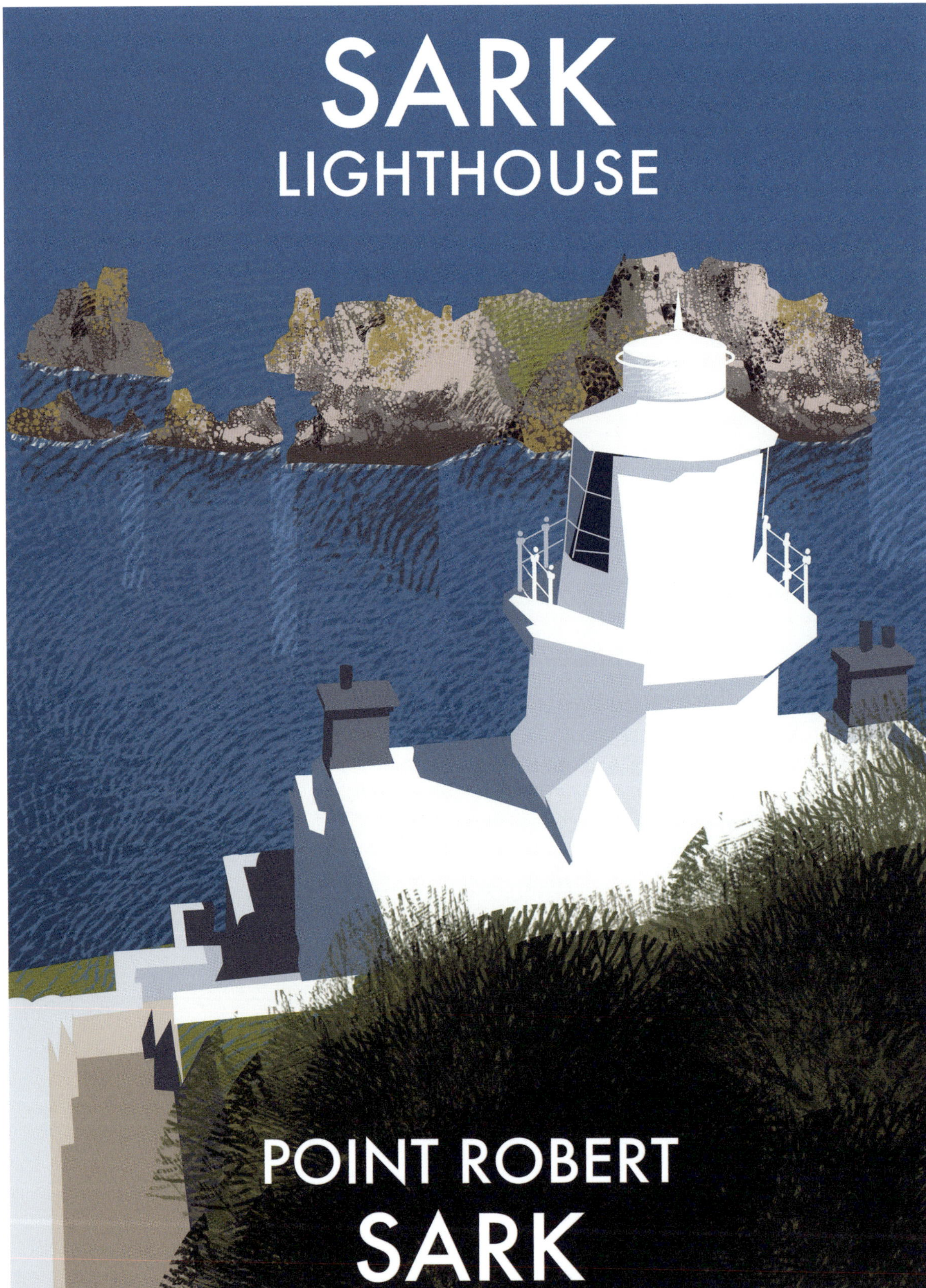
SARK
LIGHTHOUSE
POINT ROBERT
SARK

SARK

LOCATION: 49°26′11″N, 2°20′44″W
ELEVATION: 65m (213ft)
CHARACTER: Fl 15s
RANGE: 33km (21 miles)

Sark is the smallest of the Channel Islands located to the east of Guernsey and, although a Crown property, was the last feudal territory in Europe to be ruled by a seigneur (i.e. feudal lord of manor) until its constitution was reformed in 2008. It is a mere 5km (3 miles) long and 3km (2 miles) wide, the north and south parts being almost separate islands that are attached only by a narrow strip of land known as La Coupée.

The stories of coastal communities in Devon, Cornwall and the Channel Islands are full of smugglers, buccaneers and pirates – and Sark is no exception. In fact, of all the coastlines in this part of the world, piracy has had perhaps the most profound and long-lasting effect on that of Sark. In the Middle Ages, various monastic communities sought solace on Sark, but by the 16th century, they had either abandoned the island or been driven away by pirates; ironically including one known as Eustace the Monk, who used the island as a base. Things got so bad that, in 1565, Helier de Carteret, Seigneur of St Ouen in Jersey, was granted Sark in perpetuity by Elizabeth I on condition that he kept the island free of pirates. Legend has it that the island was regained by a small band of his men who anchored offshore and persuaded the pirates to let them bury a deceased colleague in the grounds of St Magloire's Chapel. Once the pirates had searched them to establish that they were unarmed, the band of sailors were left alone in the chapel, where they broke open the coffin and extracted their hidden cache of weapons and put the pirates to the sword. Whatever the truth of the story, de Carteret regained control of the island and was granted the fiefdom, which remained until 2008.

Sark was also the scene of a coup of sorts in 1990, when a Frenchman by the name of André Gardes invaded the island via the ferry from Guernsey and, armed with a semi-automatic weapon, bill-posted up the declaration that he was the rightful heir to the feudal principality. The island's only volunteer policeman approached him while he was resting on a bench and enquired as to whether the weapon was any good. When Gardes decided to show him how the magazine was changed, the constable overpowered him and placed him under arrest. The miscreant was given seven days in jail and told not to return to the island. The following year he tried again, but was refused a ticket on the ferry and slunk home defeated.

Sark's lighthouse is located on the cliffside at Point Robert in the northeast of the island and guides vessels passing through the Channel Islands away from Blanchard Rock, which lies several miles to the east. Built in 1913 and comprising a white, stone-built octagonal tower rising from flat-roofed service rooms and cottages, the station is accessed via a steep flight of steps from the top of the cliff.

Sark was a popular posting for lighthouse keepers. Officially, it was considered a rock station and thus the pay scale was higher than for onshore lighthouses, but it was not as remote as other lighthouses in that category. With the help of a bicycle or a willing horse, it might have been the only rock station where the keepers could go to the pub when not working.

The lighthouse was automated in 1994 and re-engineered in 2017, when the rotating optic was removed and replaced by two LED lights, one above the other to provide a main light and a standby backup. Interestingly, the light that ensures safety for vessels is one of the few showing at night on the island. In 2011, Sark was designated as a Dark Sky Community and was to become the first Dark Sky Island in the world.

La Coupée is an 80m (263ft) high causeway, which is about 3m (10ft) wide and 100m (328ft) long. The ridge connects Big and Little Sark, but it is gradually being eroded and Little Sark will eventually become an island.

LES HANOIS

LOCATION: 49°26′06″N, 2°42′08″W
ELEVATION: 33m (108ft)
CHARACTER: Fl (2) 13s
RANGE: 37km (23 miles)

Les Hanois lighthouse stands off Guernsey's southwest coast on the rock known as Le Biseau, or Le Bisé, part of the reef Les Hanois, where it can be clearly seen from the headland 1.6km (1 mile away) at Pleinmont. It was built because of the increasing number of shipwrecks on the hazardous rocks off the western coast of Guernsey. It is estimated that over a hundred ships met their end on the reefs around Les Hanois between 1734 and 1978, despite the addition of the lighthouse and the relocation of shipping lanes further offshore in the 1970s.

In 1817, Trinity House was petitioned about the placement of a lighthouse on the headland at Pleinmont. Apparently mistaking this as a request for a signal light for channel shipping rather than for a warning light, the request was declined. Their argument was that the lights at Casquets just off the coast of Alderney and on Portland on the Dorset coast were sufficient, and that as a result mariners could adequately navigate the English Channel. However, those stations lie 45km (28 miles) and 125km (78 miles) respectively from Les Hanois and neither can be seen from the south of Guernsey. Following the loss of three more ships on the rocks in the 1820s and 1830s, the proposal was reconsidered and plans were made to build a lighthouse on the reef.

Kayakers at the lighthouse.

Designed by James Douglass and built between 1860 and 1862 by Cornish stonemasons, Les Hanois became the template on which all subsequent rock lighthouses would be based, on account of the unique arrangement of its constituent blocks. This was the culmination of various methods developed over the centuries. John Smeaton had earlier developed the use of granite blocks for rock towers, connecting them together with metal pins and marble dowels. A similar method had been used by Alan Stevenson in the

LES HANOIS
LIGHTHOUSE
LE BISEAU
GUERNSEY

construction of the Skerryvore lighthouse, while his father, Robert Stevenson, had laid the blocks of each course in the Bell Rock lighthouse in a way that formed a series of dovetails. This way, each course was locked together into a solid single unit, and the courses were then pinned together. The Douglass method saw the stones dovetailed to-gether both laterally and vertically, while a course of cement mortar in the joint between the faces meant that the stones could not be separated without being broken, thereby giving the whole structure enormous strength.

The completed tower was 36m (118ft) tall with seven storeys of accommodation and storerooms. A spiral staircase connected the different levels. The original lantern was a first-order optic built by Chance Brothers of Smethwick, near Birmingham, and it displayed a red flash every 45 seconds and was visible at 24km (15 miles). The red colour was achieved by fitting a ruby glass chimney over the oil lamp at the centre of the lens.

During World War II, Les Hanois was occupied by German forces and the lighthouse served as a prison for solitary confinement. There is rumoured to be a bullet hole in the ceiling of one of the rooms where a despairing prisoner shot himself. The lantern room also suffered quite a bit of damage due to gunfire but was quickly repaired at the war's end. In 1964, electricity arrived and the light was replaced by a fourth-order catadioptric optic. The year 1979 saw the weathervane removed from the lantern room, to be replaced by a helipad, thus ensuring easier access to this remote station. In 1996, the lighthouse became the first rock lighthouse to be operated by solar power and the lighthouse was eventually automated and the keepers retired.

The Table des Pions fairy ring close to Fort Pezeries on the Pleinmont headland.

LA CORBIÉRE
LIGHTHOUSE
ST BRÉLADE
JERSEY

LA CORBIÈRE

LOCATION: 49°10′47″N, 2°14′59″W
OS GRID: N/A
ELEVATION: 36m (118ft)
CHARACTER: Iso WR 5s
RANGE: White 33km (21 miles); Red 30km (19 miles)

La Corbière lighthouse sits on an islet just off the southwestern point of Jersey and is connected to the main island via a tidal causeway. The location is certainly picturesque and the lighthouse is a particular favourite of photographers looking for the perfect sunset shot.

The tower, 10km (6 miles) east of St Helier, overlooks the shipping routes between Guernsey and Britain. The name La Corbière, deriving from *corbeau*, the French word for "crow", is first recorded in 1309 as meaning "the place of the crows".

Derek Tristram's sculpture commemorates the successful rescue of passengers from a catamaran called the Saint-Malo, which hit a rock near La Corbière in 1995.

There's often an ice cream van parked near the causeway, and if you opt for a 99 ice cream, you'll notice crows in short supply, but herring gulls aplenty and very intent on sharing your cone.

Completed in 1873 to a design by Sir John Coode, the 19m (62ft) lighthouse was the first in these isles to be built of concrete, though it was rendered to look like it had been made of stone. All the materials used in the construction were ferried to the site by barge and landed at a lower working platform by cable hoist. A temporary inclined narrow rail was then built to transport the mixed concrete up to the site and the tower was cast in situ. The lighthouse, like its contemporaries, originally operated using paraffin, but it upgraded to electric operation in 1970, at which point the keepers were retired. The light is isophase, with red and white sectors alternating every five seconds.

When German forces landed in Guernsey on 30 June 1940, it heralded the longest period of darkness for La Corbière since its inception, only ending five years later when the light was finally restored on 19

La Corbière Radio Tower was built as an observation post during World War II by occupying German forces. After the war, it became a radio tower and now it has been converted into holiday accommodation

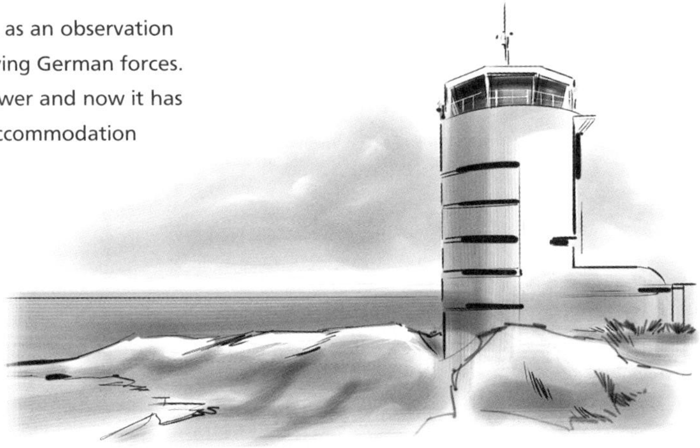

May 1945. Just a year later, tragedy struck when one of the keepers, Peter Edwin Larbalestier, was drowned while attempting to rescue a tourist who, having ignored the tide warning, had got stuck on rocks between the lighthouse and the shore. On the wall of the former lightkeepers' cottage at the entrance to the causeway, a plaque commemorates Larbalestier's bravery. These days, there is an alarm to warn visitors to head back to the main island as the waters rise, but it's still advisable to check the tide charts lest you get stuck on the wrong side of the causeway.

The lighthouse takes us about as far south as these isles go, but just 15km (9 miles) south of La Corbière lie Les Minquiers, a group of minuscule reefs and islands. On the tiny islet of Maîtresse Île sits a lonely outdoor toilet, the most southerly building in these isles! A sign fastened to it reads: "Please use with care! As the nearest alternative is Jersey 11 miles, Chausey 10 miles."

EUROPA POINT, GIBRALTAR

LOCATION: 36°06′35″N, 5°20′41″W
ELEVATION: 49m (161ft)
CHARACTER: Iso W 10s
RANGE: 33km (21 miles)

Built in 1841, the Europa Point lighthouse is a modern-day pillar of Hercules, guarding the entrance to the Mediterranean from the Atlantic Ocean.

An Act of Parliament in 1838 entrusted Trinity House with responsibility for aids to navigation in the territory, and under the Merchant Shipping Act of 1894, the corporation became the General Lighthouse Authority for Gibraltar. Europa Point is the only lighthouse outside of these islands that is operated by Trinity House.

In the centuries before Europa Point was built, navigators in the bay were dependent on the light emanating from the Shrine of Our Lady of Europe, which had originally been a mosque. Its conversion to a Catholic sanctuary took place after the victory of King Ferdinand IV of Spain over the Moors at the siege of 1309. The locals expressed their gratitude by leaving supplies of oil at the chapel, which also encouraged the continued burning of the lights.

One of the natives enjoying the sun.

The new light at Gibraltar was first exhibited in 1841 in a ceremony witnessed by 10,000 onlookers. At first, a fixed light was exhibited using a single-wick oil lamp amplified by catoptric mirrors and then focused through a dioptric fixed lens. This was later improved by fitting a four-wick burner, with a new lens incorporating a red arc to indicate the Pearl Rock, a dangerous group of jagged rocks on the western edge of the entrance to Gibraltar Bay. Eleven years later, the light was improved once again when the range and incandescence were enhanced.

The lighthouse stands 19m (62ft) tall including lantern and gallery. "La Farola", or "the lamp post", as it is known in Gibraltar's spoken vernacular, is painted white with a single broad red band in the middle. In 1994, the station was automated and then converted to LED operation in 2016.

EUROPA POINT
LIGHTHOUSE
EUROPA POINT
GIBRALTAR

Europa Point escaped World War II relatively unscathed, at a time when the security of Gibraltar itself was in serious jeopardy. On 18 July 1940, after the British attack on the French fleet at Mers El Kébir, the Vichy government retaliated by authorizing a number of bombing raids on Gibraltar. Little damage was reported as it appeared that the majority of the bombs had been deliberately dropped short of their target, but the South Mole (one of a trio of breakwaters) was heavily damaged, as were a number of ships.

The history of wartime Gibraltar is fascinating in its own right and the network of tunnels dug to house the defence of the rock can be explored to some extent by interested visitors. One of the more bizarre defensive scenarios, Operation Tracer, would have tested even the hardiest of rock station lighthouse veterans. If Gibraltar fell, six men were to be sealed into a cave with enough supplies for seven years. Their job was to observe shipping through a 30cm by 15cm (12in by 6in) slit cut in the side of the rock and report back to the Admiralty. Should anyone die during the operation, they were simply to be embalmed and cemented into the floor. Lovely. Anyone who endured lockdown during the Covid-19 crisis is, I'm sure, wondering just how six men would live together underground on emergency rations for perhaps years on end in a space about the size of a small bungalow without going completely gaga!

The Gibraltar cable car takes you to the top of the rock in six minutes.

In February 2014, plans were announced to build a football stadium on Europa Point. Although the lighthouse would not have been demolished, its beam would have been obstructed by the stadium. As a result, it was suggested that the light be moved to a location atop the stadium. In September 2015, the government, under heavy pressure from a Save Europa Point movement, found another location for the stadium.

FURTHER READING

Roger O'Reilly, *Lighthouses of Ireland*, Gill Books, 2018

Bella Bathurst, *The Lighthouse Stevensons*, Flamingo, 1999

Tony Denton and Nicholas Leach, *Lighthouses of England and Wales*, The History Press, 2018

R G Grant, *Sentinels of the Sea*, Thames & Hudson, 2018

Sarah Kerr, *The British Lighthouse Trail*, Whittles Publishing, 2019

Jo Kerrigan and Richard Mills, *Stories from the Sea*, O'Brien Press, 2021

Sharma Krauskopf, *Scottish Lighthouses*, Appletree Press, 2001

Bill Long, *Bright Light, White Water*, New Island Books, 1997

R W Munro, *Scottish Lighthouses*, Thule Press, 1979

Donald S Murray, *For the Safety of All: A Story of Scotland's Lighthouses*, Historic Environment Scotland, 2021

Tom Nancollas, *Seashaken Houses*, Particular Publishing, 2018

Christopher Nicholson, *Postcards from the Edge*, Whittles Publishing, 2010

—, *Rock Lighthouses of Britain*, Whittles Publishing, 2015

Michael A W Strachan, *Scottish Lighthouses: An Illustrated History*, Amberley Books, 2016

Kenneth Sutton Jones, *Pharos: The Lighthouse Yesterday, Today and Tomorrow*, Michael Russell Publishing, 1985

Richard Woodman and Jane Wilson, *The Lighthouses of Trinity House*, Thomas Reed Publications, 2002

Websites

The Northern Lighthouse Board: www.nlb.org.uk

Trinity House: www.trinityhouse.co.uk

USEFUL ADDRESSES

Here is a selection of the lighthouses listed in this book that provide tours and accommodation for those who fancy a wild night away (of a different sort!).
This is just a short list and by no means exhaustive.

LIGHTHOUSE TOURS

England

- Lizard Point: www.trinityhouse.co.uk/lighthouse-visitor-centres
- Roker: https://rokerpier.co.uk/
- Souter: www.nationaltrust.org.uk/visit/north-east/souter-lighthouse-and-the-leas
- Flamborough Head: www.trinityhouse.co.uk/lighthouse-visitor-centres
- Southwold: www.trinityhouse.co.uk/lighthouse-visitor-centres
- Portland Bill: www.trinityhouse.co.uk/lighthouse-visitor-centres
- Start Point: www.trinityhouse.co.uk/lighthouse-visitor-centres

Wales

- South Stack: www.trinityhouse.co.uk/lighthouse-visitor-centres

Scotland

- Mull of Galloway: https://mull-of-galloway.co.uk/mull-of-galloway-experience
- Ardnamurchan: www.ardnamurchanlighthouse.com/the-lighthouse
- North Ronaldsay: www.northronaldsay.co.uk/lighthouses.html
- Sumburgh Head: www.sumburghhead.com
- Museum of Scottish Lighthouses, Kinnaird Head: https://lighthousemuseum.org.uk
- Isle of May: www.isleofmayferry.com

LIGHTHOUSE ACCOMMODATION

- Sally Port Cottage, St Anthony: www.coolstays.com/property/sally-port-cottage/18064
- Trevose Head: www.trinityhouse.co.uk/lighthouse-cottage-rental/trevose-head-holiday-cottages

- The Old Light, Lundy: www.landmarktrust.org.uk
- Belle Tout: www.belletout.co.uk
- Lynmouth Foreland: www.nationaltrust.org.uk/holidays/devon/foreland-lighthouse-keepers-cottage
- Cromer: www.trinityhouse.co.uk/lighthouse-cottage-rental/cromer-lighthouse-cottages
- Portland Bill: www.oldhigherlighthouse.com

Wales

- Point Lynas: www.pointlynaslighthouse.com

Scotland

- Dunnet Head: https://dunnetheadlighthouse.com
- North Ronaldsay: https://northronaldsaytrust.com/2017/06/21/lighthousekeepers-cottages/

INDEX

A

B

C

D

E

I

J

K

L

M

N

O

P

Q

R

S

T

U

V